SOARING AND SETTLING

Soaring and Settling

Buddhist Perspectives on Contemporary Social and Religious Issues

≈

Rita M. Gross

CONTINUUM NEW YORK

1998
The Continuum Publishing Company
370 Lexington Avenue
New York, NY 10017

Printed in the Unite⁻ ⁻ ⁻tes of America

Library of Congress Cataloging-in-Publication Data

Gross, Rita M.
    Soaring and settling : Buddhist perspectives on contemporary
social and religious issues / Rita M. Gross.
        p. cm.
    Includes bibliographical references and index.
    ISBN 0-8264-1113-4
    1. Buddhism—Social aspects. 2. Feminism—Religious aspects—
Buddhism. 3. Woman (Buddhism) I. Title.
    BQ4570.S6G76 1998   98-30086
    294.3'37—dc21   CIP

*In gratitude and respect, this book is dedicated to
my Buddhist teachers,
Vidyadhara,
the Venerable Chogyam Trungpa, Rinpoche,
the Venerable Khandro, Rinpoche,
and the Venerable Sakyong Mipham, Rinpoche*

Contents

Overview: Buddhist Practice, Feminism, and Social Concern

BUDDHISM IS MORE than a set of texts to be translated and studied using the methods of Buddhalogy and philology. It is a living, vibrant tradition of great relevance to millions of contemporary people. Buddhism is not merely a "given," an unalterable set of Asian beliefs and practices. It is an evolving spiritual discipline and worldview that is shaped by modernity and, especially in its Western forms, by the concerns that are particularly urgent to Westerners, such as feminism, ecology, and social activism. And Buddhism is far more than an exotic philosophy relevant to "others," to Asians perhaps, that should be studied by outsiders whose lives are not formed by the Buddhist worldview and Buddhist values. It is a set of values and ideals by which many Westerners live and which needs to be part of ongoing conversations concerning the issues and dilemmas that inform our lives. Buddhism is not merely something to think *about*, to study and analyze; it is also a set of values, practices, and beliefs *with which* to think about our lives, with which to make decisions about how to proceed in difficult situations.

All the essays in this volume are informed by the conviction that Buddhist perspectives and values can and should be brought into discussions of the issues that confront us today. But these essays are informed also by the conviction that Buddhism itself is a creatively open-ended value system and praxis. Such Buddhist "theology"—deliberately normative and creative thinking within Buddhist parameters—is still somewhat unusual. More often Buddhism is regarded as a foreign intellectual and spiritual system, to be studied as such but not to be utilized in making decisions about our own direction. Even those Westerners who regard themselves as Buddhists and live by its orientation often regard Buddhism as a complete, finished work which they attempt to assimilate rather than as an evolving system whose development they can influence and for which they are responsible. Furthermore, such Buddhists do not always suggest or apply Buddhist solutions to contemporary social issues. But as I have become more at home in the Buddhist worldview through the years, I have come to feel an increasing urgency to think about the world and its issues in Buddhist terms, to bring the wisdom of the Buddhist tradition into discussions of issues such as feminism, ecology, and social change in general. At the same time, however, I have felt an equal urgency to think critically about my Buddhist religion and to suggest appropriate modifications of that tradition. Thus, this volume and all the essays contained in it share this double agenda as I work as a Buddhist "theologian." I use Buddhism as a tool with which to think about the contemporary situation at the same time as I suggest modifications to and interpretations of Buddhism that are particular to Western feminist Buddhism at the turn of the millennium.

The Buddhist wisdom for which I am so profoundly grateful and which has had so much impact on my own views and my own responses to contemporary issues is not merely an intellectual system. It is intimately connected with Buddhist spiritual disciplines and derives almost completely from them. I do not believe that the wisdom of Buddhism is really available apart from meditation, apart from the spiritual disciplines recommended by all Buddhists of all sects, times, and cultures. Much as I respect book learning and intellectual discipline, by themselves, I do not believe that they are powerful enough to effect the personal transformations I see as necessary to make a difference in the complex contemporary situation. My recommendation of Buddhist wisdom as a relevant resource for thinking about contemporary issues is conditioned by my insistence that that resource include meditation practice and spiritual discipline. Every chapter of this book reflects, in one way or another, what I have learned from Buddhist practice, even though this book is not a meditation manual and does not contain direct instructions on how to meditate. It is, rather, a plea to take Buddhism seriously as a stance relevant to the contemporary world that is also a plea to take Buddhism in its entirety. Buddhism, as I discovered long ago, is not just an ethical and philosophical system, even though my early academic training predisposed me to that error. It is also a meditational system. These three together—worldview, ethics, and meditation (*prajna*, *shila*, and *samadhi* in Buddhist jargon)—have *always* been the foundations of Buddhist life. They are also the basis for every chapter in this book.

Feminism, which I have defined for many years as "the radical practice of the co-humanity of women and men," is dealt with directly in the first and third parts of this book and indirectly in the second part. As is narrated in the first chapter, Buddhist practice has had a profound impact on my presentation of feminism. I can no longer imagine being the kind of ideological, angry feminist I was before my consciousness was impacted by Buddhist meditation. Nevertheless, in my work as a Buddhist constructive theologian, feminism contributes the most to suggested new Buddhist constructions. The third part of this book, especially the last four chapters, detail some of the issues with which I have been most concerned in my Buddhist feminist theology, namely, feminine sacred images and women teachers. In the middle section, which deals most directly with social issues and social change, feminism is a semisilent partner in the discussions. On occasion, when some issue calls for explicitly feminist commentary, it is provided. But for the most part, I simply discuss issues related to consumerism, pro-natalism, children's rights, family, friendship, community, and so on, as a commentator whose vision includes feminism would discuss such concerns. As feminism matures and becomes an inevitable part of our moral landscape, such assumed feminism may become more possible and frequent, which would be a most welcome development.

This is a book about Buddhist practice, feminism, and social change; I see it in the stream of emerging discussions from the Engaged Buddhist movement. These essays, however, focus on themes not often emphasized in the Engaged Buddhist movement, beginning with feminism itself. Engaged Buddhism often directs its comments and critiques outside, toward large systems of development, colonialism, and globalization. But internal critiques, such as those brought up by Buddhist feminists concerning patterns within Buddhism itself, are less likely to find a voice within the Engaged Buddhist movement. Such blindness to internal problems is often characteristic of movements of social protest and criticism. Nevertheless, I regard Buddhist feminism and its agenda within Buddhism itself as part of the necessary program for Engaged Buddhism, one of the issues with which Engaged Buddhists need to be deal.

The particular emphasis I bring to discussions of social change is the conviction that successful movements for social change must pay attention to internal individual states of mind and emotion. This perspective also courses through all the essays of this book, whether they focus more on social issues or on religious issues. (Religious issues are clearly not irrelevant to social issues and social change; therefore, one should not assume that the second and third sections of this book are on different topics.) Especially regarding the interdependent forces of consumerism and pro-natalism that drive so much of the current degradation of the planet, it is necessary to look into the psychological factors that compel people to consume and to reproduce more than is wise, against their better interests. It is, of course, equally necessary to seek psychological and spiritual antidotes to the compulsions that fuel consumerism and pro-natalism. Without such interior, individual transformations of heart and mind, policies and recommendations are likely to be resisted, no matter how sensible they may be.

Much of the dissatisfaction that drives people into patterns of over-consumption surely is connected with the lack of community, the difficulty of finding meaningful relationships and support systems, that has become so endemic to our lives in North America today. Thus, some chapters address questions of friendship and community as issues for Engaged Buddhists. Dissatisfaction, cravings, alienation, loneliness—seemingly internal individual issues—are critical to my perspectives on social change, as is finding equanimity, finding some peacefulness in the midst of all the inadequacies and frustrations we encounter. Buddhism, I claim, is uniquely suited to address such problems. And, equally, I claim that without addressing these seemingly personal individual issues, we are not likely to make much progress toward the social changes that are so desperately needed in our rapidly failing ecosystem, which is so overburdened with so many people consuming or wanting to consume so much. Focusing on these internal states of mind and heart may be a uniquely Buddhist perspective; focusing on the personal as political is a uniquely feminist stance. Together they bring a powerful perspective to Engaged Buddhism and to contemporary social and religious issues.

Almost all the essays that make up this book were written recently, after I published *Buddhism after Patriarchy* in 1993. Many of the essays were written in response to invitations I received as a result of that book. As my repertoire of essays regarding Buddhist perspectives on contemporary social and religious issues grew, I wished to bring them together so that readers could be aware of the variety and depth of Buddhist perspectives on such issues without having to consult a number of scattered publications, some of them difficult to obtain. I am grateful to my editor at Continuum, Frank Oveis, who provided that opportunity and guided the process of putting together this collection. I am also grateful to those whose invitations first inspired me to write many of the chapters of this book. Harold Coward's invitations are responsible for four of the essays in this collection: "Interdependence and Detachment: Toward a Buddhist Environmental Ethic," "Buddhist Values for Overcoming Pro-natalism and Consumerism," "Children, Children's Rights, and Family Well-being in Buddhist Perspective," and "Life-giving Images in Vajrayana Buddhist Ritual." Kenneth Tanaka's invitation to contribute to a series of presentations on Buddhism in America resulted in the chapter entitled "Helping the Iron Bird Fly: Western Buddhists and Issues of Authority." The Zen Center of San Francisco's invitation to participate in a lecture series resulted in "Finding Renunciation and Balance in Western Buddhist Practice: Work, Family, Community, and Friendship." Women of the Buddhist community of Halifax, Nova Scotia, extended the invitation that resulted in "The Female Body and Precious Human Birth: An Essay on Anger and Meditation." The Lewis and Clark graduating class of 1993 invited me to give their baccalaureate address, "Soaring and Settling: Riding the Winds of Change," which also provided the title for this collection. Suwanda Suganasiri organized a conference on *Buddhism after Patriarchy* in Toronto in 1995; "Passion and Peril" was my opening address for that conference. "Some Buddhist Perspectives on the Goddess" was my invited presentation to the Goddess Conference held at Claremont Graduate University and organized by Karen Torjesen in 1992. "The Feminine Principle in Tibetan Vajrayana Buddhism: Reflections of a Buddhist Feminist," the earliest essay included in this collection, was presented at one of the first conferences on women and Buddhism, held at the Naropa Institute and organized by Judith Simmer-Brown in 1982. The only other chapter that predates the writing of *Buddhism after Patriarchy* is "I Will Never Forget to Visualize That Vajrayogini Is My Body and Mind," an American Academy of Religion paper in 1985. The other chapters of this book all began as conference papers, all of them for the American Academy of Religion except "Crying in the Prophetic Voice as a Buddhist Feminist." That paper was a plenary address at the International Buddhist-Christian Dialogue Conference held in Boston in 1992. Earlier versions of all these essays, with the exception of "Soaring and Settling" and "Life-giving Images in Vajrayana Buddhist Ritual," have been published or are in the process of being published elsewhere. I am grateful as well for those earlier opportunities to publish these reflections.

Permission to reprint the following chapters in revised form is gratefully acknowledged:

Chapter 1: "Anger and Meditation," in *Being Bodies*, edited by Lenore Friedman and Susan Moon. © 1997 by Lenore Friedman and Susan Moon. Published by arrangement with Shambhala Publications, Inc., Boston.

Chapter 2: "Autobiography, Mutual Transformation, and the Prophetic Voice in Buddhist Feminism," *Buddhist-Christian Studies*, vol. 13. © University of Hawaii Press, 1991.

Chapter 3: "Why Me? Methodological-Autobiographical Reflections of a Wisconsin Farm Girl Who Became a Buddhist Theologian When She Grew Up," *Journal of Feminist Studies in Religion* 13/2 (Fall 1997): 103–18.

PART 1

The Road Less Chosen: Becoming a Feminist Buddhist Scholar-Practitioner

Introduction: Autobiography and Feminist Method

Buddhist feminist scholar-practitioners are as rare in North America as they are in the rest of the world. This combination of identities is made, not born; no family or culture deliberately seeks to socialize its children into that composite. Buddhist cultures, to be sure, attempt to reproduce Buddhists, but this Western Buddhist is a first-generation convert who has become quite outspoken in her vision of "Buddhism after Patriarchy," to quote the title of my best-known book. Feminism, which I define as the "radical practice of the co-humanity of women and men," is by no means a culture-wide norm, either among Buddhists or in the West, though some families and subcultures now do encourage its development. In current academic culture, it is anathema to try to unite scholarship and practice, especially as a Buddhist. What previous cultures had often seen as a "both-and" proposition, Western intellectuals often regard as an "either-or" choice. And for girls to grow up to define themselves primarily as scholars or practitioners, and to succeed in doing so, has been relatively rare in both East and West.

How does this unusual combination come to pass? In the articles that follow, I do not narrate my autobiography event by event. But in keeping with the feminist academic ethic of self-disclosure, I have frequently used autobiography as an element in making a case or explaining my stance. Feminist theologians and scholars are much more likely to be autobiographical in their professional writing than are their more conventional colleagues, who find self-disclosure embarrassing and feel that reason alone should be used to express one's position. Feminists, however, have strong and cogent reasons for their autobiographical acts. Having painfully discovered that conventional scholarship, which billed itself as objective

3

and claimed to speak for and from the human perspective, was in fact androcentrically selective, feminists have argued that ignoring our stories and our "situatedness" only creates false universalism. We experienced strongly that our specific situations as women in patriarchal societies affected our interests, our concerns, and the results of our scholarship; we also saw quite clearly that the methods and values that our male mentors and colleagues assumed to be universally valid actually depended to some extent on their experiences as men. Eventually we also came to see that not only gender but also race, class, culture, sexual orientation, and the like, had their impact on scholarship. Therefore, we are unlikely ever again to be naive enough to believe that the scholar's experience does not affect her scholarship.

Instead, we advocate stating openly the generative experiences for our particular scholarly or theological stances. We take certain positions, for which we give cogent rational arguments, rather than other positions, in part because of formative experiences, not solely on the basis of logic and rationality. So do all other scholars. Scholarly honesty and completeness are served by expounding the experience as well as the logic that leads us to our stances. This does not mean that acknowledging and reflecting on the specific "situated" places from which we *know* undoes our concern for rationality, objectivity, neutrality, and good scholarship and theology. On the contrary, it means that we are more likely to be aware of the limits of these goals and of the need to make good, cogent arguments for the positions that arise out of our specific situations. Such introspective self-disclosure may also lead to interesting insights. In my own case, since I believe that I am the only Wisconsin farm girl who has ever grown up to be a Buddhist theologian, it seems obvious that logic alone could not explain my stance, and that bound up in the experiences that led me to my position are interesting insights about religion and society. Therefore, all the chapters in this book, but particularly those in this section, come with a warning—"The author will engage in the kind of autobiographical act typical of contemporary feminist theology"—but only in the service of clarifying a position, not for self-display.

The reader will notice recurring formative events in these chapters: early experiences of poverty and cultural deprivation, early fundamentalist and exclusivist religious indoctrination, early rebellion against gender roles being presented to me, especially dislike of what I could look forward to as a female in patriarchal society and religion. The reader will also notice a recurring "naivete" about academic, intellectual, and spiritual pursuits—a love of learning and spiritual cultivation for their own sake and surprise that such virtues are not very highly regarded. The high costs of scholarly innovation, of being on the cutting edge of a paradigm shift the academy did not particularly want to accommodate, also figure into these stories. I have paid dearly for my uniqueness as a Buddhist feminist scholar-practitioner. Key stories—how and why I first began to question the androcentric norms which I had previously accepted without question, why I first began to *practice* Buddhist spiritual disciplines, as opposed to simply studying Buddhism—are narrated briefly in appropriate contexts.

Each of these four chapters was first an oral presentation in a highly charged environment. In each case, the self-disclosure and the information I revealed about myself were challenging and I was emotionally drained by the event. In each case, I wanted to make an important point about feminism, scholarship, theology, or Buddhism and felt that my points were strengthened by speaking from the heart in autobiographical self-revelation.

The chapter entitled "The Female Body and Precious Human Birth: An Essay on Anger and Meditation" was delivered in Halifax, Nova Scotia, in 1995 during events surrounding the enthronement of one my principal Buddhist teachers, the Sakyong Mipham, Rinpoche, eldest son of my root guru, Chogyam Trungpa, Rinpoche. My talk was not one of the officially scheduled events in the week-long celebration; instead, Buddhist women in Halifax, frustrated by the all-too-familiar male dominance in our Buddhist organization, asked me to give a talk and made the arrangements. Publicity was haphazard and I went to the talk quite uncertain of what would happen. A standing-room-only crowd turned out, and the talk was quite successful, gratifying, and well received. Later I made a transcript from my notes (the attempt at taping was not successful), and the talk was published in the *Shambhala Sun*, a widely read Buddhist periodical, where it generated letters to the editor for months. It has also been published in *Being Bodies: Buddhist Women on the Paradox of Embodiment* (Boston: Shambhala, 1997).

The next chapter, on the "prophetic voice in Buddhism," a concept I developed and introduced in *Buddhism after Patriarchy*, was a presidential plenary address at the Fourth International Buddhist-Christian Dialogue Conference in Boston in 1992. To speak so autobiographically in such an academic setting was challenging, and I had never before publicly discussed my excommunication from Christianity and its effects on my thinking and my life. To discuss those experiences before so many prominent Christian theologians was unnerving, but I saw no other way to contextualize the points I wanted to make about the tyranny of absolute truth claims in doctrinal matters. An earlier version of this chapter has been published in volume 13 of *Buddhist-Christian Studies*.

The chapter entitled "Why Me?" is the most complex methodologically. In it I seek both to explain and to justify my dual stance as a historian of religions and a theologian, showing how my experiences as an outsider-woman in an androcentric academic environment first led me to question the sharp division between normative and descriptive studies in religion. Many scholars of religion accept that dichotomy without question, arguing that a scholar can do one or the other, but not both. By contrast, I argue that it is impossible really to separate the two approaches to religion and the study of religion completely. I was reluctantly led to that conclusion by experiences in the late 1960s and early 1970s as a graduate student and young scholar that first caused me to question prevailing androcentric methods. This paper was first presented at the annual meeting of the American Academy of Religion in 1992 and has been published in the *Journal of Feminist Studies in Religion*.

Finally, "Passion and Peril" was my opening address at a conference on my book *Buddhism after Patriarchy* held at Trinity College of the University of Toronto in 1995. While in some ways such a conference represents great achievement and acclaim, it also means, in the folkways of academic culture, that it's "open season" on one's best efforts. Such a hyper-competitive academic culture is one of the "perils" I discuss in that chapter. In my opening address, I wanted to "let it all hang out" in discussing the context of my book. For, indeed, I had transgressed many sacred boundaries in writing *Buddhism after Patriarchy*, and I wanted to discuss each of those "transgressions" intimately. This chapter represents the most complete overview of my methodology and my stances, to date. Because Randi Warne has been invited to guest edit a volume on women and religion for Toronto University's journal *Method and Theory in the Study of Religion*, this article will be published there. It is highly ironic for such an unorthodox article to wind up in one of the most conventional journals in religious studies; without the sisterhood of feminist scholars it would never have happened.

CHAPTER 1

The Female Body
and Precious Human Birth:
An Essay on Anger and Meditation

H UMAN BIRTH IS PRECIOUS in Buddhism because the human body is the basis for the practices that facilitate realization. Without the human body, it is impossible to do such practices. In Vajrayana traditions, we are encouraged to contemplate: "Precious human body, free and well favored, difficult to obtain, easy to lose, now I must do something useful." Such contemplation on the worthiness of the body contrasts significantly with the devaluation and fear of the body found in so many religious systems, including those with which most of us grew up. Such body affirmation is part of the refreshing emphasis on the basic goodness of human beings and the world that is so central to Buddhism.

Nevertheless, traditional Buddhism also contains contradictory teachings which suggest that when the precious human birth occurs in a female body, that birth is less precious. Female rebirth, said to result from the negative karma of misdeeds in previous lives, was thought to be unfortunate. Women's spiritual and intellectual capabilities were considered to be lower than those of men and their female bodies not disposed to dharma practice. Because it was thought that women did not deserve to be involved in religious learning and teaching, they were allotted many fewer opportunities to practice the dharma than men.

To correct this problematic situation, women were given practices such as piety, conventional morality, deference, and specific prayers that would enable them to be reborn as men in their next life. With male bodies they would then more easily become enlightened. (At the most extreme, some Buddhist texts declare that a Buddha would never appear in a female body.) Thus, Buddhism, like many other traditions, declares that men are the

7

really normal human beings, while women are odd, not full-fledged representatives of the human species.

This stark assessment of the effects on precious human birth of having a female body elicits two observations. First, it is based on circular reasoning. Women are not trained in Buddhist meditation and philosophy because they have been evaluated as inferior human beings, but then their lack of achievement in philosophy or meditation is used to justify not providing them with opportunities for training. Second, such evaluations of the worth of one's precious human birth have a devastating effect on one's self-acceptance, one's *maitri*, or loving-kindness, in Buddhist terms. Many Buddhist practices encourage us to "start where we are" and to accept who we are as human beings, but this is difficult if we also believe what we've been told about our inferiority and want to start over with male bodies.

For me, feminism is a powerful antidote to such teachings, whether in Western or in Buddhist guise. Since I define feminism as the "radical practice of the co-humanity of women and men," feminism is about cherishing precious human birth in a female body. When we talk about feminism in the context of spiritual practice, we are talking about taking the Buddha nature of women as seriously as we have always taken the Buddha nature of men, including finding and training young women to be our next generation of teachers, just as we have always been willing to accept young men as teachers.

Unfortunately, the more one knows about Buddhist history and some contemporary forms of Buddhism, the more we realize how much we need feminism. Many people do not realize how much negativity toward women is in the Buddhist heritage. This is why it is so important to be aware and critical of residues of such attitudes that are still found in current iconographies and liturgies. Feminism is an *upaya*, or skillful means, appropriate to counter such negativity toward women. I cannot imagine taking my bodhisattva vow seriously or working to promote an enlightened society without being a feminist.

When I was a child growing up in the 1950s, before the second wave of feminism, I hated being female, with good reason. I was taught that all the things I wanted to do with my life were not what girls did. I wanted to explore the world, to read, to think, to discover reality. Most decidedly, I did not want to be limited to doing what girls and women did—enabling others, especially men and children, so that their lives could proceed smoothly, at the cost of my own life. Every girl who rebels against the prison of gender roles has her own version of what she will *not* spend her life doing; for me it was dusting lamps. I wanted to spend my life reading, thinking, and writing, not dusting lamps. (I now have many beautiful antique lamps which I dust every now and then, but I dust them because

I like them, not because it is my preordained gender role. And because my life includes much more than dusting lamps, doing so isn't imprisoning.)

The human activity that I value most is naming reality especially in religious and spiritual ways. The activity of putting raw, inchoate perceptions into words that others may find helpful has always beckoned me. But every direction in which I tried to go was marked by a sign that read "Stop! No girls allowed." My patriarchal culture insisted that such exploration and spiritual development were not my gender role. The patriarchal prison of gender roles not only teaches that women are not quite real human beings; it also teaches that women should willingly accept having their reality named for them by others.

What do you do in a situation like that? As a child you don't understand that the problem is with the system, not with you—a girl who wants to think about reality. So you accept it as a fact that there's something wrong with you. Either my desire to think about reality was wrong or my female body was wrong. My desire to explore the world was too persistent for me to give that up, so for years as a child, I hated my female body because it was the impediment to being the human being I wanted to become.

I don't quite know how it happened, but sometime in my late teens, I had one of those sudden "Aha" experiences that save your life if you can remember them and not fall back into habitual patterns. While dancing between the milk cans in our shoestring dairy operation, I experienced a very strong realization: "It's not me. I'm not what's wrong; there's nothing wrong with my female body. It's the system—the system!" I have a strong body memory of how I felt at that moment. I felt powerful synchronization of body and mind—mental delight meshed with physical alertness—and a sensation of freedom and empowerment. The insight was very brief, almost instantaneous, but I don't believe I ever again said, "If only I weren't female! Why did I have to be female."

Years later when I learned Buddhist names for experiences, I realized that this was the first time I had experienced self-acceptance, or *maitri*. And, years later, when I encountered Buddhist beliefs that my female body needed to be traded in for a male one before I could truly practice, the memory of this experience kept me from taking that doctrine seriously. I knew that in this *female* body I could learn, I could name reality and create culture, I could become a teacher. I knew I did not have to wait around until I had a male body.

That insight was followed by years of what I would now characterize as complaint and aggression, which, though painful in its own way, was a lot healthier than the previous self-rejection. I was a pioneer in my field, the feminist study of religion. I was also angry because I was punished professionally rather than rewarded for my feminist insights. I responded to the academic establishment with verbal aggression and sarcasm at every opportunity. If on a daily basis you are having your life taken away from you because of your gender, from a conventional point of view it would be logical to be angry about that. If you are going to get angry about anything, that's something worth getting angry about. In terms of Buddhist psychology, I am describing unenlightened *vajra* energy, and I lived with that for many years.

Many people, and particularly those with a meditative practice, dismiss feminism because of the anger they see displayed. While it is true that feminists who do not have a meditation practice often become ideological and aggressive, it's helpful to look at the situation using some basic Buddhist tools instead of glibly writing off feminism as "too aggressive." According to Mahayana teachings, aggression always arises from pain. The angry feminists who are such a turnoff are expressing their pain at having their lives taken away from them by a sex/gender system that doesn't work. Usually as Buddhists we try to understand the source of a person's aggression, and also the critical intelligence that is always present within aggression, but feminists are often dismissed—and quite aggressively! What does this dismissal say about women's precious human birth?

For Buddhists to be unwilling, even aggressively unwilling, to examine conventional habitual patterns, such as gender roles, is rather odd. This may be the only realm in which ignorance is not only tolerated but actually encouraged. And this occurs at all levels, from the language of our liturgies all the way to our Buddhist leadership. For example, within my own Vajradhatu *sangha*, daily chants still use generic masculine language and the shrine room is often devoid of feminine imagery and female lineage holders and *tulku*s are quite rare in Tibetan Buddhism. Those who criticize this situation are often subjected to dismissal and isolation themselves. It is very strange and sad that this continues to happen.

I was already well schooled in feminism and the academic study of Buddhism when I began meditation practice. I had no idea how profoundly meditation would affect my self-righteous feminist anger. Observing that effect over more than twenty years has been an interesting journey. At first my feminist friends thought I had lost it. It's one thing to *inherit* a patriarchal religion and try to work with it. Many of my feminist friends were making that choice. But to *convert* to a patriarchal religion was incomprehensible. No wonder they questioned my basic sanity.

My Buddhist friends were not much help either. The generic line was something like, "That's okay, Rita. When you get to be a real Buddhist practitioner, you won't care about feminism any more because you'll be detached." It was okay from their point of view to care about jobs and families or about Buddhist practice, but not to care about the politics of affirming the preciousness of human birth in a female body. So basically I found myself between two factions, both asking what was the matter with me.

What happened was not what either faction predicted, which is where the magic connecting feminism and the path of practice occurs. After being involved in serious meditation practice for several years, I began to discover that I simply didn't find anger so satisfying any longer. Previously I always experienced emotional relief through venting verbally, often with extreme sarcasm and cutting intellect, when I was overwhelmed by misogyny and patriarchy. But I no longer found it so appealing to get mad when gender issues arose, because the relief was not as reliable and I began to see that in any case my anger was not doing anything to alleviate the general misery brought about by patriarchy and misogyny. I began to realize personally the Buddhist teaching that aggressive speech and actions always produce negative counterreactions. I began to see that people tuned out when I vented my angry feelings, that my fits of aggressive rhetoric only caused further mutual entrenchment rather than any significant change in those whom I confronted. I wanted to do something more helpful.

These changes were very scary at first because I feared that I *was* ceasing to care about concerns that had been central to my life for years. Maybe my Buddhist friends were correct and practitioners are not involved in "causes." But something else was also happening. With practice, the anger that had been so much a part of my feminism had started to transmute. I no longer experienced so much of the time that painful state in which clarity and anger are totally mixed up. The clarity remained but the anger started to settle. My body no longer tensed with hot, explosive energy; instead I began to hold a relaxed body state that has nothing to do with giving in and everything to do with furthering communication. Now I test myself on issues. If I find that I explode into emotionalism, felt in the body as cloudy rage, I know that I must work further with that issue by myself before I am fit for public communication about it.

As my anger became less urgent, my clarity concerning gender issues and the dharma increased proportionately and my skill in expressing my convictions without polarizing the situation also increased. I was actually becoming a much more effective spokesperson for feminism. I was not ceasing to care about feminism, as my Buddhist friends had been encouraging me to do, but ceasing to nurse my anger. I did not stop saying the same things that I always had, but when I expressed myself less aggressively, people could hear what I was saying. I discovered a middle path between aggressive expression and passive acquiescence, and sometimes I have been able to bring about major changes in a meditation program because I simply maintained my position without aggression.

One does not have to choose between either confronting someone or getting rolled over, even though that's what the conventional world teaches us. Thereby, some measure of victory over warfare may be achieved, because one cannot be so easily dismissed when one does not respond aggressively to provocation. This middle path is very hard to maintain. It takes a lot of being with each moment, moment by moment to avoid getting rolled over or becoming confrontational, but that is the magic of the Middle Way. The point of feminism is not to fight wars but to alleviate the suffering caused by conventional gender roles. Practice can tame the anger and unleash the clarity of feminism so that communication is more possible.

Not only does meditation unlock the power of feminism; it also sustains feminism in the long haul. I don't see any way that, more than thirty years after I began to advocate feminism, I could still be talking about it if I had not begun to practice meditation. If you really want to work with the world on something you care about, practice provides the staying power to avoid burnout, precisely because meditation tames anger and makes it workable. Practice seems to be the foundation for caring about the world without becoming exhausted. It is the foundation of a movement that people are beginning to call Engaged Buddhism—and Buddhist feminism will be part of that movement.

CHAPTER 2

Crying in the Prophetic Voice
as a Buddhist Feminist

IN MY WORK AS A BUDDHIST FEMINIST, I have often suggested that Buddhism needs to utilize what I call "the prophetic voice" as a method and resource for critiquing and reconstructing Buddhist sexism and patriarchy. Though Buddhism includes ethical teachings such as "non-harming" and "compassion," which serve well as self-correctives to Buddhist sexism, I argue that the prophetic categories of "righteousness" and "justice" are useful and appropriate tools for Buddhists. Additionally, I argue that the prophetic inclination to seek social change through activism, demonstration, and organization is a necessary balance to the Buddhist tendency to seek tranquillity in the midst of whatever conditions one faces, no matter how unpleasant. I also try to demonstrate how "compassion" and "righteousness" complement each other, how when used together, each is a corrective for the problems that can be generated by the other.

This discussion of how a Buddhist could utilize values such as "righteousness" and "justice" is grounded in discussion of dialogue and mutual transformation, specifically in a conversation with John Cobb at the 1985 Buddhist-Christian Theological Encounter. He stated that he was convinced that my being the kind of Buddhist I am—namely, a strongly and self-consciously *feminist* Buddhist—owed something to my having been initially trained religiously and spiritually in a Western religion. He challenged me to acknowledge the Western roots of my Buddhist feminism, a challenge that has had a significant impact on me. His suggestion makes a great deal of sense.

Though the prophets of the monotheistic religions engaged in their share of misogyny and patriarchy, that dimension of their work is surely part of their human frailty, not part of their prophetic vision and voice.

13

Feminism is one of the great contemporary manifestations of the prophetic voice shorn of outmoded and outdated cultural biases. Since we are constituted by our history, including our personal histories, and since I had received significant academic and religious training in the prophetic voice as articulated in, not one, but two of the Western monotheistic religions, it might seem that part of Western religion came with me into my incarnation as a Buddhist feminist theologian—the prophetic voice. Superficially, everything fits very well.

I still find some cogency in that explanation of the genesis of the kind of thinking I engage in as a Buddhist feminist, but I am not fully satisfied with it. Wisconsin farm girls, especially those who grow up in poverty and cultural deprivation, rarely become theologians, but if they do, they usually become *Christian* rather than *Buddhist* theologians. Clearly, in my case something more complex than mutual transformation due to a Buddhist encounter with Christianity explains my use of the prophetic voice; my ethnicity and my personal history would normally result in my using the prophetic voice as a Christian rather than as a Buddhist.

But much more important, if I am honest, I must state that I never really experienced the prophetic voice within Christianity until I began to engage in Buddhist–Christian dialogue as a Buddhist. What I encountered instead has been the cause of deep personal wounding and a lifelong search for a positive personal experience with Christianity. Therefore, superficially at least, my early training in Christianity is not the source of my use of the prophetic voice. Nor, in my view, can my use of the prophetic voice be attributed to my training in Judaism. I believe that my involvement with Judaism, beginning only in my late teens and early twenties, came too late in my life to be responsible for my use of the prophetic voice. So where did the prophetic voice come from?

A Buddhist might simply attribute it to *karma*. What is the karma (which literally means the action or the cause) that led me to become a Buddhist theologian instead of a Christian theologian? It is the same karma that led me to become so involved in Buddhist–Christian dialogue and encounter, namely, the lack of previous positive personal experiences with Christianity. Explaining that statement requires me to name the dimensions of Christianity, as I encountered it, that entailed such poverty; furthermore, I would claim that naming those dimensions of Christianity is itself a manifestation of the prophetic voice.

My Christian training was in a denomination that shall not be named; I believe that my particular experiences are possible, even likely, in any religious system that makes exclusive truth claims, which is to say throughout most of Christianity, if not the entirety of monotheism. I look back upon that training with anger, frustration, and longing. Obviously, I came through these experiences, but I would not wish them on anyone. From my vantage point of adulthood and lifelong pursuit of academic and spiritual disciplines, I recognize that as a child, I received systematic training in scorn and arrogance, masked as certainty about the one true faith. Curiosity was anathema. That one might appreciate pluralism rather than hating it was completely unheard-of. And because we alone had the truth, according to what I was taught, it was necessary to refute and denigrate all other points of view, in the process of bringing "the truth" to everyone else. It is hard for me to avoid the conclusion that I was given systematic training in hatred parading as religious conviction and faith. I find it difficult to imagine who would train a sensitive and thoughtful child in such thought patterns. Yet I know that my experience is by no means unique; many students come to my classroom still carrying such training deeply imprinted into their minds.

Needless to say, the training did not take. I now believe that my first articulation of the prophetic voice was to stand against that training, timidly and tentatively at first as a teenager. My suggestion, made before I began my academic study of religion, that all religions worship the same deity called by different names, was dismissed, and I was instructed again that all other namings of ultimate reality are false, evil, and dangerous to those who hold them. Subjected to public castigation for my wayward theology at my mother's funeral, I was soon thereafter excommunicated and confidently declared to be someone whose future residence was hell. I was given the word in writing, in case I had any doubts. In that letter, I was lumped with "a brood of pseudo-intellectuals and higher critics" to whom, I was told, I had sold my soul "for a mess of 'academic pottage.'"

Trauma and longing best express my reactions, even so many years later. The fact that I am allergic to doctrinal dogmatism surely stems from the trauma of these experiences. I expect never fully to recover from the traumatizing effects of such religious brainwashing; I hope only to transmute those experiences into some positive contribution to the development of religious thought. But the longing for some positive personal experience of Christianity has never left either. Much of my Buddhist feminist theology is composed to the accompaniment of Christian liturgical music while a votive candle burns, and I have a finely tuned appreciation of Christian myth, symbolism, and ritual. Though the dogma and exclusive truth claims that so often accompany Christian myth and ritual are deeply troubling, dangerous, and destructive, nevertheless, a profound symbol system is tangled up with those problematic tendencies. Somewhere, I tell myself, that profound symbol system must be translated into a social reality that is not narrow-minded and does not claim unique relevance for itself—a social reality that is compassionate, kind, and inclusive. I have not found it yet, except in the context of Buddhist–Christian dialogue.

My involvement in Buddhist–Christian dialogue grows out of my longing to encounter Christianity positively and to lend my energies to the emergence of a Christianity that articulates the prophetic voice without exclusive truth claims. That motivation was very clear to me many years ago when I attended the first conference on Buddhist–Christian dialogue in 1980, and it has remained with me ever since. I treasure experiences of Christian ritual and sacrament that have occurred in some Buddhist–Christian encounters, for they are as close as I have ever come to having my longings fulfilled. Furthermore, any contributions I might make to the emergence of a Christianity that is wiser and more compassionate than the versions of Christianity I have encountered throughout my life would occur most readily within the context of Buddhist–Christian dialogue and exchange.

Why do I tell these stories about the emergence of my prophetic voice? Feminist method uses autobiography as a tool, not as an end in itself. I would like to make it as clear as I can just how painful, traumatic, damaging, and wounding exclusive truth claims about matters of symbols and doctrines can be. That message is part of my use of the prophetic voice, which today needs to be heard, first and foremost, in a self-purification of those aspects of itself that have been damaging, that lack understanding and compassion. Turned on itself in such a manner, the prophetic voice would surely proclaim that no symbol, myth, and ritual system, including monotheistic systems, loses any of its power and beauty when it lays down its claims to exclusive truth.

In fact, if anything, when a symbol system is seen as an enterprise more akin to poetry than to science or history, religion is grounded in its own proper mode of discourse. People recognize readily that there will never be agreement on the most beautiful poem in existence. People also recognize readily that one is in no danger, temporal or eternal, if one focuses on a different poem as one's favorite, as the poem that speaks most evocatively to one, rather than on one's own favorite poem. While it may be educational and entertaining to debate the pros and cons of one poem versus another, only someone with psychological problems would insist that it matters ultimately if others do not select the same favorite poem. So with the symbols, myths, and rituals of religious and spiritual systems. They have incredible power and beauty until they are literalized and subjected to tests of empiricism. Since nothing of value is lost and much is gained by renouncing exclusive truth claims, it is hard to understand why children are still being traumatized by training such as I received.

The matter has been put perhaps most succinctly by Paul Griffiths when discussing Buddhist ideas about religious truth. "There is a methodological principle that has to do with the nature of religious doctrines. Briefly and rather crudely, this principle suggests that religious doctrines have utility rather than truth; that their importance lies in the effects they have upon those who believe in them."[1] While I agree that this is in fact the Buddhist position, the importance of this principle is not that it is Buddhist rather than Christian in its origins. The importance of this principle lies rather in its eminent common sense and compassion. Surely the whole point of religious doctrines is to humanize those who hold them, to help them become gentle, compassionate, and vulnerable, rather than aggressive, scornful, and arrogant. If one evaluated religious doctrines on their utility, surely the first doctrine to be abandoned would be exclusive truth claims about matters of symbol and doctrine, simply because the effect of such claims is so injurious and damaging. I can think of no instance in which a religion or its adherents have been improved by exclusive truth claims and many in which the results have been aggression, oppression, hostility, and arrogance. Nothing valuable is lost in such renunciation and much is gained.

If we wish to seek truth rather than utility, we should not seek it in religious doctrines and symbols, which by their very nature are neither true nor false, but meaningful or meaningless. Instead we might reserve the quest for truth to ethical questions, to the domain of interpersonal interactions and our treatment of each other. For while I am arguing for relativism vis-à-vis doctrines and symbols, I most definitely do not think that complete moral or ethical relativism possesses either truth or utility. Some ways of treating other people, such as those to which I was subjected under the reign of exclusive truth claims, are inappropriate, injurious, and despicable. That is why there is no hesitation or equivocation in my feminism, why I argue that the world cannot be repaired until patriarchy has lost its hold on people's psyches and social realities, even though I would never argue that the world cannot be a better place until there are more Buddhists in it. To me, nothing more clearly enunciates the prophetic voice for our time than that combination of doctrinal flexibility and moral urgency.

What of the initial question about the genesis of the prophetic voice in someone who grew up to be Buddhist theologian when all the odds would favor her becoming a Christian theologian, though the odds against her becoming any kind of theologian were very high? One could propose two solutions. Perhaps the prophetic voice rang through, despite all the arrogance and dogmatism with which it was muffled. Perhaps I was lucky enough to retain that call in spite of all the static surrounding it. Or perhaps my articulation of the prophetic voice as a Buddhist *is* a matter of karma, of fulfilling certain bodhisattva commitments through this strange autobiography. For no Buddhist could more creditably make the plea for Christians to drop exclusive truth claims than an ex-Christian Buddhist who has suffered what I have suffered. And other Buddhists would not usually have the generative experiences that make the case so clear-cut to me.

In a way, the latter explanation makes more sense to me, for by all odds, my life should have been simpler, my story line straighter. And I experience many of the stances I now embody as choiceless; I certainly never planned on becoming a Buddhist feminist theologian immersed in Buddhist–Christian dialogue and encounter, nor do I think I could possibly have figured out such an articulation of the prophetic voice. But it happened. We can never have certain answers as to which explanatory framework is correct. In fact the question as to which explanatory framework accounts for my use of the prophetic voice barely makes sense. But by telling the stories, we can inch the transformation forward.

CHAPTER 3

Why Me?
Reflections of a Wisconsin Farm Girl
Who Became a Buddhist Theologian
When She Grew Up

URING MY MANY YEARS of teaching Buddhism at a provincial Mid-western university, I have been faced with two opposing demands or questions from students. Some have wanted to be taught Buddhism, "not filtered through the lens of Western perspectives but the way an Asian Buddhist [culture unspecified] would experience it." Others have asked, unbelievingly, whether anyone born in the West could ever understand Buddhism. One student commented about a film that included scenes of some Western Buddhists doing a complicated Tibetan *sadhana*, "The film was okay except when the whites tried to meditate. You could tell that they couldn't possibly do it."

Admittedly, the first demand occurred more frequently in the early seventies, while the latter skepticism characterizes students of more recent vintage. Nevertheless, they were equally dissatisfied with my responses. The former felt that if I were a good enough teacher, I should be able to undo their (and my) immersion in Western culture and enable them to "feel" like "real Buddhists," that is, Asian Buddhists. The latter simply refused to concede when I tried to explain that the ability to understand Buddhist teachings or engage in Buddhist meditation is not encoded on one's genes, like hair color or eye shape, and that, therefore, Westerners could perfectly well learn to meditate and could understand Buddhism.

These conflicting student expectations reflect in a naive way major methodological issues about who can study religion and how much or what we can understand. Some insist on a rigid separation between theology, or constructive work, and history of religions, or descriptive work. Such demands permit a scholar either immersion in one's subject matter or distance from it, but do not accept the possibility that one could self-consciously and contemplatively move between these two stances. I maintain that the most significant contemporary religious scholarship, whether feminist or not, refuses to buy the false dichotomy between descriptive scholarship and reflective world construction. One does not have to choose between accurate scholarship about religious phenomena and passionate, personal involvement with those same phenomena. By routinely combining disclosure and autobiography with reflection and analysis, one can ride that supposed dichotomy without pretending to more universality than is appropriate.

In my own work, I am both a Buddhist feminist theologian and a historian of religions. These two sides of my being are, according to some, as incompatible as my students' opposing expectations. My history-of-religions training tried to teach me that "whites can't meditate," or at least shouldn't meditate if they wanted to be good students of religions. But I am also a Buddhist "theologian," an oxymoron I use to indicate that I do not confine my discussions of Buddhism to reports about Buddhist history and doctrine, but insist on doing reflective world construction, mainly in a feminist vein, with the explicit aim of contributing to the development of Buddhism. Therefore, I have learned to meditate, despite my white skin. Rather than choosing one identity and rejecting the other, I attend to the dialogue between them and to what this dialogue teaches me about attending to religion, whether to study, to understand, or to participate in religion. As feminists usually understand, the dialogue often plays itself out in story, in tracing the developments that lead to one's unique stance, which is presented as an offering and example to others. In this we differ from conventional scholars who try to convince us that the results of their thinking are independent of personal experience and are applicable universally.

∾ Then and Now

Nothing in my cultural background as an impoverished, highly provincial Wisconsin farm girl growing up before both feminism and awareness of pluralism should predispose me to become a Buddhist theologian, or a historian of religions, for that matter. But the cultural distance between my hayfields and the meditation caves of Tibet is even greater than the cultural distance between a girlhood spent milking cows by hand and young adulthood spent studying Sanskrit in the Swift Hall Library of the Divinity School at the University of Chicago. It is hard even for me to imagine traveling those distances, for the world of my childhood was very small and impoverished, both economically and culturally. Being familiar only with an outhouse in my early years, the first time I found myself alone with a flush toilet, at about age seven, I didn't know how to use it. My parents barely had grade school educations and did not value education. Indeed, the opposite was often true. There were no books at home, and my library privileges were taken from me because my parents didn't pay property taxes to the county that supported the nearest library. We did not receive a daily newspaper or have a telephone, and in the summer my only contact with the world was an AM radio. When I left for college, I had never been out of the state of Wisconsin and had rarely been more than seventy-five miles from home. The meditation caves of Tibet could hardly have been farther away. And yet I am sure I remember correctly that in the summer of 1959, I heard on the AM news about the Chinese takeover of Tibet and the flight of the Dalai Lama—and that I *understood* what was going on.

Many years later, I did join the meditation caves of Tibet with that spot where I grew up. I still own the twenty-by-twenty-foot log cabin in which I grew up. It has been abandoned for thirty years, except for my occasional visits, but in recent years I returned there to complete a meditation practice in the sequence I am doing as a Vajrayana Buddhist that requires total isolation. The road in to the cabin has now become a trail indiscernible to most eyes. Once my supplies are inside, I lock the gate behind me; since no one has seen me arrive, no one knows I am there or what I am doing, which is as it should be. I set up the shrines facing east, looking out a window at a tree I have watched for almost fifty years. The shrines are in the place that used to be my parents' bedroom and my meditation seat may well be over the spot on which I was conceived. Days of ceaseless effort turn into weeks. But for the fact that I am chanting in English, I could just as well be in Tibet, given what I am doing. And they say whites can't meditate!

But that is ahead of my story. I became a Buddhist theologian only after first becoming a historian of religions. In my circumstances, the leap straight from milking cows to meditating was too great to be possible. My route out of the provincialism and extreme religious dogmatism that I experienced in my early life was to study the history of religions at the University of Chicago. As I have already said, nothing that I learned as a historian of religions predisposed me or even gave me a hint of permission to become a Buddhist theologian. The opposite was true. Every message I received insisted that whites shouldn't meditate because then they wouldn't be good (read "objective") scholars. So how is it that I became a Buddhist theologian, not only against the odds that any Wisconsin farm girl would become a Buddhist theologian, but also against the explicit scholarly training that I received? If there is an explanation, I suspect it may well lie in the differences and difficulties entailed by being a woman in my field, especially at the time when I entered graduate school (1965) and experienced my formative years as an academic. I suspect that my unwillingness to buy into the "normative-descriptive" dichotomy that most of my male colleagues insist upon so adamantly has everything to do with what I experienced as a female in the field.

∿ The Education of a Feminist Historian of Religions

The chain of cause and effect that links the girl milking cows with me (whoever that might be), what remains constant in that karmic continuum, is the desire to be a good student of religions. That meant then, and still means, two things. It means that I want to understand, as much as possible, the infinite variety and wonder of religion as it has appeared in human life through time and across space. It also means that I want to understand, as much as I can, "which end is up and what makes the world go round." In other words, I want both to understand "the other" as best one can and to explore questions of meaning and truth, to engage in world construction. Furthermore, I cannot really separate the two tasks and goals. Nor can I imagine anyone caring about religion enough to go through the horrors of obtaining a Ph.D. in the field unmotivated by both visions simultaneously.

Very early on, I realized that neither task could be well performed if I confined myself to the study of religion as it had appeared in the culture of my birth. Therefore, I chose graduate work in the history of religions. At that time, my conviction that I could never be an adequate student of religions if I remained culture-bound did not involve any intention whatsoever to become a Buddhist theologian. I chose the discipline of history of religions over the discipline of theology because the impulse to study religion cross-culturally was more intense and overriding than the desire to publicly engage questions of meaning, truth, or world construction. Initially, I was willing to abide by the division of labor that stated that my task was to study *homo religiosus*, not to *be homo religiosus*. I tried to agree that any such inclinations toward being *homo religiosus* were irrelevant to scholarship and best kept private, lest one incur the dreaded label "crypto-theologian," more damning by far than "feeble-minded." In fact, my theological heart and my history-of-religions head[1] remained separated for quite some time—until I had safely completed graduate school, though they reunited before I had gotten a "good job" (one that rewards scholarly activities and allows for graduate students), a "mistake" for which I have

paid a certain price, albeit less of a price, I believe, than remaining methodologically schizophrenic would have entailed.

I believe that what eventually promoted the reunification of my
history-of-religions head with my theological heart was the formative
event of my entire scholarly life, probably of my entire life—my lonely discovery of feminist methodology early in graduate work. During the spring
of 1967, I wrote a massive paper for Mircea Eliade on "The Role of Women
in Australian and Melanesian Religion." Though I strictly listened to my
history-of-religions head in my research and analysis, that paper was motivated, at least in part, by my theological heart. I was heartsick over the
limited roles allowed to me in any culturally available Western religion.
These included both Christianity, from which I had already been excommunicated for heresy when a senior in college (I was a philosophy major
who took historical scholarship about the Bible seriously), and Judaism, to
which I had already converted as a more intellectually and spiritually wel-
coming refuge from which I could ask questions of meaning and truth. I
wanted to find out "if things were that bad elsewhere." In part, that project became so formative because Mircea Eliade liked the paper very much
and insisted that I should continue such research, both because it was
important and because I, a woman, was seeing things in the materials that
he had not seen earlier. His insistence and encouragement were literally
life-shaping.

Even more formative about that project, however, was the discovery I
began to make through doing that research. I did not really answer my
question about whether things were as bad in Australia and Melanesia as
in Christianity and Judaism. What I started to discover was even more
shattering—the methodology of history of religions was at least "that
bad"; in fact it was devastatingly worse. Women were mainly omitted
from descriptions, but when they were included, they were dealt with as
objects exterior to "mankind," to be analyzed, described, classified, and
prescribed for. Their own religious lives and meanings were never considered, never thought interesting or important. Important elements of
today's sophisticated feminist methodology were searing themselves into
my consciousness, without adequate linguistic and conceptual tools or a
community of discourse in which these insights could be grounded, in the
midst of an academic environment that, with very few exceptions, was
hostile to me because of what I was discovering.

But I did realize that I was an outsider, not only to the culture or religion that I might be studying, which is the common fate of good historians of religions, whether male or female, but also an outsider to my own
discipline in a way that was different from what any male historian of religions would ever experience. That experience reunited my theological

heart and my history-of-religions head because I had to engage in world-constructive thinking in order to survive in the world I had chosen to inhabit—the world of scholarship in the history of religions. I might have been able to consider myself an outsider to the class of "all Australians," studying them phenomenologically, but my heart would not permit me to perpetuate scholarship in which Australian women were presented as less human that Australian men. Before I could proceed with my research and analysis about the role of women anywhere, I had to reconstruct the questions and methods of the field to be able to deal with women as real human beings, not merely as objects, whether to male Australians or to Western androcentric scholars.

Through the exceedingly head-oriented task of thinking past the inadequacies of the androcentric model of humanity guiding the research process and into more adequate methods and models of humanity, I grew used to critiquing and reconstructing worldviews as a necessary part of my task. Furthermore, since, in order to be a historian of religions, I had to deconstruct and reconstruct worlds, I no longer bought the division of labor that said I, as a historian of religions, studied the worlds of others, while the task of world construction was left to theologians. That distinction simply made no sense to me, given the world construction I had to do to be able to work as a historian of religions. Many years elapsed before I became a Buddhist theologian, but the fateful steps in that direction had already been taken. Having been the primordial outsider to the androcentric world of Western scholarship, in gender, in class, and in prior education, but having found a way to let myself into the world of scholarship by circumventing its androcentrism, other worlds did not seem more inaccessible or incomprehensible. I grew used to moving between worlds, between the world of my supposed cultural origins and the many worlds that became my worlds as I became more familiar with some of them than I had even been with the world of my supposed cultural origins.

I think it is no accident that as soon as I had completed my methodological demonstration of the necessity of feminist methodology in the history of religions in my dissertation on Australian women, I began to traffic between theology and the history of religions, developing both simultaneously. My early publications in Jewish feminist theology, including "Female God Language in a Jewish Context,"[2] coincided with my early publications on feminist methodology in the history of religions and on the role of women in Australian aboriginal religion. Nor is it an accident that the traffic has moved in both directions. I have used materials from "other" worlds to deconstruct and reconstruct the world of Western theistic discourse, especially in my suggestions that Hindu goddess imagery might be inspiring to those seeking a corrective to male monotheism. Likewise, I have used prophetic methods originally at home in Western discourse to deconstruct and reconstruct Buddhism, which is now my own world as much as, or more than, Western religious discourse ever was.

If there is a surprise in this simultaneous pursuit of theology and the history of religions, as I sought to reunite my theological heart with my history-of-religions head, it is that my major "theological" work has been done as a Buddhist rather than as a monotheist. Why me? Why should a farm girl from northern Wisconsin end up as one of the first Western Buddhist feminist theologians? To narrate that story fully would take us too far from the methodological issues central to this paper. But, clearly, both my history-of-religions head and my theological heart were involved, for I would never have known enough about Buddhism to convert myself to Buddhism, but for my academic training in and teaching of that religion. Suffice it to narrate that in September 1973, I was walking across the parking lot toward my office on the kind of unbearably beautiful fall day that makes living so far north so pleasurable, thinking about how to teach the Four Noble Truths, which I didn't think I understood very well, in my upcoming Buddhism class. I was also quite miserable, for I had spent the previous year living with the grief and trauma of discovering that the young philosopher with whom I was in love had a terminal brain tumor. I had just moved to Eau Claire after my first teaching appointment, truly a "job from hell," and, though I knew no one in Eau Claire, it was already apparent to me that I was far too scholarly and far too radical religiously to find much collegiality at the University of Wisconsin, Eau Claire. So there I was, experiencing at one and the same time both intense misery at my own situation and intense appreciation for the beauty in which I was immersed. Clearly, by conventional standards, one of these experiences was "desirable" and the other was "undesirable," but their co-emergence rather than their contrast impressed itself upon me. Something suddenly snapped in my mind and I said to myself in wonder, "The Four Noble Truths are true!" This experience was not superficial or short-lived, for it motivated me to seek out Buddhist meditation disciplines and sent my life onto a course that previously I had never deemed possible or appealing.

Yet, because I am a Western, academically trained historian of religions engaging in Buddhist world construction, I have no obvious single home and few companions in my questings. I have yet to see a job ad for a Buddhist feminist theologian; those who hire people to teach Buddhist studies generally are suspicious of people who understand Buddhism well enough to engage in Buddhist world construction, while it never occurs to those interested in hiring a feminist theologian that she might do feminist theology in an Asian rather than an Abrahamic context.

Some contend that my lack of "success" is due to the fact that I have improperly mixed my media. Historians of religions should not become the "other," should not be influenced by what they study, it is often claimed, because that messes up their scholarship. Besides, according to some of my students, quoted earlier, "whites can't meditate." In other words, I shouldn't work as a Buddhist theologian because I can't become the other, however much my other students wanted me to do that for them. I would contend, however, that, while I have, indeed, mixed my media—my worlds or the symbol systems in which I discourse—nevertheless, my more basic heresy is the way in which I nave mixed my disciplines, the descriptive history of religions and world construction or theology. Furthermore, I will contend that such mixing, though unconventional, is not off base.

∽ Mixing Media: Becoming a Western Buddhist Theologian

The first question is that of mixing media, of using Buddhist constructs in my own world construction, of utilizing Indian symbols constructively in Western feminist thought, or of bringing the prophetic voice into Buddhist feminist discourse.[3] The objection made by some is that such exercises inappropriately mix symbols from different religious milieus. It is claimed that instead of confining myself to studying and reporting on the other, I use the other's symbols to think with, and that appropriation of otherness is improper, as well as impossible, since "whites can't meditate." If I want to do world construction—not the task of a historian of religions anyway— I should confine myself to my own cultural milieu, rather than borrowing from others.

In dealing with these issues, I want to appeal to certain Buddhist understandings of "otherness," which are quite different from the usual feminist understanding of "otherness," and to Buddhist understandings of the process of interaction between self and other. In certain Buddhist psychological interpretations of the process of ego formation, of the *skandha*s, we literally constitute ourselves by means of the other. That is to say, the first *skandha*, of form, of the sense of being centralized in our bodies, does not really establish ego. What begins to establish ego is the experience of "that," of "other." The second *skandha*, with its vague, preconceptual perception of otherness, confirms ego. "If that is there, I must be here," is the logic by which ego becomes more solidified. But without "that," "this" is very shaky, so that self does not emerge and evolve alone, but only in interdependence with "that." Of course, ego formation involves problems in Buddhist thought, but ego formation is also inevitable in having "precious human birth," as well as the working basis for enlightenment. The relevant point here is that "other" is not really extrinsic to "self" but the raw material that confirms and constitutes self.[4]

That we literally constitute ourselves by means of the other strikes me as an incredibly accurate description of how a mature, educated, reflective person actually becomes whoever she may be. Throughout our lives, if we continue to reflect, we become who we are by incorporating symbols and concepts into our worldview, our understanding, our manner and mode of being in the world, through the method of contemplative study. In the kind of world we live in today, no cogent argument can be made that those concepts and symbols must somehow belong to the culture into which we were born. Interpreted narrowly, such a claim would mean that I should never transcend the culture of poverty, provincialism, and religious conservatism. Interpreted more usually, such a claim would mean that as my cultural horizons expanded, they should have expanded into the world of European high culture and liberal Christianity, rather than into the world of Asian religion and Buddhism. Such a claim constitutes cultural imperialism at its worst. Being disinherited from androcentric European high culture, in terms of both gender and class, it did not in any way appear self-evident to me that that was the world I should embrace in order to constitute myself. And I would contend that the world of Asian religion and Buddhism was in no significant way more "other" to me than the world of European high culture, that it was as learnable as the world of European high culture and, to me, more interesting and valuable.

Several issues still remain, however. While we inevitably constitute ourselves by means of the other, that task can be done well or poorly, sloppily and lazily, or with class and clarity. In suggesting that it is proper for me to constitute myself through Buddhism rather than through liberal Christianity, I am not suggesting that I be excused from the hard work of learning Buddhism well, accurately, and thoroughly. The great drawback of people constituting themselves by means of any "other" is the spectacle of someone who simply doesn't understand what that other is saying sounding off about their newfound and lightly worn philosophy of life. Like any well-trained historian of religions, I am made extremely uncomfortable by blatant misinterpretations, by cheap syncretism and mindless shopping the great spiritual supermarket. We must also recognize, however, that any symbol system can be, and frequently is, thus misappropriated, not merely those of "exotic," non-Western origins.

We must return to my students once more—both those who wanted me to immerse them completely in Asian religion and those who claimed that "whites can't meditate." If one constitutes one's self by any set of symbols and concepts, how much does one distort the "original" meaning? Again, I believe the problem is the same, whether the appropriated symbols derive from one's own culture, Western culture, broadly defined, or whether they derive from an Asian culture, but the problems are perhaps more obvious when dealing with a culture that many Westerners regard as exotic. One must ask whether the symbols and concepts even have any original meaning, whether we are not in fact dealing with nothing but mirrors, interpretation influenced by interpretation, rather than an "original meaning" and distortions of that meaning by cultural outsiders.

Let us assume that both sets of students are looking at Tibetan Vajrayana Buddhism. Some of them wish to merge completely into this religious phenomenon, and others say that whites simply cannot comprehend it, by virtue of their genes. Certainly Tibetan Vajrayana Buddhism is both "other" and "exotic." It is helpful to distinguish what makes it exotic from what makes it other, for what is other may become something through which I may eventually constitute myself, while what makes it exotic will probably always remain culturally foreign and "not-me."

Though I can come to understand more about *Tibetan* Vajrayana Buddhism, I can never become a *Tibetan* Vajrayana Buddhist because my memories are of milking cows in Wisconsin, not dreys in Tibet, and no amount of study or fieldwork can ever change that basic fact. But, though white, I can meditate. Therefore, I can perfectly well constitute myself as a *Vajrayana* Buddhist, though an *American* Vajrayana Buddhist, not a *Tibetan* Vajrayana Buddhist. When talking about otherness, it is important to distinguish what is unassimilable from what is now other but could become that through which I constitute myself. It is also important to remember that symbols and concepts that originate in Asia are no more inherently other than symbols or concepts that originate in ancient Israel or Greece, in Europe, or even in America. The only thing that differentiates them is attitude toward them as "exotic" or "familiar," and the seriousness and frequency with which they are taught to the general public. Thus, my students who demanded that I teach them Asian Buddhism as Asians would experience it simply did not understand that, though one may be changed by assimilating what is "other," one cannot merge with or become that other. Likewise, my students who insisted that whites like me couldn't meditate because it's not in our heritage do not understand the extent to which each of us constitutes ourselves by assimilating that which is originally "other," whether it derives from ancient Israel, ancient Greece, or somewhere else.

Finally, it is also important, to me at least, to discuss the charge that constituting myself as a Buddhist somehow makes me incapable of doing good scholarship on Buddhism. Clearly, there is some realistic base to this fear, for many adherents of Asian religions seem to be mere apologists for their traditions when subjected to the canons of Western academic scholarship. But this tone is due, I believe, not to their adherence to an Asian religion but to their lack of training in or commitment to the standards of Western scholarship. A historian of religions who constitutes herself partially through Buddhism does not automatically sell out on the standards of Western academic scholarship any more than does one who does not so constitute herself.

Furthermore, I would contend that the best kind of historian of religions needs to be not only an outsider, in the way that someone who really pays attention to academic analysis is always an outsider to traditions, but, in some sense, also an insider to the tradition being studied. By this I do not mean that only card-carrying members of non-Western religions can do history of religions, but that a good historian of religions must somehow be able to participate in that which is being studied, must be able to "feel with," not just to know about that which is being studied. Choosing to constitute oneself by means of what one studies is not required, though it is no inherent obstacle to good scholarship. However, deep experience of and empathy with what one studies are required. To achieve those, I think it helps to be an outsider to the normative culture—to have not inherited white, male, elite, Western European culture. If one thinks about it, most great recent historians of religions have, in fact, been outsiders to the culture that defines itself as the norm.

So much for mixing media, for using Asian symbols and concepts with which to think my thought, and also for using Western values with which to reconstruct Buddhism. Though mixing media is important to my interface between studying Eastern religions and being a Western woman, I think that what constitutes my stamp is the manner in which I mix disciplines. This mixing of disciplines is also what is unconventional, for if I had merely privately constituted myself by means of Buddhism, but continued to confine my scholarly writing to the methods, techniques, and issues of history of religions only, my career might have been very different. I might have a good job by now, but I would not have reunited my theological heart with my history-of-religions head—and I would not undo that path.

∼ Mixing Disciplines: Making Judgments as a Historian of Religions

The justification for mixing disciplines is already clear from my story. No matter what anyone may claim, the history of religions is willy-nilly a world-constructive discipline in any case. This realization forced itself upon me with my discovery of the androcentric construction of the history of religions, as I had been introduced to it, and was doubly reinforced by the reactions to that discovery. It was an intensely radicalizing experience to have mentors resist adamantly the claim that history of religions could be flawed by androcentric methods and practices. Obviously, they were working out of a particular but unacknowledged and unadmitted world construction in their intense but largely unexamined commitment to the androcentric model of humanity. Ever since then, I have been convinced that, since history of religions depends on a specific way of constructing the world, we might as well be self-conscious about world construction, admit that we do it, and try to do it well.

And so how do we do it well? That project begins when we realize that to understand religion in the manner that is routine in the history of religions intellectually prohibits some methods of being religious or of understanding religions and promotes others.[5] Furthermore, historically such understandings of religion have not been appreciated by many religious authorities. Thus, positions about religion common to many historians of religions involve theological or world-constructive judgments. Having inevitably taken such a step, there is no cogent reason to advocate shyness or denial of the values and choices that guide one's work as a historian of religions. Since we are all crypto-theologians anyway, we might as well try to become theologians who know what we are saying and have something worth saying without losing our stance as historians of religions.

In my view, however, there is a definite procedure that should be followed by those who mix disciplines, by those who want to adhere to the scholarly requirements for doing history of religions but who also choose to be responsible for the inevitably value-laden character of their work. I would argue that the only responsible basis for engaging in evaluative, world-constructive judgments is a thorough grounding in the cross-cultural descriptive study of religion. Thus, one's work as a theologian is best preceded by a thorough and ongoing apprenticeship in the history of religions, because such an apprenticeship is the most effective safeguard of which I am aware against doctrinal and cultural chauvinism and imperialism. And that dimension of one's work must be guided by the conventional historian of religion's values—objectivity and empathy.

When we mix disciplines, "objectivity" is still important, but the limits of objectivity must be clearly conceded. Objectivity cannot mean that the scholar has no stance, outlook, or limits that guide and inform his work and color his conclusions. That is impossible, as we have seen already. Nor does objectivity mean that the scholar has no interest or involvement in her sub-

ject matter. Rather, objectivity involves several things about those interests and involvements. The first and central meaning of objectivity turns
on the scholar's own methodological self-awareness. She declares her
methodologies and interests clearly, rather than hiding behind a facade of
being value-free. Second, objectivity means that the scholar does strive for
what Ninian Smart has called "descriptive success,"[6] which means that
she does not function as an apologist for her point of view. To achieve
some descriptive success and not function as an apologist, she must consistently apply what I call "the unity of methodology rule." This involves
using the same standards to describe all positions and points of view,
whether or not one finds them palatable. Thus, while pure objectivity is
not possible, neutrality should be cultivated at the descriptive stage of
one's work. A scholar does not suppress negative information or highlight
positive information concerning her own evaluative or confessional stance.
We do not engage in hierarchic evaluations or rankings of religions. We do
not use one standard when talking about "us" and another when talking
about "them." We are more interested in accuracy than in promoting any
specific religion or point of view. We have a deeper loyalty to honesty than
to any specific religion or philosophy. Because we value such honesty, we
do not pretend that we can present "the objective picture," which brings us
what level of objectivity we can have. Without partisan apologetic loyalties, we state, "This is the point of view, the story out of which I work.
These are the values central to me as a scholar of religion and these are my
analyses and conclusions, derived in the following manner."

Protecting and promoting the development of genuine objectivity even
further is the most central and critical value necessary for any student of
religion—empathy. Empathy both deabsolutizes every symbol system and
creates a powerful tool for understanding any symbol system, which is
why it is so basic. To quote the definition I use in my introductory classes,
empathy involves "mentally entering into the spirit of a person or thing
and developing appreciative understanding of that phenomenon." Any
good scholar of religions should have developed the ability to speak in
many voices, or from the point of view of many different outlooks and
symbols. She should be able to speak convincingly from any of these positions and should be able to switch from one to another readily. She should
also be able to translate between the voices or positions. And in all these
vocalizations, her own voice should be quite hidden. The historian of religions who is competent in the requirement to be nonapologetic can present with great empathy points of view that she may find personally
unappealing. It is difficult to overemphasize this need to develop skill in
empathy in order to do good work in religious studies. It is also impossible

to recount the number of failures to do so; lack of empathy is probably the most serious failing in most discussions of religion and most teaching methods in the field.

Eschewing apologetics and practicing empathy are widely recognized values for historians of religions, and most practitioners of the discipline pay some attention to them. However, rather than being content with them as a sufficient orientation, I regard them as the necessary foundation for doing constructive, reflective thinking about religion relevant to the crisis situation of our world. This is the point at which one truly begins to mix disciplines, to cross forbidden lines, and to risk one's reputation as a reputable scholar. But, if I am correct, such a step only makes explicit what is already implicit—all scholars have their agendas.

The distinguishing trait of history of religions among the subdisciplines of religious studies is its insistence that the scholar be familiar with and trained in a number of religious traditions and able to engage in comparative studies. These capabilities point to the critical, constructive tasks that are especially relevant for the engaged historian of religions. They also point out the additional perspectives that such a scholar may have that the more traditional theologian, trained in only his or her own tradition, may lack.

That we live in a world of competing, conflicting, multiple religious symbol systems is news to no historian of religions. That the historian of religions has some responsibility to think constructively and ethically about that situation would be debated by many. Yet no task is more central than somehow finding, promoting, and fostering genuine pluralism in our world. To think and to act critically and constructively about such issues are not usually considered part of the job assignment of a historian of religions because dealing with competing truth claims is usually thought to be a theological task. But if we do not accept that dichotomy, what happens? Then we might recognize that no one is in a better position to say something intelligent and helpful about the problems of living with diversity and pluralism than someone whose life training involves empathy for diverse and various symbol systems. What else justifies the expenditure of time, resources, and energy spent on cross-cultural studies? That explains, at least in part, another chapter in my life, my work in interreligious dialogue and in the theory and practice of religious pluralism[7]—a task that most of my more conventional colleagues in the history of religions avoid.

Finally, I make a suggestion that goes far beyond the usual agenda of conventional history of religions, though it will not seem very radical to a feminist. An advanced task of the fully engaged historian of religions involves taking a critical stance against some values espoused in some of the symbol systems one studies. This task is far more delicate when one works as a historian of religions and an outsider than when one works only as a theologian and an insider. Even within feminist studies of religions, we have discovered how difficult it is to make fair judgments that do not derive from or promote ethnocentrism and chauvinism. The example of the bitterness that has developed between some Jewish and Christian feminists all too clearly demonstrates that it is difficult to critically assess religious systems that one does not claim as one's own.

Nevertheless, some traditional values studied by the comparative scholar do undermine the dignity of some members of that religion, such as, for example, the patriarchal values common to many religions. Some traditional values of a religion studied by the comparativist may directly contradict the vision of genuine pluralism in a global village by promoting militancy or hostility toward "the others." Someone has to name such tenets for what they are, rather than simply presenting them as neutral options in a religious smorgasbord. Not all the points of view that one can describe and understand deserve to survive. To describe the negative effects of some values in the symbol systems one studies is essential to the task of the historian of religions. If the well-trained and empathetic comparativist is too timid to speak out, who can speak with wisdom and authority? But, had I not been pushed into making judgments about the inadequacy of androcentrism and patriarchy long ago, I too might well shirk the task of making such judgments part of my job as an engaged historian of religions. A feminist cannot afford such luxury.

Obviously, it is important to avoid ethnocentrism and colonialism when one takes up this difficult critical task of making evaluations. Here again, the "unity of methodology" rule and a nonapologetic stance are necessary. And, once again, empathy enters the picture. For example, to be able to explain the worldview of patriarchy with empathy is a required assignment. To do scholarship that extends, perpetuates, legitimates, or justifies patriarchy is not acceptable. In order to meet that double assignment, one must not only describe but expose patriarchy, militarism, fundamentalism, or other deeply held but destructive traditional religious values. The great fear and danger are that many give themselves permission to engage in critical world construction without first engaging in objective and empathetic cross-cultural study. That problem is not remedied by disallowing or discouraging those who continuously pursue objective and empathetic study of the many competing worldviews from critical world construction, for the world remains quite unfinished and incomplete without their input.

CHAPTER 4

Passion and Peril:
Transgressing Boundaries as a
Feminist Buddhist Scholar-Practitioner

IN THE FALL OF 1992, the imminent publication of my *Buddhism after Patriarchy* brought to the fore a "double bind" facing scholars like myself who transgress traditional boundaries. The text offers a reconstruction of Buddhist tradition and understanding that decenters androcentric privilege. This bold move would not be appreciated, I feared, by any of the constituencies that the book might reasonably be expected to address. Some historians of religion, persuaded by the possibility of "objective" (i.e., unsituated) scholarship could dismiss the book because I am a practicing Buddhist. Eurocentric feminist scholars would consider it too "foreign" and therefore not "relevant," and might possibly also argue that reconstructing Asian patriarchy was a waste of time. Buddhists would not consider it important because it falls outside of the parameters of previously established authority. These concerns were not passing ones, nor stray fears.

Rather, this nightmare was the result of frequent experiences of the perils involved in crossing boundaries dear to those more firmly entrenched within only one of the major concerns that inform my work and my life. But for me, such boundary transgressions have always seemed unavoidable and inevitable. My scholarship as a comparative scholar of religion, my life as a feminist, and my spiritual practice as a Buddhist are not three separate aspects of my experience, sealed off from each other in separate compartments of my brain and my being, but an integrated mosaic whose different parts are always interacting with and affecting each other. In fact, it is not even accurate to limit my academic concerns to comparative scholarship, nor my major life issue to feminism, nor my spiritual practice to Buddhism. Rather, all these concerns always intersect and interpenetrate, so that scholarship, core issues, and spiritual practice form a seamless web; I cannot imagine it to be otherwise.

I cannot understand people who idealize scholarship as a realm set apart, people whose spiritual life and politics do not influence their scholarship. Nor do I understand well people who are involved in a spiritual discipline but do not bring it to bear upon urgent social and political issues, such as those brought up by feminism. Finally, I cannot separate the clarity and compelling urgency of my feminist vision from what I want to see actualized in academia and in my religious community. Sometimes I wonder if my conviction that it makes no sense to separate out one's ultimate concerns into separate pursuits is due to my being a Caucasian female in a culture in which women of my race are typically more interested in a network of integrated relationships, while Caucasian men are more interested in autonomy and control, having greater freedom to think of their lives as a series of separate compartments. I do not know if such is the case, but I do know that I regard weaving scholarship, spirituality, and politics into a seamless garment as infinitely more mature and healthy psychologically, emotionally, and spiritually than is its alternative. Thus, it was inevitable that my book would integrate rather than fragment my life concerns. And, in the long run, taking the chance involved in writing such an unconventional book was more compelling to me than the potential perils inherent in so many boundary crossings.

∼ The Generating Passions

Buddhism after Patriarchy was written much more as a love child than as a career-building enterprise, in keeping with the ethic of following my heart and the lifestyle of risk taking that have always guided my choices. From my perspective, the book cannot be understood apart from the passions that led me to something so superficially surprising, given my origins. Looking at my life as a factual narrative, it might well seem preposterous for a Wisconsin farm girl to write Buddhist feminist theology, especially on the immodest scale of *Buddhism after Patriarchy*. From my internal vantage point, it feels like a natural unfolding, even though even I sometimes shake my head in disbelief that I could have made such a journey in a few short years.

The passions that led to writing *Buddhism after Patriarchy* began with sheer love of reading and thinking in a culture that respected and encouraged neither, especially in girls. Inadequate as were the schools I attended, with no programs for gifted students, extremely limited libraries, and few imaginative teachers, they were the key out of a life characterized by prejudice, intolerance, narrow-mindedness, and anti-intellectualism on the part of parents and religious authorities. Had I not been able to use that key to get out, I would probably still be living in poverty milking cows and indoctrinating yet another generation the way I was indoctrinated. But I found extreme pleasure and freedom in thinking about ultimate questions and in reading (when I could, which was infrequently); therefore I envisioned the ideal life as dedicated to these activities despite a mother who ridiculed me for thinking I could make a living reading books and a pastor who regarded my questioning spirit as evil. I did not especially envision escaping poverty to lead a middle-class existence, but escaping ignorance and prejudice to live a life of reflection and contemplation based on learning. Thus, I took a philosophy major followed by graduate work in the history of religions as an odd but straight path from milking cows to writing Buddhist feminist theology.

My conscious life plan certainly never included deliberately becoming a Buddhist. It obviously was not a good professional move in terms of its effects on my career as a feminist and as a historian of religions. Let me just say that while no rational cause-and-effect explanation makes much sense, being Buddhist feels to me like the most natural unfolding possible. If there are such things as rebirth and karma, they offer as cogent an explanation as any for the sense of fit, of being home, that has been my strong gut feeling about my Buddhist identity.

However, that straight path between milking cows and writing Buddhist feminist theology includes not only the longing *for* the life of contemplation but also very strong longings *against* certain things that, though I successfully resisted their imprinting, were forcefully inculcated into me in my early life. These rebellious visions are also directly in the chain of cause and effect leading to my being a feminist and a historian of religions.

Early on, I saw that the female gender role in mid-America in the mid-fifties was a dead end that would curtail any attempt to live a life of contemplation and creative activity. I was horrified by the fate that would be mine unless I could resist that role, and I made avoiding it one of my foremost goals, an isolating desire before the second wave of feminism brought home the damaging and destructive character of gender roles in patriarchal culture. Very early on, I also developed an antipathy toward the kind of religious prejudice, chauvinism, exclusivism, and absolutism into which I had been indoctrinated. I deliberately chose a life of studying and teaching the comparative study of religion as an antidote to that mind-set and as a way to do something to undercut religious prejudice and hatred.

In part, then, the underlying formula that leads to *Buddhism after Patriarchy* consists of passion to contemplate reality and to live a useful life, mingled with conviction that there had to be a more sane and humane way to live than the prison of gender roles in patriarchal society. This passion and this conviction are grounded in the vision of religion as a compassionate, peace-promoting, life-affirming enterprise, not a repressive, ideological straitjacket. But the rest of the formula is even harder to speak of openly in an academic context because such passion is so frowned upon. Ultimately, I wrote *Buddhism after Patriarchy* because it was the most useful and helpful thing I could imagine ever doing in my life. It is not only a love child but what I can do to try to fulfill my bodhisattva vows, what I can do to alleviate the suffering inherent in imprisonment in patriarchy and gender roles. I have often thought of it as an offering, born of my own suffering, to try to chip away at *samsara*, at pain-laced conventional life. And it is the way that I can live out the Confucian ideal of the sage who does what is right in any case at all costs, even if it is not profitable, as well as my version of Hindu *karma yoga*, the discipline of working for the rightness of the task rather than the rewards. It is what prophetic message I have to offer.

Such passion is not well received in academic circles; it is met with embarrassed silence. Academics rarely talk about life-and-death issues that matter ultimately and that change people's lives. But for me, very early in my life, education was the antidote to a narrow-minded, dead-end lifestyle, and that has never changed in my vision of what academics should do in the classroom and in their publications.

∿ Perils of the Academic Life

College teaching is one obvious career choice for financial support of a life of contemplation, questioning, reading, and writing. But academia is actually a relatively conservative, conventional place. It is easy to go too far, as anyone who crosses boundaries or strays from academic fashions finds out. Moreover, it is also still, in many many ways, dominated by the values of androcentric culture, which makes academia a perilous and difficult environment for women, apart from the dangers inherent in transgressing boundaries.

In my generation, simply being a female academic, especially in the field of religious studies, was the first serious boundary transgression. My most valued college mentor, a woman professor of English pleaded with me to enter a field like English, where a woman might have some chance of survival, rather than religious studies, in which she felt women had no chance of survival. Given the statistics in the mid-sixties when I entered graduate school, she was right. The year that I entered the Divinity School

of the University of Chicago (1965), the number of women students dou-
bled, from six to twelve among a student body of over four hundred; the
all-male faculty worried to us about how all these women would change
the Divinity School and what could possibly be done with so many women.
My college mentor, however, was not as altogether discouraging as another
well-meaning mentor who tried to dissuade me from thinking I might win
a Woodrow Wilson Fellowship. When I was a college senior with an outstanding record, he assured me that I could not hope to win such a fellowship: "You've got to understand that they simply can't give that kind of
fellowship to you. You're an attractive woman; you'll get married and
waste it." (I did receive a Woodrow Wilson Fellowship, nevertheless.) His
projections were matched by the graduate school dean, who said to me
after I became engaged, "I assume you'll be dropping out now," and abandoned his mentoring role when I did not. These are not unique experiences, to which numerous publications on women in academic life amply
attest.[1] These experiences, however, do illustrate the ubiquity of nonaca-
demic criteria in determining *who* gets credentialed and thus who may be
recognized as an authoritative speaker in our culture.

Far worse were the attitudes attendant upon my entering the job mar-
ket. A conversation I had with a dean of students from my graduate institution that occurred shortly after I had taken my obscure, marginal
position at the University of Wisconsin in Eau Claire is quite revealing. At
the time, I was finishing the first religious studies dissertation in North
America to use feminist methods, and, in all probability, the first in the
world; my dissertation exposed the presence and limitations of androcentrism in the history of religions. The dean of students was telling me that
he had high hopes of placing a male student in a "good" position because
"he really deserves such a position. His dissertation contains a major new
insight into the theology of H. Richard Niebuhr." I was dumbstruck;
despite the originality of my dissertation, I had not been deemed worthy
of a "good position." In retrospect, however, this experience reinforces my
assessment of the academy as a profoundly conservative site, far more
comfortable with little additions to conventional and possibly outmoded
frameworks than with major shifts of perspective requiring whole new
ways of looking at the world and doing our scholarly work. That I am a
woman and that my dissertation was feminist simply added to the threat.

Nor are the practical effects of such perils minimal. I have spent my
entire career teaching at an institution where I will never have a single
graduate student, an institution where I cannot even assign articles I have
written that are widely used at other colleges and universities, because the
level of courses I am restricted to teaching is too elementary. I have long
mused that if I had done work less threatening to the male establishment,

my career would probably have been much more full of academic possibility and reward. It is hard not to draw the conclusion that in academia, sheer quality and creativity count for relatively little. Those who pursue conventional subject matters following conventional methodologies are much more likely to be superficially successful than those who challenge preexisting boundaries of scholarly thought. This is not merely a personal issue and complaint. Many feminist scholars have been similarly treated, with the net effect that the next generation of professors of religious studies is not being trained in the single most innovative and important intellectual development in our field in our lifetimes because very few of the current leaders of feminist scholarship in religion are employed by Ph.D.-granting institutions.

Other perils come with a position in an institution such as the one at which I teach. The lack of collegiality and subtle exclusion that go with being the only woman in a department of older married men for most of the twenty-five years I spent at Eau Claire took a high toll. When I arrived at Eau Claire, thirty and single, I found myself in an older, more conservative, mainly married, mainly male faculty. I cannot put into words how difficult it was until retirements in the last seven or eight years brought women to other departments on campus. Almost immediately upon moving into my office, I sensed male camaraderie and male bonding, from which I was excluded, occurring up and down the halls. It culminated one day when, after particularly offensive banter, one of my department members exclaimed, "Poor Rita! You live in a male locker room."

Even more harmful has been the lack of collegial conversation. For all the difficulties of graduate school, there were always satisfying and stimulating conversations about matters of mutual professional interest, an experience that continues at the many conferences I attend. I had always assumed that such collegial interactions would be a lifelong bonus of being an academic, but these are absent in the hallways in which our department is located. Instead, football and family, golf and gambling, dominate the conversations, and backslapping horseplay the interactions. Nor is there much emotional support during difficult times, or, for that matter, much congratulation and rejoicing over professional triumphs. Usually I do not even tell department members about a new publication or some other professional achievement because I have been told once too often that such behavior constitutes bragging. It is not an exaggeration to say that I have often been punished for my academic achievements, which are not valued by most of my colleagues. The only thing that has eased the situation is the recent development of a support network among other women who are also active scholars and researchers. One of the purposes of this group is to celebrate one another's achievements. Among them, I am something of a role model who has proved that it is possible to maintain one's scholarly activity despite little support, emotional or financial, for research and publication.[2] (To be fair to my institution, I must also report that very recently, since the publication of *Buddhism after Patriarchy*, I have received more financial support for research and publication than earlier, though the level of emotional support is still very low.)

Other perils of the academic life stem from the wrong kind of collegial interchange. Scholarship sometimes takes on the aura of competitive sports. Withering debate, confrontative responses, and sarcastically critical deconstruction of any work that tries to fathom the larger picture are the norm, and following this norm brings prestige to the nastiest critic. This style of academic discourse is often difficult for women for several reasons, including prior socialization.[3]

Dislike of this conventionally male style of academic discourse has led many women to seek out alternative spaces and forums for presenting our hard-won, boundary-transgressing insights. In my case, all the academic groups to which I have devoted considerable organizational efforts and loyalties have been alternative forums in which competitive academic gamesmanship was not the norm. Some years ago, the Women and Religion section of the American Academy of Religion was such a forum, in which many highly innovative early papers on feminist method and theory in religious studies were presented in an environment where people were encouraged rather than discouraged from such efforts. Likewise, the world of Buddhist–Christian dialogue has largely been a safe and supportive environment, peopled by thinkers more interested in fostering insight and understanding than in scoring points. Buddhist–Christian dialogue has the added advantage of being a forum in which both men and women participate, which I prefer for feminist reasons. (In the long run, feminism is about women and men sharing and cooperating equitably, not about separatism.)

I must also note with irony, however, that both academic enterprises— feminist scholarship and Buddhist–Christian dialogue—are widely criticized as not being genuinely scholarly. Part of this evaluation results from the fact that those who take part in them care about the issues and have some existential involvement in them, which causes some to recoil in horror. To them, advocacy is an activity that is incompatible with scholarship, although clearly it is not, since scholars advance points of view all the time. It is lamentable that an academic enterprise that asks serious and probably unanswerable questions about fundamental issues is dismissed as "unscholarly," while arcane historical or philological research into data that are safely contained within conventional boundaries gains its author a scholarly reputation. It is also a mistake to assume that those conventional data gatherers are uninvolved in the worldview within which they work. Rather, because they are not methodologically introspective, they mistake their specific methodology and worldview for a universal and necessary standpoint.[4]

∿ Allegiances and Boundary Crossings

In my pre-publication nightmare, I dreaded the effects of the numerous boundary crossings involved in working simultaneously with my three major allegiances—the cross-cultural comparative study of religions that I had been taught as the history of religions at the University of Chicago, the feminism I had discovered on my own and to my peril as a graduate student, and the Buddhism that had unexpectedly complicated my allegiance to both the history of religions and to feminism, even as it clarified all aspects of my life and my work. By combining these three perspectives in *Buddhism after Patriarchy*, I violated boundaries sacred to each perspective and developed each in ways that were heretical to mainstream discourse within that perspective. That is why I imagined that others more firmly entrenched within these perspectives would dismiss my work and that it would "fall through the cracks," as so often happens to scholars whose work does not fit into any of the established academic niches or pastures.

Before I explore these boundaries and their transgressions in more detail, I want to relate that I was somewhat amused when I noticed, much later, that worries about offending Buddhalogists had not entered my nightmare, even in the slightest. Given the vividness of my nightmare, I am grateful that it did not occur to me to include Buddhalogists in it! But why not? That Buddhalogists had not haunted my nightmare is probably due to the fact that I feel no allegiance to that particular academic camp and therefore I was not so worried about their responses.

After all, I do not follow their methods of detailed text study, translation, and historical reconstruction, nor do I agree with their claims that these are the only or the privileged means to understand Buddhism. Furthermore, I reject completely the implicit premise of the most conservative wing of Buddhalogy—the claim that non-Buddhist scholars are those best prepared to understand Buddhism because of their distance and unbiased "objectivity." While I believe that non-Buddhist Buddhalogists can render important services to the study of Buddhism, I reject out of hand the claim that Buddhists can't really do accurate or worthy scholarship about Buddhism because of their personal involvement in the tradition.

In the context of scholarship on Christianity or Judaism, many of the most reputable scholars also have some involvement with the tradition. Furthermore, in Native American studies, one is almost required to be an insider to be considered capable of doing accurate scholarly work. Current scholarly sensitivities to questions of appropriation and situated knowledge suggest that claims of "objectivity" via noninvolvement in any particular tradition are at best simplistic. Finally, I do not think that Buddhalogists, especially non-Buddhist Buddhalogists, are well prepared to evaluate what I tried to do in *Buddhism after Patriarchy*, because what I tried to do is existentially irrelevant to them. Their potential negative evaluations, in fact, would seem to amount to nothing more than horror that a Western woman would speak as a Buddhist insider or imperialistic claims that no scholar should approach Buddhism with the questions and concerns that were mine. Sometimes I want to ask such purists *what* they would study if everyone had always observed their rules of being outsiders interested only in historical scholarship, philology, and translation!

One who crosses boundaries between allegiances is both an insider and outsider, and therefore, in some senses, neither an outsider nor and insider, which is why such activity can be perilous. Because one has crossed a boundary, one is no longer an insider in the same way as are those who feel no urge to roam. Those who feel no urge to roam often upbraid the one who crosses boundaries, even though that one roams out of loyalty rather than disloyalty to the allegiance in question. But the roamer also feels that compatriots who stay contentedly within the fold have missed something vital. Therefore, transgressing boundaries creates a dissonance, both in terms of disapproval coming from one's colleagues and in terms of not feeling fully on the same wave length with one's colleagues.

As someone who has often transgressed boundaries, I regard it not as a task that anyone would willingly seek out but as something choiceless, as something that had to be done to answer the questions I was asking. Pursuing these questions has meant that I was often at variance with current academic fashions and unique in my choices of scholarly methods and subject matter. While this has meant that my work has been truly original, it has also meant that I often lacked the scholarly community available to those more comfortable with following the broken track.

～ Allegiances and Boundary Crossings
   in the Comparative Study of Religion

Of all my allegiances, dedication to comparative study in religion is the most basic. In my view, nothing is more helpful to an intelligent understanding and practice of religion than comparative knowledge. One might say that I am a "true believer" in Max Muller's famous paraphrase, "To know one religion is to know none." In my view, a key problem with the work of other feminist scholars of religion and other Buddhists is their insufficient attention to comparative methods. This is true even of the Women and Religion section of the American Academy of Religion, of which I was section chair for five years, where few papers on non-Christian or comparative topics are ever read. I am just as frustrated that many Caucasian Buddhists, reasonably sophisticated in their assessments of certain elements of Christian tradition that are woefully out of date, will believe anything as long as it is said by a Tibetan lama. Such double standards have no place in mature religious practice or religious studies scholarship.

Nevertheless, I also transgress boundaries sacred to the history of religions, and have done so almost from the beginning. When I was just starting out as a comparative scholar, there was a strong preference in the field for translators *cum* area studies specialists. I pursued the large normative and philosophical questions that first led me into the academic study of religion. For years, my "theological" (or evaluative and constructive) work, the way in which I use materials studied as a comparative scholar in constructing a point of view, and the way in which I evaluate certain aspects of the religions I study, especially Buddhism, have been dismissed as "inappropriate" by some scholars. Nor is this heresy really due to my being a Buddhist, though that identity has intensified my tendency to engage in constructive or "theological" work.

Because I became a feminist before I began to publish, I was primed to do feminist constructive work drawing on my expertise as a historian of religions and did so in early publications before I became a Buddhist.[5] My early experiences as a feminist led me to many of the methodological claims that make me such a heretic among historians of religion. I question completely the conventional division of labor between "religious studies" and "theology" because I learned very early that supposedly neutral and objective scholars of religion, who claimed to be different from "theologians," with their personal investments in their subject matter, were in fact fully invested in maintaining a self-serving androcentrism, which dictated what data they saw and how they interpreted them. Furthermore, their hostility to feminist methodological criticism showed just how invested they truly were. That discovery cured me, once and for all, of the fiction that scholars can approach their subject matter with a value-free or neutral methodology and convinced me that it is impossible to avoid evaluation and a constructive element in one's discussions of religious studies. Therefore, I have long argued that religious studies scholars need not try to be "neutral," whatever that might be, but instead should be extremely self-conscious and self-reflective about their own methodological choices and interpretive strategies. With many other feminists, I argue for the need to contextualize one's conclusions within one's own history and experience, thereby avoiding the false universalism of a supposedly "neutral" standpoint that only ignores the effects of one's gender, class, race, culture, or sexual orientation on one's scholarship.[6] In addition to their naïveté, I find scholars' claims about their own neutrality arrogant, self-centered, and egotistical in the extreme.

∽ Allegiances and Boundary Crossings as a Feminist

My work has been more fully received in the area of feminist studies in religion than in the history of religions, in part because I was working on the issues so early and in part because I am a less heretical feminist than historian of religions. I have been intrigued and pleased to discover that some Christian feminist theologians are using *Buddhism after Patriarchy* in their theology classes, not to teach Buddhism but to teach feminist method in theology. They report great success with their students, and I have received a few invitations to lecture at theological seminaries that are serious about feminist method in theology. Nevertheless, my cross-cultural and comparative orientation and my primary interests in non-Western religions have meant that I am among a distinct minority in feminist studies in religion. It appears that a number of my feminist colleagues feel that it is just "too much bother" to do the required apprenticeship in an unfamiliar religion, a position I believe limits their scholarly horizons drastically. In my recently published *Feminism and Religion: An Introduction*, I evaluated the intensely Western focus of most feminist theology and scholarship in religion as the weak link in that enterprise. I also observed that many of the efforts to diversify feminist studies in religion and to include previously marginalized perspectives have been rather inadequate, since the major effort has been to include more diversity of race, class, culture, and sexual orientation *within* Christianity, rather than to include more *religious diversity*.

I suspect that my work falls "between the cracks" precisely because of this particular boundary transgression away from conventional feminism. As a feminist, I cannot avoid constructive and evaluative discussion of the religions I study. Thus, I write, especially about Buddhism, in an evaluative and constructive way. But those hiring someone to teach Buddhism do not usually want to hire someone who understands Buddhism well enough to do Buddhist "theology" or world construction. A theology position might appear to be more appropriate, but I have strayed outside the usual boundaries of "relevant" religious traditions for feminist theology. Those who hire feminist theologians always hire people who comment on a major Western tradition; they do not consider seriously that their resident feminist might theologize out of an Asian rather than an Abrahamic tradition. Feminists whose religious affiliations and whose work, no matter how radical, are closest to the interests of the Eurocentric Christian mainstream of the discipline do best in securing and retaining positions. Feminists who speak out of and for Jewish, wiccan, post-Christian, or Buddhist positions do not have very successful employment track records, which indicates how perilous it is to be the "wrong" kind of religious feminist.

~ Allegiances and Boundary Crossings as a Buddhist

Clearly, my identity as a Buddhist has complicated my allegiances to both comparative religious studies and feminism. If I were only a feminist historian of religions, at least I would not have to deal so directly with being an "insider"—a position taboo to most historians of religion. As a Buddhist, I cannot avoid the complications of being an insider in a field that claims to prefer outsiders.[7] Furthermore, it is heterodox enough to bring a constructive and critical stance such as feminism to the history of religions and to claim that religious studies is a world-constructive discipline, which I do because of what I experienced as a feminist in that field. But to be a *Buddhist* feminist "theologian" and scholar of religious studies is triply complicated.

Feminists do not have problems with someone being an "insider"; in fact, feminists tend to privilege information from "insiders," rightly in my view. But, as indicated above, I'm the wrong kind of insider—a white Buddhist. In fact, once in a while, a young Caucasian feminist goes so far as to suggest that a white woman shouldn't or can't speak as a Buddhist, claiming that to do so is appropriation. But since Buddhism is not a culturally based religion, this accusation is not very serious. Others don't want a Westerner doing theology for an Asian tradition, but Buddhism is not a tradition limited to Asia. I agree that *Asians* must do *Asian* Buddhist feminist criticism and analysis, but I would suggest that Western Buddhist feminist analysis and criticism might be insightful and useful to those doing such work. To those who want to forbid Westerners or whites to speak *as* Buddhists and to do constructive Buddhist thought because of our ethnic or cultural limitations, I reply that then the reverse must also be true; blacks or Asians can't do Christian theology because historically

Christianity is not their native tradition. Most people recoil swiftly from such an assertion because of its obvious racism; its reverse should therefore be seen as equally problematic.

The more conventional the historian of religions, however, the more skeptical she will be of "insiders," especially if they are "insiders" but not "natives." Not able to see her own perspective as a *perspective* rather than objectivity, she often dismisses the non-native insider as not understanding the difference between scholarship and advocacy, as someone incapable of genuine scholarship. I make a reverse claim—that some aspects of some religious traditions *cannot* be adequately understood unless one has access to the "insider" point of view. This claim irritates the religious studies scholar who believes that objectivity is possible and desirable. But certainly regarding the tradition about which I write most directly— Vajrayana Buddhism—a claim that one must have access to "insider" information is more than accurate. Like any tradition that emphasizes initiation and does not "publish the password," Vajrayana Buddhism studied only from the "outside" is limited because critical aspects of the tradition are simply inaccessible to the uninitiated outsider-scholar. Once I realized this fact because of my initiation into a tradition to which I had become a genuine insider, I vowed never to do more research on the tradition about which I had done my doctoral work—aboriginal Australia. I came to the conclusion that initiation is so central to aboriginal Australian religious practices that all I could do as an outsider was to participate in European debates about how to interpret what outsiders could see. I no longer had any interest in that enterprise, despite my passion to correct the androcentric interpretations Europeans had imposed on these materials.

But what impact does my being a feminist and a religious studies scholar have on my allegiance to Buddhism? Again, a triple allegiance makes for complications, for a simultaneous stance as heretic and adherent, insider and outsider. Initially many colleagues, whether feminist or Buddhist, predicted that feminism and Buddhism would prove to be incompatible. My feminist colleagues thought I had sold out when I became involved in yet another religion they saw as hopelessly patriarchal; worse, it was a form of patriarchy I had *chosen*, rather than one I had *inherited*. My Buddhist friends assured me that once I became a more seasoned Buddhist practitioner, I would lose all interest in any cause and become detached, seeing feminism as an attachment to be shunned. As I have become a leading spokesperson for Buddhist feminism, my feminist colleagues have lost their initial fears. But what about the Western Buddhist establishment, especially Shambhala, the Buddhist organization of which I am a member? There is no question that I feel the usual feminist frustration with "institutional drag," that I feel there is no excuse for moving so slowly on some very basic issues, like gender-neutral language in English-language chants and texts and more female imagery in the main meditation halls. Probably I feel the old adage that a prophet is without honor in her own country more keenly in connection with Buddhism than in connection with any other of my multiple allegiances. Such experiences sadden me, but they don't anger me too much. Being part of the particular religious lineage that I am part of is choiceless, but I am a loyal critic rather than a true believer and will continue to do what I can to move the establishment. In the wider Buddhist world, I feel that my work is simply part of the sea change that must happen to all major religions if they are to continue to have any relevance to humanity.

Being a scholar of religions also makes for some discomfort with aspects of the Buddhist establishment. As a scholar, I cannot take seriously the kind of religious declarations that I find so preposterous in the context of any other religion simply because they are made by someone in my religion instead. I expect some basic sophistication regarding religion in general from American Buddhist leaders. I expect them to know how religions work, and I expect them not to claim that Buddhism is any more free of human limitations than any other religion. I expect them to be skeptical of Buddhist claims to radically superior insight or relevance, of Buddhist claims to supernatural intervention in human politics and history, and to Buddhist miracle stories. I am disappointed when they recommend such beliefs about Buddhism to their followers. Therefore, in my view, some of the political controversies about apparent corruption in high places that are now tearing apart some Western Buddhist communities have a largely unrecognized positive side effect. These all-too-human corruptions and controversies demonstrate that Buddhism is a religion like any other religion, with the same pitfalls and problems.

∼ Peril in Buddhist and Feminist Perspective

Some might say that the kind of edge provided by the danger involved in transgressing boundaries is actually of long-term benefit because adversity and struggle make one tough. Such opinions are rather commonplace in our culture. However, as a Buddhist, I really don't see it that way. In my opinion, the popular notion that adversity and lack of emotional support are good for one comes out of the Western view of humanity, with its notions of original sin and its mistrust of the human and natural worlds. Slowly, Mahayana Buddhism has nurtured in me another sense of how things work. People who prosper with adversity do so not because of but in spite of adversity. Because people are basically good at the core and endowed with Buddha nature; they do not need to be whipped into shape before they are willing to give their best efforts to living and to helping others. They need a safe, supportive, nurturing environment in which feedback is accurate but not combative. It is true that I have accomplished a great deal. But what would be the story if I had had more collegiality, some graduate students, more financial and emotional support for writing, and, most important of all, *a lot less loneliness?* Given the extent of my work without such supports, why would one not suppose that a more collegial, emotionally supportive environment, and a teaching position with more appreciation for research and writing would have led to more?

But the bottom line is my appreciation for the life I have been able to lead. On some levels, I am very successful; I make an adequate living doing work that I love and I am well respected and well known. Things could be much worse. I did manage to avoid many, though not all, of the horrors of the female gender role in a patriarchal society, and I have managed to spend my life pursuing and fulfilling my vision and my dream. When I look back at how my efforts have helped the world, I do not have to wonder if I have wasted my life; I could die tonight feeling that I haven't squandered my life. I would not make other choices if I had it to do over again, but I would change responses to academic passion and creativity if I could, making them less perilous for the scholar whose questions move her beyond the beaten track of easy conventionality.

PART 2

Soaring and Settling: Buddhism Engaged in Contemporary Social Issues

Introduction: Meditation, Impermanence, and Social Change

THE SEVEN ESSAYS IN THIS SECTION all deal with contemporary social issues from a Buddhist point of view nurtured by my many years of Buddhist meditation and ongoing contemplation of basic Buddhist teachings. A dual perspective informs all these essays. On the one hand, I believe that Buddhists need to think about contemporary issues in Buddhist terms and to offer the wisdom of the Buddhist tradition to the cause of helping solve our current dilemmas much more frequently than they do. Hence, the term "engaged" in this section's title, as I link myself with the emerging international movement of Engaged Buddhists. On the other hand, I believe that Buddhism has unique wisdom to offer the contemporary world, some pieces missing from the puzzle of nonaggressive social action. Hence, the terms "meditation" and "impermanence" in the title of the introduction to this section.

Like Engaged Buddhists, I see Buddhism as, among other things, a potent force for social criticism and social change, not only as a path for developing personal serenity. In fact, I would argue that Buddhism itself teaches that personal serenity should lead to social criticism, to concern for how to change the world for the better, though that it is not a traditional way of talking about Mahayana Buddhism and the bodhisattva path. Thus, most of these articles are highly critical of the status quo and suggest somewhat radical changes to which many would object. However, unlike typical offerings from Engaged Buddhists to date, many of these essays deal with issues that are social and psychological rather than political and economic—family, friendship, relationships, community issues, work habits that are negative to personal well-being. Even the essays that deal with more directly political and economic issues, such as population,

51

consumerism, and ecology, delve deeply into the personal transformations that must be part of the solution to these problems.

In fact, not only the Engaged Buddhist but social commentators of other persuasions might balk at the idea that the articles in this section are primarily about social issues. The titles and the content might strike some as more personal than social, and every article talks in depth about personal issues, attitudes, and opinions and recommends significant and unconventional changes in outlook on some topics that many would consider intensely personal—reproduction, friendship, relationship choices. . . . But, as feminists said long ago, "The personal is political." Seemingly private individual "choices" (which often are much more the result of social manipulation than most like to admit) add up to a healthy society, or a sick society, or a sexist society, or an egalitarian society. If we are social critics, if we want to encourage social change out of commitment to Buddhist vows of compassion for all sentient beings (or other deeply held ethical commitments), where do we start but with individual "private" attitudes and the internal personal transformations that defuse loneliness, consumerism, pro-natalism, and the myriad of personal issues that color the fabric of society, so often so negatively. Furthermore, as is suggested in several of these chapters, deep personal transformation of problematic personal patterns is one of Buddhism's strengths. So when we Buddhists address the sufferings of society and seek some methods to alleviate them, why would we not include first our most highly developed resources? My emphasis on the centrality of inner, individual transformation, however, should not be misconstrued to mean that I am suggesting that individual will power is sufficient or that individuals can "just say no" to system-wide social pressures and all will be well. Systemic injustice and oppression are very real and too powerful for most individuals to combat by themselves; system-wide changes are necessary. What I am suggesting is that working for systemic change, by itself, will not be sufficient either. Social critics need to pay more attention to ways to effect deep personal transformation, including one of the most effective techniques for personal change—spiritual disciplines.

The lack of such emphases in the Engaged Buddhist movement is unfortunate in my view, for I believe it limits the effectiveness of the Engaged Buddhist movement. I suspect that my different emphases owe much to the way in which feminism, which is often overlooked and ignored by Engaged Buddhists, informs all my thinking. Feminism is not in the foreground of these essays, but its values and its vision of life free from "the prison of gender roles" for both women and men are always crucial to my conclusions and suggestions. I hope that the model that I have presented in these chapters of how feminism can inform social criticism without dominating the discourse becomes more characteristic of Engaged Buddhist social criticism, indeed social criticism in general, in the future.

But I also believe that Buddhism brings some things to social concern that I have not found elsewhere. Foremost among them is the fruition of long-term meditation—some measure of detachment and tranquillity. For, as I demonstrated in the lead essay of this collection, "The Female Body and Precious Human Birth: An Essay on Anger and Meditation," growing detachment translates not into apathy but into nonaggressive concern and action, into a less fixated and less ideological but more effective presence. Therefore, many of the essays in this section include considerable discussion of meditation practice, beginning with the first essay, "Soaring and Settling," which also provides the book's title. The meditation instruction of "touch and go" discussed in that essay is, in my view, integral to negotiating complex and difficult issues. The perspective articulated in that essay is the background of every chapter and every issue discussed in this book. I also emphasize meditation practice because of its power to effect inner personal transformation. Let me say again that I do not see how the social changes necessary to reverse current ecologically devastating habits will occur without profound inner personal transformation, individual by individual. Because the habits fueled by consumerism and pro-natalism are not easily amenable to legislation, I have emphasized contemplative and meditative practices especially in the articles dealing with environmental issues. I have also emphasized meditation practices because even individuals who rationally see a need for change in personal behaviors may have difficulty implementing such changes because of the force of habitual patterns of desire and attachment. Meditation and contemplation often prove quite effective in promoting such changes.

Another gift Buddhism brings to the arena of social concerns are profound teachings on impermanence and finitude. Hence, I choose to pair "impermanence" with "meditation" as key topics for introducing this section on "Buddhism Engaged in Contemporary Social Issues." Nothing is more key or more basic to the Buddhist worldview than the observation that ceaseless, universal impermanence, from which nothing is exempt, is the bottom line. The implications of this teaching, especially for ecological issues, are most clearly spelled out in the final chapter of this section, which is a contemplation on death and grieving. But the reality of ceaseless change also provides another useful perspective for social critics. Since change is inevitable, resisting change in the name of "tradition" and "traditional values," which are often code words for preserving an oppressive, extravagant, or wasteful status quo, is rather pointless. Rather, it makes more sense to ascertain which changes are compassionately useful and which would be counterproductive, to "ride the winds of change," rather than be driven about by them. Since changes are required in patterns of work, family life, and the politics of relationship in order to diminish the alienation and loneliness that so often fuel negative social practices, and since people so often resist changes precisely in these so-called personal areas, contemplating the reality of ceaseless change could be a powerful tool. Ceaseless change, however, can be frightening, can be something people resist mightily unless we can "find our ease in impermanence"—to quote the phrase that governs much of the first and the last chapters of this section. And how do we find our ease in impermanence? We are led once again to the topic of meditation, the place of spiritual discipline in social action and social change. For I do not believe there are any genuinely Buddhist perspectives on social issues that do not always refer to spiritual discipline and inner transformation as being at the heart of the matter.

All of these articles were written after I had finished my first major piece of Buddhist social commentary, *Buddhism after Patriarchy*. Most of them were responses to invitations I received as a result of that book. Through such feminist Buddhist reconstructions, people became more aware that Buddhism is a contemporary thought system that could comment on and be changed by current events, not just a set of classical texts to be exegeted by Buddhalogists or a foreign point of view inaccessible to Westerners. I hope (insofar as a Buddhist is permitted to hope) that Westerners will become much more aware of that living Buddhism in the next years and decades. I am grateful for the encouragement to continue to bring the wisdom of the Buddhist tradition to bear upon issues that are so urgent to survival and well-being at the turn of the century. I am also grateful for the opportunity to collect and revise these articles for publication together, since previously they were scattered in a many different publications and unlikely to be viewed as parts of a larger whole. I hope that this example will demonstrate the need for ongoing, thoroughgoing, and systematic Buddhist social commentary on current issues. I hope that other Buddhists will become more willing to use Buddhism as a resource with which to think about contemporary issues and that non-Buddhists come to expect thoughtful and challenging analyses of these same issues from Buddhists.

CHAPTER 5

Soaring and Settling:
Riding the Winds of Change

S INCE I HAVE BEEN ASKED TO COMMENT on the theme "Communities in Motion: Creating the Winds of Discovery," I will discuss change as understood in Buddhist tradition. "The winds of discovery" is a romantic and appealing phrase. Who could resist wanting to plunge into such excitement and stimulation! Nevertheless, change is frightening to some people, and chaos is never pleasant, though sometimes it is unavoidable. Both the positive and the negative aspects of change are aptly captured in the metaphor of "wind" as wind is understood in Vajrayana Buddhism.

In common with many esoteric traditions, both Asian and Western, in Tibetan Buddhist perspective, wind or air is one of the five basic elements out of which the phenomenal world is constituted, one of the five atoms of early atomic theory. The other four are earth, fire, water, and space. Any composite entity can be analyzed in terms of these five components, according to such esoteric traditions. In Tibetan Buddhism, these elements or atoms are understood psychologically as much as, or even more than, they are understood to be material elements. Air, earth, fire, water, and space—each has its distinctive "feel," a distinctive psychological manifestation or quality. Therefore, every experience has its earthy element, its fiery element, its watery aspect, its spacious or accommodating nature, and its windy or airy dimension. Introspection into one's own personality styles or those of one's friends or enemies is greatly enhanced by analyzing our experiences to see which of these elements are present.

The element of wind, or air, is, quite predictably, connected with energy, with exertion, accomplishment, and activity. It is that quality in people or in experiences that sets goals, acts with discipline and dispatch, and, quite literally, moves mountains with its unrelenting, forceful activity. But such energy is morally neutral, in and of itself. According to Tibetan Buddhism, each of the basic elements can manifest itself either in deluded or enlightened form, depending on the context and on the skill and maturity of the person releasing the energy. Wind can blow in fertilizing, refreshing rain clouds, or it can blow in hurricanes and tornadoes. Wind is wind, and its nature is to blow, to move things. Sometimes that motion is beneficent and creative; sometimes it is destructive and chaotic, but the motion itself is simply neutral power and energy. Likewise, "windy" people or experiences can be tremendously effective, accomplishing great deeds; or they can be extremely pushy, critical, and competitive. The element, the energy is neutral; its manifestation depends on the skill and wisdom of those who set the winds in motion, who blow on the situation. So it is not enough merely to create winds of change. One needs to know how to work with the wind to create something useful and beneficent rather than something chaotic and destructive.

The meditative traditions of Buddhism and Shambhala include a great deal of practical wisdom concerning how to work with the elements of the phenomenal world in an intelligent, sane manner, rather than in a counterproductive, deluded fashion. While it is difficult fully to apply this wisdom from the viewpoint of theory only, without actual training and experience in meditative disciplines, contemplation of a few basic themes arising out of meditation practices can be very helpful. I will devote the remainder of my comments to two basic guidelines. The first of them is that the basic fact of life is all-pervading impermanence, and the second is that the way to work with impermanence is with the technique of "touch and go."

"Impermanence" is a word that has a good deal less romantic appeal than "change," even though, devoid of connotations, the two words mean the same thing. But people often connect impermanence with losing valuable things, like life and relationships, which means that impermanence is feared, while people often look forward to change. A change of pace, of scenery, of wardrobe or residence or job or partner will fix what is wrong with the present situation, in the perspective of conventional hope. Nevertheless, when the matter is contemplated carefully, it becomes clear that there not one iota of difference between experiencing the results of feared impermanence or hoped-for change. Therefore, Buddhists are fond of saying that hope and fear are merely two sides of the same coin, a statement that often infuriates or mystifies others. We hope that things will go a certain way and we're afraid that they won't. But they will change in any case. So, from a certain point of view there is no need to create the winds of change; they will happen. The point is to ride those winds of change well and in a manner that benefits the world.

To be able to ride the winds of change well, for the benefit of the world, the first requirement is simply to concede that impermanence is the first, middle, and last word about the human condition and the circumstances of our lives. Everything is always changing moment by moment, from tectonic plates and mountain ranges to the ongoing, ceaseless flickering of our emotional and intellectual lives. Thus, change is simply the basic fact of life; whether human beings approve of change is irrelevant and beside the point. Because everything is always changing, all that really happens is the razor's edge of nowness, of this immediate moment. That is the razor's edge we must balance upon to ride the winds of change well. The sharp and penetrating insistence that, *without exception*, everything is always changing, is probably responsible, more than anything else, for the mystification of Asian wisdom traditions among many outside those traditions, and for the expectation that those who live within those traditions must be gloomy and downcast. But inside the Buddhist perspective, it is very clear that impermanence itself has never caused a single human problem or instance of suffering. Rather, all problems and suffering are generated by resistance to relentless, unavoidable impermanence and change. The matter is quite simple. If change is relentless, unavoidable, and ever present, trying to fix one's anchors in a place that seems satisfactory can only lead to pain and anguish. The anchors will not hold, no matter how hard one tries.

The other side of the coin, however, is that to find one's ease in impermanence is an incredibly fruitful, fulfilling, and joyous experience. Strange as it sounds to minds habituated to thinking that finding some changeless substratum beneath life's fickle vagaries would be trustworthy and fulfilling, many Asian wisdom traditions explain that, since there is only that thin edge of nowness, experiencing it fully, completely, and intensely is fulfilling and joyous—beyond that provided by belief in permanence to which one might cling. Experiencing no problem with change or impermanence, one can experience life as it happens fully and productively. That is the meaning of freedom in Buddhism and in many other Asian wisdom traditions.

To ride the winds of change in such a manner is, of course, easier said than done, which is where the actual traditions of meditation come into the picture. In my specific training, the root advice on how to ride the winds of change is to practice "touch and go" constantly, without ceasing. That means that each moment needs to be touched, fully, completely, intensely, without barrier or hesitation, whether it be a moment of pleasure or pain, an experience we seek or one we would prefer to avoid. At this moment, whatever it is, it is that razor's edge of nowness which is always the immediate context and content of our lives. But then, it is just as important to "go," to release, as it was to touch. The habitual tendency is instead to fixate, to cling, even to present moments that are less than perfect, out of fear of impermanence. But, gently, without passion or aggression, one needs to relinquish that moment to the next. Then, again, it is necessary to touch, simply, gently, to touch, rather than to grasp, or seize, or attempt to ward off that next moment. Touch and go, or soaring and settling. Settle onto the edge of nowness, soar off that edge, settle and soar ceaselessly . . . .

Learning to ride one's mind, to soar and settle with the winds of change in this manner, is not an end in itself. Perhaps the single greatest misperception about the Asian wisdom traditions is that they advocate mental stability and fearlessness merely for individual relief, for individual comfort, and that meditation requires withdrawal from the world. Rather, however, in the long run, though not necessarily the short run, learning to ride the winds of change results in fruitful and beneficent interactions with one's world, with the interpersonal and natural context of our lives. In fact, from the Buddhist point of view, the most effective way to interact peacefully and productively with one's world is through learning to stay with the flexibility and immediacy of present impermanent nowness. If one can ride the winds of change, then one does not have to retreat from the world into withdrawal or dogmatism, because the winds of change are not a threat or a destabilizing force.

For "communities in motion," this insight is particularly appropriate and compelling. All modern communities, it seems to me, are communities in motion. Global communication networks and mobility force an interdependence among communities and constituencies within communities heretofore unknown and impossible. As a result the only communities possible today are pluralistic communities—communities built out of divergence and diversity—and communities constantly in motion, constituting and reconstituting themselves. Furthermore, as we begin to realize the finitude of our planet and its resources, we must change deeply held conventional views and values about our habits of reproduction and consumption. To support such changes, we must also discover new patterns of work, friendship, family life, and community, since the old familiar patterns produce pro-natalism and consumerism, practices that we can no longer afford as a global community.

Encountering diversity and divergence and living in a world that demands the development of new lifestyles continually brings us face to face with impermanence and instability. These challenges indeed involve "communities in motion" experiencing "the winds of discovery." Conventionally, people resist such changes because of their provocative challenge to seemingly settled and permanent opinions and stances. That is why many people seek a monolithic community rather than a diverse community and regard it as an imposition that such communities are vanishing. That is why politicians and conservative religious voices decry new forms of family and community, new lifestyles and new kinds of relationships and friendships, regarding as an imposition the fact that we must take into account the finite and interdependent character of our planet. But monolithic communities, built out of sameness and lack of variety, are no longer really a possibility, and communities encouraging pro-natalism and consumerism are no longer ethically valid. Some mourn these changes, these "winds of discovery" as losses, but I think that is rather timid and uninspired.

Nevertheless, we will need all our skills, including the meditative skills of being able to "touch and go," as we soar and settle into these new situations and lifestyles. Developing the tools to regard pluralism as a resource rather than as a problem within community is definitely one of the riddles and challenges of our time. Resisting pro-natalism and consumerism, building satisfying support networks of friendship and community that do not demand and depend on growth and consumption, is an equal challenge. These invitations to become "communities in motion" involve deep structural external challenges, but I think the deeper issue lies within. Resistance to these challenges, which is widespread, stems from a habitual tendency to resist change, to experience dis-ease with impermanence. A monolithic community not in motion and lacking diversity can seem to be lulling, to provide a safe, unchanging environment. A static community not in motion and not exploring lifestyles that overcome pro-natalism and consumerism can seem "traditional," and thus comforting. Such perceptions are, of course, illusions from the point of view of an Asian wisdom tradition not at war with impermanence. To live in a community in motion, a community that is continually changing, continually reconstituting itself by including different pluralities and points of view, requires members who have learned to find their ease in impermanence, who have learned to soar and settle, constantly and unceasingly with the winds of change and discovery. Come, let us dance on the razor's edge of nowness, ceasing our war with impermanence, and celebrating, rather than decrying, our increasingly diverse communities in motion, both locally and globally. For we must realize that, like the element of wind, the interdependent and pluralistic matrix of our existence is neutral and powerful. What makes the difference is whether we work with that energy wisely and skillfully, riding the winds of change and impermanence.

CHAPTER 6

Helping the Iron Bird Fly:[1]
Western Buddhists and
Issues of Authority

TRADITIONALLY, BUDDHISTS GIVE spiritual authorities great respect. Yet this practice clashes with Western feminist and democratic mistrust of hierarchy and authority. In my view, no issue is more crucial to the successful transmission of Buddhism to the West and to women's involvement in that transmission than successfully negotiating that impasse. My suggestions concerning this problem will circle around two issues. First I will discuss alleged misuse of authority by currently empowered spiritual teachers, mainly men—an issue that I consider to be more specific and short-term. This analysis of alleged abuse of power will be balanced in the second half of this chapter by suggestions regarding models and concepts of spiritual authority appropriate for Western Buddhism, including especially the relationship between women and authority. This latter discussion is far more critical for the long term, in my view.

∾ Sexual Behaviors of Male Buddhist
Teachers and Sexual Misconduct

I take up the issue of alleged "sexual misconduct" on the part of male Buddhist teachers—a topic that I had thus far successfully avoided discussing publicly—with extreme reluctance. (Though the misconduct issue involves a whole host of behaviors, including use of drugs and alcohol, misappropriation of funds, and general abuse of power, I will focus on the sexual misconduct charge because it is the most volatile and the most central to women, and also because no other alleged abuse has touched exposed nerves of American Buddhists so sharply or caused so much anguish for so long in the American Buddhist community.) Yet I would also argue that excessive attention to the topic of teachers' alleged misconduct is diverting much-needed energy from more basic issues that must be adequately attended to if Buddhism is to be transmitted to the West and if genuine Western Buddhism, rather than Asian Buddhism hothoused in the West, is ever to emerge.

While those more attuned to academic Buddhist studies might be relatively unaware of, or at least emotionally distant from, the turmoil swirling around many major Buddhist teachers in the West, no Buddhist practitioner involved in any major Western Buddhist community can be unaware of this phenomenon. Nor are most Western Buddhists without opinion on this topic; indeed, some show more dogmatism on this topic than any other issue facing Western Buddhists. Since the early eighties it has torn apart many prospering North American Buddhist organizations, including, among others, the Zen Center of San Francisco, by then headed by Richard Baker, Roshi; Vajradhatu, the international association of meditation centers founded by Vajracharya the Venerable Chogyam Trungpa, Rinpoche, and headed by the Vajra Regent Osel Tendzin during its most difficult phase; the Los Angeles Zen Center headed by Maisumi Roshi; and the New York Zen Center headed by Eido Roshi. Though most of these communities are now picking up the pieces and regrouping, controversy and bad feelings have not abated, and many students abandoned long-term association with a dharma center, apparently for good.

In March 1993, a meeting between selected Western dharma teachers and the Dalai Lama resulted in a statement that gives the impression that there is only one correct opinion regarding the issue. The behaviors alleged to be misconduct, including sexual misconduct, are indeed misconduct and should be exposed and criticized as such. Western Buddhist teachers then met at Spirit Rock near San Francisco in September 1993 to continue the discussion. At this meeting, which was facilitated largely by non-Buddhist therapists, some Western dharma teachers engaged in highly emotional expressions of disapproval of their own Asian dharma teachers. Some found the whole event cathartic and others found it appalling. A few months later, in March 1994, another conference with the Dalai Lama was held. According to some reports, he distanced himself from the whole issue at that time. Then, in later 1994, a large suit for damages for alleged sexual misconduct was brought against Tsogyel Rinpoche, the author of the popular *Tibetan Book of Living and Dying*. Undoubtedly, this is not the last event in the story, but only the most recent at the time of this writing. As an indication of how much emotional force the issue still packs, one can note that almost half of the issues of the new Buddhist journal of opinion *Tricycle* have carried some content devoted to the sexual behaviors of teachers, if only in the form of letters to the editor.[2]

If it is not already clear, it will quickly become obvious that I do *not* share the horror felt by some people about these Buddhist teachers' alleged sexual misconduct. However, my central concern is not to condone, justify, or explain the sexual behaviors of some male teachers either. My central point is that, while I do not have a strong opinion regarding the sexual behaviors of male Buddhist teachers, most especially my own teacher, Chogyam Trungpa, I do feel very strongly that other issues need our attention far more. This view runs counter to that of many articulate female and feminist Buddhists; therefore, I will try to explain why I take the stand that I do.

First, it is important to answer the charge that blind loyalty to my own teacher keeps me from being appalled by the sexual activities of male teachers. On the contrary, I am known within Vajradhatu as something of a rebel and a troublemaker, someone who has a mind of her own, because of my consistent advocacy of a feminist agenda within Buddhism. If I were convinced that the sexual behavior of teachers was an overriding concern for the transmission of post-patriarchal Buddhism to the West, I doubt that loyalty to my teacher would keep me from speaking out, since my loyalties, which are very deep, have not deterred me on other issues.

However, probably my stance is in part dependent on my being the student of Chogyam Trungpa rather than of some other teacher. I say this because in my view, the crisis-precipitating conduct has not been the sexual behaviors themselves, but *secrecy surrounding sexual behaviors.* Certainly when Vajradhatu fell apart, in 1988–1990, it was not over Trungpa's womanizing and drinking, which had been totally common knowledge for years, but over secrecy surrounding sexual activities of his dharma heir, the Vajra Regent Osel Tendzin. Perhaps I would have been more stung and hurt by the sexual conduct of my teacher if I had been the student of a teacher who gave one appearance in public but acted differently in private. When I was deciding whether or not to become Trungpa's student, I knew about his behaviors, though I was never in the inner circle of students who witnessed or participated in them. Quite frankly, initially I was more distressed by his ostentatious and pretentious lifestyle and its cost to his students, who, as a group, are not wealthy. I literally had to make a decision as to whether my discomfort with his expensive lifestyle should keep me from his brilliance as a dharma teacher and his ability to illumine mind to me. I think everyone who accepts a spiritual teacher has to make such a decision, though the specifics are different for each teacher–student relationship.

My reasons for not pouncing on teachers' alleged misconduct as the central problem for Buddhist women circle around two issues. The first is the question of what a guru or spiritual teacher is or is not, which is closely connected with the question of what a guru could be expected to provide for students. Second, I will question whether one can suggest that women should not or cannot consent to certain kinds of sexual activities if they also want to function as self-determining adults.

WHAT A GURU ISN'T

Being a feminist before I became a Buddhist has perhaps stood me in good stead in not expecting too much from a guru, in not expecting someone I can completely model myself after, someone who will never disappoint me, or someone who is always all wise. Since very few gurus thoroughly understand, manifest, or have assimilated feminism into their being, it has always been obvious to me that the guru is not the perfect, infallible authority on all issues. On this point we have the most complete example from Buddhist tradition and history that we could possibly have or want. Even the Buddha was not all wise on every social issue, as is clear from his handling of the founding of the nuns' sangha and his insistence on the eight special rules.[3]

If even the Buddha is not a perfect role model, why should we expect it of the men and women who have enough spiritual insight to function as gurus today? This principle, that the guru is not an authority on all issues, needs to be much more thoroughly assimilated, for in my view much of the disappointment many people express about their teachers' conduct results from theistic expectations of the guru, from confusing the guru with God or from longing for him or her to be the perfect mummy or daddy one never had. It is also my view that the demand for a perfect guru is, in practice language, an aspect of resistance, a phenomenon well known to every meditator and meditation instructor, as one of the tricks of habitual mind or "ego," in the Buddhist sense, to protect itself from deconstruction and freedom. The demand for a perfect guru is resistance, in the form of the statement, "unless I find a guru and a spiritual scene that I totally approve of, I won't practice meditation with them." I do not think there is a spiritual teacher out there who is also a perfect, flawless role model in every regard, whatever that might be. I would suggest that the quest and the demand for such a teacher are quite immature and that the student's rejection of a teacher who is not "perfect" says more about the student than about the teacher.

If teachers are not authorities on all issues and cannot be expected to be perfect role models, in what areas are they authorities and role models? As

I understand it, a teacher understands the nature of mind and can point that out to the student. If one doubts the teacher's insight into that sharp nameless quality, one should abandon the teacher forthwith. Every teacher with whom I have worked would say the same thing in his or her own words. A teacher also understands the skillful means, the meditation practices, to bring a student to penetrating insight into his or her own unsullied mind, can transmit those practices, and can instruct the student regarding them. These are the things I sought and seek from my teachers, for my feminist view and practices did not give me sufficient access to them. In fact, I first met my teachers as a skeptic who doubted that so-called spiritual teachers knew any more than I did. But in a penetrating non-verbal interchange, it become immediately obvious to me that this was the only person I had ever met who knew something I wanted to know that I didn't and wouldn't learn easily, if at all, by myself. His Mercedes became small potatoes in that context. I do not have to approve of every nuance of a teacher's behavior to respect and learn from that person, because I do not expect a teacher to be all-wise; nor do I expect a teacher to model for me all aspects of my life.

This middle path of revering the spiritual teacher as an authority on mind-to-mind transmission but not necessarily an all-wise or all-perfect role model guards against excessive attention to a teacher's everyday actions at the same time as it protects the heart of the teacher–student bond. My questioning, or even my disapproval, of certain actions taken by a teacher does not harden into ideology or fixed mind. To me, the ideological fixation and conventional moralism of those who insist that teachers' sexual misconduct is an overriding concern send up red flags. More than anything else, such persons' self-righteousness and moral rigidity make me suspicious and wary. My experience of Buddhist meditation practice is precisely that it enhances a quality of flexibility, humor, and non-judgment that has nothing to do with being passive and manipulable. When I encounter ideological moralism instead, I am not inclined to take the complaints too seriously. And I fear that the energy exhausted by grief and ideology over teachers' disapproved behaviors is seriously depleting Western Buddhism at a critical time.

Likewise, my assertion that the guru is not the authority on all issues does not conflict with devotion to the guru, which is so important in Vajrayana Buddhism and some other forms of Buddhism. One is required to appreciate and follow the guru's meditation instructions, but one is not required to worship or imitate his or her lifestyle. Devotion is not blind hero worship but intelligent application of the teacher's methods and messages, which is why I am completely confident when confronted by some Buddhists, usually men, who object to my feminist Buddhist teaching as disloyalty to my guru. Some discrimination regarding devotion is especially important. If one confuses devotion to the guru with imitation of the guru, rather unfortunate behaviors result, as was the case with many of Trungpa's students, who imitated his lifestyle in rather unhealthy ways. The ridiculous results of confusing devotion and imitation are aptly summed up by the reprimands some self-righteous imitators of Trungpa directed at me, suggesting that I was being disloyal to my guru, since I like cats very much and he, reportedly, hated cats, in keeping with widespread Asian prejudice. Even now, students sometimes ask me why he disliked cats so much and I reply, "because he was wrong on that point, which has nothing to do with his reliability as a teacher." To be unable to differ from the teacher, to imitate the teacher's every behavior is the flip side of requiring the teacher to fulfill one's own expectations of morality. Both are serious misunderstandings of devotion and the absolute bond that holds a student to a teacher in Vajrayana Buddhism.[4]

For these reasons, I reject the frequent comparison of sexual encounters between spiritual teachers and their students to sexual contacts between bosses and secretaries or between professors and students. Most especially, I reject the comparison of the guru–student relationship to the therapist–client relationship, which is so inegalitarian that sexual relationships would almost always be exploitative. I reject both elements in this comparison. The guru is not a therapist and the meditation student is not a therapy client. While I am sure others have had more positive experiences of therapy, in my experience therapists see themselves as experts and their clients as incompetent and in need of fixing. If the client questions a therapist's conclusions or advice, the client is said to be in denial, which puts the client in a double-bind situation in which she is encouraged to mistrust her own intelligence. Gurus, at least the ones I have worked with, do not treat their students in such a fashion but encourage students to test a guru before committing to the relationship and then encourage students to discover their own basic goodness and intelligence. Furthermore, I do not see a meditation student as a needy client in a dependent therapeutic relationship but as someone capable of rejecting sexual propositions from teachers if the terms are not acceptable. Certainly in the community in which I participate, such rejections occurred.

Because the guru is not an all-wise absolute authority and the student is not a needy, immature person in need of fixing up by such an authority, it cannot be claimed that a sexual relationship between a spiritual teacher and a student *must* be inappropriate and exploitative, though under certain conditions such a relationship *might* be exploitative and inappropriate. Such a relationship could also be mutual and mutually enriching, and in some cases surely is, as has been attested by some women I know. (I

have the same reservation about absolute rules prohibiting sexual relationships between most other "unequal" partners, such as professors and
students, or deans and professors, as well.) Finally, however, difficult as it
may be to understand the sexual behavior of someone like Trungpa, with
his numerous partners, I have never thought his behaviors were motivated
by the obvious egotism and personal neediness that motivates some well-
known womanizers in politics or entertainment. I cannot make the same
claim about other teachers, with whom I had no connection. Their own
students would have to make that judgement.

SEXUAL PARTNERS AS MORAL AGENTS, NOT VICTIMS

Many women for whom teachers' sexual activity is a serious problem
experienced extreme pain as a result of their own or friends' experiences of
sexual relationships with teachers. Others were not personally affected by
such a relationship but have a strong ideological position regarding sex
between supposed "unequals." They concur in labeling the teachers'
behavior "sexual misconduct" or "sexual abuse."

But I have observed, from my own experience if nothing else, that sexual relationships often eventually produce pain, even if they also, at other
times, involve deep communication and spiritual growth. Sometimes I
think that if it were not for breakthroughs that can occur through sexual
communication, no one would risk relating sexually with anyone because
of the pain that so often eventually comes. Things rarely work out as well
as one can envision in an encounter between two people. Therefore, disappointment is almost endemic. The leap from experiencing disappointment to labeling it abuse is troubling to me. Why it should be different
with teachers, if we recognize that teachers are not always all-wise, is
incomprehensible to me. Some women may have had sexual relationships
with their teachers that turned out in the long run to have been unwise
and unhealthy. That does not necessarily mean they were exploited, only
that they made decisions they later regretted.

I am extremely troubled by the development in recent feminist discourse to proclaim women as victims in such sexual encounters and to
seek to make rules that would protect women from such "victimization."
I am troubled because this move is directly counter to the basic feminist
drive to define women as adult human beings who have a right to make
their own choices. I see no way in which we can affirm both that women
are self-determining adults and that adult women cannot be trusted to
make their own decisions regarding relationships with "powerful" men,
but must be protected from sexual advances from such men. Formerly,
women were often coercively paired with powerful men; now some would

forbid such pairings under any circumstances. But either rule equally denies the agency of women; there is not much difference between telling a woman that she must become the sexual partner of a certain man and telling her that she should not or cannot become his partner. Rather than making it almost impossible for men to make sexual advances without facing the possibility of sexual harassment charges, we need to encourage women's self-esteem so that they do not feel pressured by offers that are unattractive to them. And, of course, women must be protected unconditionally from the negative consequences that can come from refusing a sexual proposition in a patriarchal contest.

But if a spiritual teacher and his or her student accept each other's invitation to sexual activity, it is quite unfair for the student later to claim that he or she was a victim of sexual abuse. Nor could the student claim that he or she expected the relationship to proceed in the manner of a conventional romance. Only the most naive person could have begun a sexual liaison with someone like Trungpa expecting that he was entering into a permanent romantic relationship with her.

For these reasons, I am reluctant to make blanket condemnations of teachers who have sex with their students, but would suggest that only under certain circumstances are such encounters abusive and inappropriate. If teachers are bound by vows of celibacy, obviously they should not be engaging in sex with their students. If a teacher were to withhold dharma instruction or transmissions unless the student engaged in sex or if the teacher were to insist that a sexual relationship is necessary to the student's spiritual practice, these would be serious problems and should be dealt with as such. They would indeed constitute sexual abuse. If the teacher has a track record of brief relationships with troubled, immature, distraught students, especially those new to dharma practice, one should be extremely suspicious. In addition, I am skeptical when the teacher practices what I call "the patriarchal politics of mate selection," which is to say that the female partner is most often young and conventionally attractive, whatever the age of the male partner.

In my view, the current Buddhist furor over teachers' sexual behaviors is in large part our own version of the moralistic backlash now sweeping our society in general, a phenomenon whose long-term effects will probably not be positive. I suggest that those who adamantly condemn sexual relationships between spiritual teachers and their students are overly reliant on conventional morality, especially conventional sex ethics, which are often erotophobic and repressive. On the one hand, there simply are too many examples of outstanding people, including religious teachers, who engage in unconventional behavior to assume that adherence to conventional sexual morality is any safe guide to judging people's worth. On the other hand, the repressiveness of conventional sexual ethics produces a great deal of pain. Since I have never been particularly impressed by conventional standards of sexual morality, I am not quick to judge or condemn the sexual activities of others. I would suggest that it is unfair and inappropriate to deny to spiritual teachers an active sex life simply because they are spiritual teachers. I do not expect my teachers to be less interested in an active, enjoyable, meaningful sex life than I am.

What troubles me most about the topic of teachers and their sexual activities is the hold it has on Buddhist practitioners and communities. Many people seem to have a great deal of trouble practicing the Buddhist virtues of equanimity and detachment when discussing their teachers' sex lives. The way in which people nurse wounds and hold grudges is not at all a Buddhist way of working the issues. Nor am I impressed by the dogmatism and absolutism that flare up in conjunction with the issue of sexual relationships between teachers and students. In my view the emotionalism that swirls around teachers and sex ethics is quite detrimental to the founding and flourishing of Buddhism in the West. While I don't feel a personal need to initiate comment on teachers' sexual behavior, I do feel, quite strongly, that too much energy is going into this issue and that this energy needs to be spent on much wiser causes and issues. I appeal to the feminist principle of choosing our battles wisely because we can't fight them all. I consider the interdependent issues of community and authority to be much more basic to the well-being of Buddhism in the West.

∾ Natural Hierarchy, Buddhism, and Feminism

One of the reactions to the scandals surrounding Buddhist teachers has been to question whether hierarchy in spiritual communities should exist and whether gurus should have spiritual authority. Many attempts to decentralize Buddhist communities and disperse authority among more people have occurred. Therefore, this is a very provocative time at which to suggest that I think the most important issue for Buddhist women is the transmission of spiritual authority to female gurus. Indeed, on some occasions when I have introduced the issue, women have adamantly insisted that guruship is an inherently corrupt phenomenon and should have no place in post-patriarchal Buddhism. And feminism is a notoriously anti-hierarchical movement. Since the importance of female gurus will be more fully discussed in later chapters, I will set the stage for those comments by discussing natural hierarchy, feminism, and Buddhism in the remainder of this chapter.

NATURAL HIERARCHY AS THE MIDDLE WAY

I would not give my life energy to a community, spiritual or secular, that was either completely authoritarian or completely democratic in its organization. My reasons for withholding support and commitment from organizations that are too authoritarian or too egalitarian are the same. Learning, discipline, accomplishment, and wisdom, qualities that I believe are essential to human well-being and should therefore be honored, are irrelevant in both authoritarian and ultra-egalitarian institutions. In fact, some ultra-democratic groups strive for leaderless communities, which strikes me as an oxymoron. In particular, I cannot imagine a spiritual community without hierarchy and leadership being very successful at effecting spiritual transformation among its members.

Among the many things I have learned as student of Chogyam Trungpa, none has been more helpful to me than the "natural hierarchy" which he taught, but not too publicly.[5] At first hearing, most people would think that this concept means that hierarchy is inevitable or inherent in human life and so we'd just better kowtow to the powers that be. The first part of that conjecture is correct, but the second part is not. Hierarchy is natural, in the sense that, for example, a tree grows best when its roots are in the ground, its branches in the sky, and its trunk joins them. Thinking that all the parts of the tree should be equal and therefore equally exposed to the earth or sky is not too helpful. But nothing in the concept of natural hierarchy assumes that whatever hierarchies we may currently experience exemplify natural hierarchy. In fact, since most conventional hierarchies we experience are based on irrelevant and arbitrary criteria, such as gender, race, class, sexual orientation, and so on, rather than on learning, discipline, accomplishment, and wisdom, they are most certainly *unnatural hierarchies.*

The term "hierarchy" seems to imply a vertical structure, a pyramid. In any specific moment, a natural hierarchy may indeed look like a pyramid, because one person or a small group of people are the focal point of activity, *for now.* But at heart, the basic geometric form that describes natural hierarchy is the circle rather than the pyramid. The more accurate picture of "natural hierarchy" is the *mandala* structure of center and fringe, in which the parts are organically connected, mutually interdependent, and in constant communication. But it is difficult to talk about authority in such a circular and interdependent manner.

Natural hierarchy has much to do with recognizing that not everyone is equally good at everything, and communities flourish when people can find the niche in which they are most comfortable, most productive, and

most able to contribute to society. Natural hierarchies are also fluid hierarchies, in the sense that no one is always in the center and most people
will be in the center at some point. In some situations I will be in a middle
position, in other situations in a bottom position, and in others at the top
of the current hierarchy. Sometimes I serve, and sometimes I direct,
depending on what needs to be done and on my abilities, achievement, and
training. All roles are valuable as learning experiences.

In living out natural hierarchy, I am grateful to have learned many
things I am sure I would otherwise have missed, such as how to serve a
table properly and how to receive such service. But more importantly, I
have learned that serving is not inherently degrading but is extremely
pleasurable and dignified. Two things make service difficult in our egalitarian setting. One is the standard interpretation of the concept of equality to mean that serving is demeaning because not everyone does the same
thing. The other is the fact that there is little fluidity in our supposedly
egalitarian society, which means that servers stay in their positions,
which builds resentment. But for myself, I would not trade for anything
the hours spent running the institutional-size dishwasher or slicing endless vegetables on work-period assignment at meditation programs. They
are the perfect counterpoint and antidote to the weekends I spend as top
dog directing programs, teaching, and being served. Without my experience of filling all positions in a fluid natural hierarchy, I suspect I could be
an arrogant and humorless director.

Natural hierarchy degenerates into unnatural hierarchy when who may
fill any niche is predetermined by irrelevant criteria, such as gender,
which is what has happened since the creation of patriarchy. Natural hierarchies also degenerate into unnatural hierarchies when their fluidity is
lost and a permanent, rigid, static pyramid emerges. By contrast, natural
hierarchy honors the abilities, experience, and achievements relevant for
authority in any particular situation, but does not limit who might have
that relevant ability, experience, and achievement. Therefore, for natural
hierarchy to be possible, the training and apprenticeship that are prerequi-
sites to having the appropriate experience and achievement must be available to everyone. When those conditions are met, natural hierarchy is the
middle way between absolutism and the kind of democracy that ignores
merit.

If, because of harsh experiences with unnatural hierarchy, we try to
insist that everyone is equally good at everything and there should be no
hierarchies at all, the only result is that we lose the gifts of the gifted,
whatever their gift may be. As a society, we seem now to be a phase in
which our belief in equality has resulted in the practice of pretending, to
quote the slogan of mythical Lake Wobegon, that "all the children are

above average." But, obviously, if *all* the children are above average, the needs of the truly above average children are not met, which was my experience forever in childhood. It didn't do the slow students any good to pretend that all have the same achievements and my own achievement was sabotaged, particularly since, as a girl, I was supposed to defer and to pretend that boys who achieved little were more worthy nevertheless.

Needless to say, in situations of genuine natural hierarchy, women would flourish. We would not be shunted into roles based on anatomy, but could find our niches in the tree of life. Some of us would become spiritual leaders, among other things. The fact that this is such a rare occurrence demonstrates quite clearly that most of the hierarchies we live are at least partially unnatural hierarchies and therefore deserve to be challenged. I suspect that the allergic reaction most feminists have to the word "hierarchy" is due to the fact that women have fared so badly under unnatural hierarchies, which have so arbitrarily, meaninglessly, and cruelly limited our flourishing. But I find the opposite, which is sometimes touted in feminist circles, equally appalling. I find the elevation of process over accomplishment enervating. I find the claim that all opinions are equally valid ludicrous. Having been trashed on a number of occasions by feminists for my allegiance to excellence, I have some understanding of the cliché that men seek to destroy the weakest among them and women seek to destroy the strongest among us. There has to be a middle way between these extremes, and I believe it is in a natural hierarchy that honors, respects, and gives authority based on experience and accomplishment, but does not limit who might have the relevant experience and the accomplishments in any way.

Women and Authority in Buddhism

Two issues predominate in a discussion of women and authority in Buddhism. One is the issue of why spiritual authority is so central in Buddhism. The other issue is why it is so crucial that women attain and exercise spiritual authority in Buddhism.

For a spiritual community to be without authorities selected by natural hierarchy is unimaginable to me. It cannot be the case that the beginning meditator should not regard the guru as an authority on meditation or that her opinions about spiritual discipline are as valid as those of the guru. But she may know more about finances and building codes, which are also relevant concerns for the exercise of authority in a dharma center. Such is the interplay of natural hierarchies as the middle way between complete authoritarianism and total lack of hierarchy.

Particularly in the case of spiritual discipline, experience and authority seem to me to be crucial, because, in Buddhist shorthand, ego is so slick and self-deception is so easy. Without guidance, most self-medicated spiritual disciplines become some version of "doing what feels good," which brings short-term satisfaction but little long-term growth and development. I have long argued with my colleagues in post-Christian feminist spirituality that it is dangerous to make up spiritual disciplines and to become one's own meditation instructor unless there are utterly no alternatives, especially during the beginning stages of a meditative discipline.

Furthermore, the long-standing Buddhist practice of progressing along a path, following the established curriculum of learning and development, and being authorized to take on different levels of authority progressively cannot be eliminated. There is nothing that can replace it, though the process needs to be constantly on guard against ossification or rigidities such as those that limit the teaching authority women may assume. Nevertheless, except in extreme circumstances, such as women authorizing each other as spiritual teachers if all else fails, such authorizations must come from the top down, not from the bottom up. Transmission is much more trustworthy than election as a way of choosing spiritual authorities. In this regard the two worlds that I inhabit, the world of Buddhist practice and the world of academia, are remarkably similar. Students do not confer Ph.D.'s on each other. People who already have a Ph.D. and teach at a Ph.D.-granting institution confer the degree on those who have successfully completed the course of training. Those of us in academia know there are cases of inhumane injustice in which people are denied the terminal degree or tenure because those in authority are wrong. The same thing happens in dharma lineages. But no system is foolproof and the alternative of self-conferred titles is even more nightmarish.

Therefore, I would argue that it is counterproductive to talk about abolishing spiritual authority or guruship because of the recent problems Western Buddhists have encountered with gurus. I would argue instead to carefully do away with the excesses to which the phenomenon is subject—namely, theistic excesses of regarding the guru as always all-wise and the near-male monopoly on the position. As for theistic excesses, in at least some cases they have as much to do with what students project onto the spiritual teacher as with what the guru expects or demands.

In patriarchal systems, by definition, women are forbidden to hold authority, though feminist research shows that they often wield considerable power nevertheless.[6] Since the defining trait of patriarchy is formal male control of society, clearly for women to hold formal authority would fundamentally contradict the system. With some exceptions, Buddhism has followed this patriarchal norm throughout its history. Thus, there is no question that Buddhism cannot become post-patriarchal until women wield authority in Buddhism—however that comes to be defined and structured eventually in Western Buddhism. That is one of the reasons why I claim that the presence of female gurus is so crucial as the central issue for Western Buddhist women.

Even viewed realistically rather than theistically, gurus are powerful and compelling presences. As I argued extensively in *Buddhism after Patriarchy*, given what we know about sex, gender, and role models, it will be transformative and powerful, for both women and men, to relate routinely to women whose presence exudes confident, compassionate *authority*. That is why one of the things I would most like see within my lifetime is a female and feminist lineage holder in my lineage. I am not too optimistic about that possibility. In general, Vajrayana Buddhism in the West seems to be well behind Zen Buddhism in the West in giving dharma transmission to women. I am not sure of the reasons for this, but I suspect that there are two major reasons. First, it seems that fewer people receive dharma transmission in Vajrayana Buddhism than in Zen Buddhism; and, second, in Vajrayana Buddhism, most of those who do are chosen in infancy as *tulku*s. As we know, the *tulku* system is controlled by Asian males, who despite the film *Little Buddha*, have not thus far been very serious about seeking female *tulku*s, or Western *tulku*s, for that matter.

Within my community, Shambhala Meditation Centers, the situation is perhaps unique. There is only one person with the status of guru or lineage holder, the Sakyong Mipham, Rinpoche.[7] I do not expect that to change anytime soon. Nevertheless, some natural hierarchy is evident within Vajradhatu. Much of the dharma teaching is done by people like myself— senior students with various levels of teaching authority. I certainly have never been muzzled despite my outspoken feminism, and I am starting to give seminars *within* Vajradhatu on Buddhism and feminism. Natural hierarchy as center and fringe is in operation as I am listened to even by people in the hierarchy whose first reaction is dismissive. Nevertheless, if someone with formal authority as a lineage holder were saying what I am saying, the same words would have much more impact. Changes necessary to end sexist practices, such as lack of female imagery in the meditation halls and generic masculine chants and texts, would quickly happen. That is the nature of authority, and that is why it so crucial to have female and feminist lineage holders.

Eventually that will happen, as Venerable Jetsun Kusho-la assured me when I discussed the issue with her. The transition point when women finally achieve authority in Western Vajrayana Buddhism is, however, fraught with another grave danger. Earlier I expressed my longing to see a female *feminist* lineage holder in my lineage within my lifetime. That second word is crucial. Unfortunately, in many systems, the first women to achieve authority are clones of the men who have always held authority, which solves almost nothing. As many in academia have learned, many a non-feminist female dean or chancellor is worse than many a male dean or chancellor. Why this is so is quite clear. A system that has functioned under unnatural hierarchy for millennia cannot be basically healthy. Therefore, merely putting a woman in charge does almost nothing. Using the analogy of the tree house with the sign "No Girls Allowed," I often suggest to my students that just getting into a messy dilapidated tree house is not enough. It needs to be cleaned up and restructured, which is why it is so critical to have not only female but feminist gurus involved in the transmission of Buddhism to the West and the transition to post-patriarchal Buddhism.

We have now come full circle. When noncelibate women become gurus, in a sense, the shoe will be on the other foot. I would predict that some of the same behaviors that are so troubling when done by men will also occur with female gurus, because the teacher–student relationship, in my view, always includes passion that can become erotic. How will we handle the inevitable yearnings that develop between teacher and student when the teacher is female and the student lover is male, or perhaps female? Conventional morality and prurience are not the answer, nor are the excesses or the secrecies of some male gurus.

CHAPTER 7

Interdependence and Detachment: Toward a Buddhist Environmental Ethic

*W*HENEVER I THINK *about issues of consumption and population, I also think about the way I lived early in my life. For my first eighteen years I lived without central heating, indoor plumbing, pesticides, processed foods, packaging, or neighbors that could be seen from our home. We carried water from a spring, cut our own firewood, grew much of our own food, and used an outhouse, even in subzero temperatures. Dragonflies, butterflies, fireflies, and many other beautiful creatures that I never see in my city lot abounded. Traffic noise was a novelty. At night one could see a million stars in the black sky.*

Major environmental problems—waste disposal, air pollution, and water pollution—were nonexistent in our lives and on our land because we were few people (a family of three) living simply. Because we were so few living in a sparsely populated rural area, we could use simple technologies and renewable resources for heat and waste management without harming the land, water, or air, even though those same technologies become extremely problematic when people live in crowded conditions. This is one of many reasons why population growth is so environmentally devastating.

Though many would evaluate such a lifestyle as unacceptably primitive and uncomfortable, in fact, it was not particularly a problem or a deprivation. Even now when I return to my cabin for meditation retreats and writing time, I do not mind that lifestyle. Electricity for lights, the laptop computer, and a boombox that plays classical music is completely sufficient for a satisfying lifestyle with low environmental impact. Environmentally sensitive lifestyles and scaling back to live such lifestyles do not really deprive people once it becomes clear that the levels of reproduction and consumption indulged in by most people are not necessary to well-being. To me, it is very clear that an environmental paradise, as well as an environmental necessity, is a situation of few people, not crowded together, living simply. In this chapter, I will explore how my religion of choice—Buddhism—might encourage people to live that lifestyle.

ᗞ Buddhism and Ecology

Currently, there is some debate about whether Buddhism can support an environmental ethic or the worldview of deep ecology and some Western scholar-observers are very skeptical of Buddhist efforts to derive an ecological ethic.[1] As a scholar of religion familiar with both historical and constructive methods, I find that question somewhat beside the point. Historically, we know that all living religions have gone through the major changes required to remain relevant in altered circumstances. There is no reason that the same thing cannot happen in response to the ecological crisis. And as a Buddhist feminist "theologian," I am more than familiar with the process of working within a traditional symbol system and worldview while doing major reconstructive work to eliminate certain problematic conventions. The question is not what *has* Buddhism said about ecology and the environment but what *could* Buddhism have to say about these subjects. In a time of unprecedented concern about the viability of the ecosystem within which we live and upon which we depend unconditionally, what insights and practices might a Buddhist bring into the discussion?

At the outset, I would suggest that Buddhism has not been especially oriented to an environmental ethic historically, though East Asian forms of Buddhism seem to be more nature oriented than South Asian Buddhisms. In my view, other religious traditions, including the indigenous traditions so often praised for their reverence for nature have not historically focused on an environmental ethic either. I make this somewhat controversial statement because of a claim that I will make many times in this chapter. To qualify as an environmental ethic, ethical guidelines must discourage excessive consumption and reproduction, even if such levels of consumption and reproduction are common in the culture and seem unproblematic to many people. By itself, a rhetoric of reverence for nature is insufficient as an environmental ethic. Too often a rhetoric of reverence for nature is combined with primitive technologies that limit human ability to damage and destroy the environment, but when more sophisticated and destructive technologies become available, they are readily adopted. Populations multiply and consumerism soars, even with a rhetoric of reverence for nature well in place. One need only look at East Asia in the twentieth century to see multiple examples of a rhetoric of reverence for nature combined with environmentally destructive practices. Therefore, to qualify as genuinely ecological, teachings and practices must require making *a choice* against excessive reproduction and consumption.

The question of whether Buddhism is compatible with deep ecology, which views all parts of the ecosystem as of equal value, is more complex. While Buddhism is not homocentric in the way that monotheistic religions are, nevertheless, most Buddhism does regard human life as more desirable than any other form of life because of the spiritual potential thought to be inherent in and limited to the human condition. Only human beings can practice meditation and become enlightened; however, Buddhism does not believe that the purpose of nonhuman nature is to serve human needs. Rather, human beings are one kind of life in an ecosystem within which all elements are affected in exactly the same way by whatever actions occur. Furthermore, in traditional Buddhist societies in which most people affirm rebirth, all sentient existence is thought to be interconnected and related by virtue of karmic ties from past lives, and rebirth in nonhuman realms is highly possible. Furthermore, whenever compassion is discussed, Buddhist ethics *always* promote compassion to all sentient beings, not just human beings. These views provide some basis for environmentally and ecologically sound practices, whether or not they could be regarded as "deep ecology."

The reason why environmental concerns are now so grave is because humans have the technologies to consume and reproduce in ways that, if not moderated, seem almost certain to destroy the ecological basis for human life. Therefore, the key question is what values and practices would convince people to consume and reproduce less when they have the technological ability to consume and reproduce more. The world's religions have not previously faced this situation, which explains why ecological ethics have not been in the forefront of religious thinking in any tradition. What we must do, then, as constructive thinkers in our various traditions, is to place the inherited values and insights of our traditions in the light of the current ecological crisis to see what resources the tradition affords us and where we need to extrapolate new visions.

It is not difficult to find Buddhist ideas and practices that could easily support an environmental ethic. At the simplest level, because non-harming is so fundamental to Buddhist ethics, once one realizes that excessive consumption and reproduction are harmful, one is obliged to limit such activities. Such advice is also in accord with the most fundamental of all Buddhist guidelines—the Middle Path between extremes. This guideline is always applied to all questions from questions about how much effort to put into one's meditation practice to how much luxury is appropriate to metaphysical questions about existence and nonexistence. Regarding both consumption and reproduction, we need to find the "Middle Way" between too much and too little. It could perhaps be argued that these simple basics—non-harming and the Middle Way—which would automatically come to mind for any Buddhist, are a sufficient basis for an environmental ethic that would encourage limited consumption and reproduction.

Unfortunately, however, regarding environmental issues, I do not believe coming up with the appropriate view is all that difficult. Most people know that we must put less stress on the environment if we want to survive, and all religions have at least an implicit ethic for doing so. The areas of practice and action are far more lacking; both individuals and groups seem to lack the practices that mandate translating views into action. That consumption and reproduction need to be severely curtailed is rather obvious, but what will convince individuals and groups to make limiting their consumption and reproduction a top priority?

When I am faced with a major intellectual puzzle, I usually contemplate it using a strategy that I learned from the oral traditions of Tibetan Buddhism—threefold logic. This strategy suggests that most sets of information can be fruitfully analyzed and organized by locating a starting point, a process of change and development, and an end product. The task of articulating a full-fledged Buddhist ethical response to the environmental crisis is daunting enough that I spent many hours going back to basic Buddhist teachings using a traditional threefold logic with which to think about what Buddhism might have to offer. The traditional system of threefold logic that offered the most insight is a system called "view, practice, and result." This particular system focuses first on the theoretical analysis appropriate to a specific issue—the view. Then, with the view well in hand, we turn to the question of what practices or spiritual disciplines will enable one to realize or internalize the view, so that it is no longer merely an intellectual theory. Finally, understanding the view and having practiced the appropriate contemplative and meditative exercises, what actions will one take when the view is fully internalized? As I apply this technique in this chapter, I will emphasize two things. First, I will appeal to simple pan-Buddhist teachings and practices for the most part, rather than to the doctrines of advanced Buddhist philosophy or the practices of esoteric forms of Buddhism. I do this so that Buddhists everywhere could find a Buddhist environmental ethic that is accessible and relevant. Second, I will emphasize practice over view. One of the reasons for working with the specific system of threefold logic that I chose is because the view—the theoretical analysis—is only the beginning of the discussion. I

have been somewhat disappointed with the current small body of literature on Buddhist environmental ethics because most authors have focused
on view or theory and have not sufficiently discussed practices promoting
environmentally sound lifestyles.

∼ The View according to Buddhism: Interdependence

When one brings the vast collection of Buddhist teachings into conversation with environmental concerns, one basic teaching stands out above all
others in its relevance. That is the Buddhist teaching of interdependence,
which is also one of the most basic aspects of the Buddhist worldview, a
teaching held in common by all forms of Buddhism. This law of interdependence is said to have been discovered by the historical Buddha on the
night of his enlightenment experience during the third watch of the night,
just before dawn and full enlightenment, the same time period during
which the Four Noble Truths were discovered. Mythically, this story indicates how basic the teaching of interdependence is to Buddhism.

Simply put, interdependence means that nothing stands alone apart
from the matrix of all else. Nothing is independent and everything is interdependent with everything else. Logically, the proof of interdependence is
that nothing can exist apart from the causes and conditions that give rise
to it, but those causes and conditions are also dependent on other causes
and conditions. Therefore, linear causality and isolating a single cause for
an event gives way to a more weblike understanding of causality in which
everything affects everything else in some way because everything is
interconnected.

Given interdependence, our very identity as isolated, separate entities
is called into serious question, and we are invited to forge a more inclusive
and extensive identity. We do not simply stop at the borders of our skin if
we are truly interdependent with our world. When we know ourselves to
be fundamentally interdependent with everything else, rather than independent entities existing in our own right, our self-centered behaviors will
be altered in very basic ways. Nothing that we do is irrelevant, without
impact on the rest of our matrix.

The implications of this profound, thoroughgoing interdependence for
ecology have already been articulated in a moving fashion by Joanna Macy
and others.[2] In fact, interdependence is the most commonly invoked concept in Buddhist environmental ethics to date. Most often it is celebrated
as a view of our relationships with our world that invites and requires ecological concern and a view that is much more emotionally satisfying and

realistic than the Western emphasis on the individual as the ultimately real and ultimately important entity. Western Buddhists especially seem to find immense relief in their discovery of what Harold Coward calls the "we-self."[3] This joy is quite understandable, given the emotional burdens concomitant with modern Western individualism.

Rather than emphasizing the lyrical beauty of interconnectedness, however, as others have already done very well, I wish to emphasize its more somber implications. First, we cannot intervene in or rearrange the ecosystem without affecting everything. Therefore, human interference in the ecosystem cannot be a glib pursuit of "progress" and "growth," two things that many view as ideals. The effects of growth and technological progress on the whole interconnected system are much more important, and these effects are often not anticipated. For example, lowering the death rate, especially the infant mortality rate, through modern medicine seems like clear progress. But failure to see the link between the death rate and the birth rate, which sanctions the continuation of reproductive practices appropriate when the death rate is high, is an important factor in the current population explosion. Similarly, the links between certain chemicals that made consumer products more desirable, a depleted ozone layer, and growing rates of skin cancer were not anticipated. Even when some people have some awareness of the effects of human intervention on the ecosystem, stopping such intervention can be difficult. Even though many are thoroughly alarmed at the global consequences of destroying the Amazon rain forest, its destruction continues because of the overwhelming power of consumerism. The reality of interdependence is sobering, as well as poetic. Each of us feels the effects of actions taken far away by people whom we do not know and whom we cannot influence directly.

If pervasive interconnectedness is an accurate view, then nothing can be delinked from anything else. Taking interdependence seriously urges us to apply "both-and" solutions, rather that "either-or" arguments to knotty problems. This applies particularly to consumption and population. When discussing environmental ethics, one of the most important but largely unrecognized moral agendas is the need to establish the fundamental similarity of the urge to consume more and the urge to reproduce more, rather than being lured into superficial arguments about whether excessive consumption or overpopulation is *the* major environmental problem, as so often happens in "North" (first world) versus "South" (third world) debates.

Excessive consumption and excessive reproduction are similar not only in their negative impact on the environment but also in the self-centered motivations from which they spring. The first similarity has been recognized to some extent, but that consumerism and pro-natalism stem from similarly *self-centered motivations* has been completely overlooked. This is the case even for Buddhist environmental ethics, where, given Buddhism's especially developed critic of ego, one would expect to find such insights. This literature contains many denunciations, on Buddhist grounds, of personal, corporate, and national greed for consumable goods and many discussions of how such greed damages the interdependent ecosystem. But there are almost no discussions of the fact that excessive population growth is at least equally devastating environmentally and would make impossible the vision articulated in many Buddhist environmental writings concerning the value of the ecosystem, of wilderness, and of nonhuman sentient beings. More important, Buddhist ecological literature includes almost no discussions of the fact that much reproductive behavior is fueled by individual or communal greed and ego and, therefore, on Buddhist grounds is just as suspect as greed for assets. Buddhist ecological literature ignores the reality that, most frequently, physiological reproduction results because patrilineages or individuals desire physical immortality, or because of the many ways in which birth control fails, not because of altruistic, non–ego-based motives.

In this regard Buddhist ecological ethics follows a tendency common in religious or moral discussions—a predisposition to regard individual greed and excessive consumption as a moral failing, while excessive reproduction is not similarly regarded as a moral failing. In fact, reproduction is idealized and romanticized. Religions often promote large families, both through their discouragement of fertility control and their patriarchal tendency to view women primarily as reproducers, while governments implement pro-natalist tax and social policies in an overpopulated world. Thus, to keep population and consumption properly linked, in religious discourse we may need to focus more on population issues. Because we can assume a moral condemnation of excessive consumption in religious ethics, such a focus will actually bring our attention to consumption and population into balance with each other.

Furthermore, if one accepts interdependence, then we must realize that many things that people regard as private individual choices, most especially choices regarding how much to consume and whether or how many children to bear actually are not private matters because of their profound implications for all sentient beings. The "we-self," in Harold Coward's terminology, has very strong interest in individual practices regarding reproduction and consumption, and its perspectives need to be taken seriously. Very strong ethical arguments that everyone must limit their consumption and reproduction follow. These arguments can be made both in terms of rights—the rights of other beings not to be infringed upon by our excessive reproduction and consumption—and in terms of responsibilities—our own responsibility not to harm other beings unnecessarily through our reproduction and consumption.

In an interdependent matrix, such moral obligations have little to do with "North" versus "South" or with whether people are rich or poor. Without a healthy environment, there will be nothing to consume and no place to reproduce for anyone, North or South, rich or poor. Therefore, the requirement to restore and preserve a healthy interdependent ecosystem has far more moral urgency than maintaining or increasing current levels of consumption and reproduction.

Rich countries, couples, and individuals have grave responsibilities to limit their fertility, arguably to less than zero population growth, precisely because their rich offspring have such a massive impact on the environment. The arguments made by many rich people that they desire more children and have the means to support them do not obviate their children's negative environmental consequences and thus have little moral cogency when interdependence is taken seriously. And poor countries, couples, and individuals have the same responsibility for different reasons. Poverty has always been evaluated as spiritually useless by Buddhists; it is a serious deviation from the Middle Way and does not afford people the moderate levels of physical and emotional security needed to progress spiritually, which is the only point or purpose of human rebirth. But achieving equitable distribution of goods and overcoming poverty is immensely complicated by rapid population growth. In fact, it will become impossible when the earth's population is greater than its capacity to support an adequate standard of living for all. And, precisely because poverty is so spiritually useless, it is ethically indefensible to demand that despite selective unwillingness to practice fertility control, consumables should be divided up evenly, no matter what happens to standards of living.

Additionally the argument popular in some feminist and liberal circles that population growth among the poor is not environmentally dangerous because of their low levels of consumption is flawed. First, even though some populations are severely deprived now, when their levels of consumption rise to appropriate levels, their large numbers will make an enormous environmental impact. What will the world look like when the per capita consumption of refrigerators or personal automobiles reaches the level that many deprived people aspire to? Or even when people in some of the poorest and most densely populated areas of the world have sufficient food, clean water, energy, and sanitation? Second, even now the environmental impact of deprived populations is often severe, despite low levels of consumption. Forced to the margins of the economy, their subsistence activities contribute to deforestation and desertification. These

environmental changes then affect global weather patterns and the productivity of distant lands.

Finally, it is important that population issues not be viewed as aimed
exclusively or primarily at women or as detrimental to women. Concern
with rapid population growth is concern for the whole environmental
matrix, not an anti-women campaign. The effects of overpopulation are
felt at least as seriously by women as by men, and probably more seriously
by women, in part because women's work usually becomes more difficult
and time-consuming when the immediate environment is degraded due to
overconsumption. It is well known that the most effective methods of limiting rapid population growth are increased education for women and a rising standard of living. Therefore, both environmental and populations
policies should focus on these factors, rather than denouncing women for
their fertility.

∼ Detachment: *The Practical Antidote to Desire*

An ecological ethic has been defined as a value system and set of practices
through which people come to appreciate the entire matrix of life enough
to limit their own consumption and reproduction for the well-being of
that matrix. These limits are adopted despite technologies and economies
that, by ignoring the big picture and the long run, foster in people the illu-
sion that having more children and consuming more material goods are
unproblematic. An effective religious environmental ethic would inspire
people willingly to limit reproduction and consumption. Buddhism, in my
view, has some important, perhaps unique, insights to offer toward developing such an ethic.

Buddhism suggests that we look into our own desires when we are confronted with problems and misery, and I believe such practices are quite
relevant for developing the kind of environmental ethic defined above.
The Four Noble Truths, often characterized as the Buddha's verbalization
of his enlightenment experience, provide the basis for developing an ethic
of adopting limits for the sake of the matrix of life. Because the Four Noble
Truths are so basic to Buddhism, an environmental ethic based on them is
not foreign to Buddhism even though these teachings may not have
applied to environmental ethics before. The First and Second Noble
Truths foster especially fruitful contemplations relevant to ecological
ethics. The First Noble Truth states that conventional lifestyles inevitably
result in suffering; the Second Noble Truth states that suffering stems
from desire rooted in ignorance. Translated into more ecological language,
a conventional lifestyle of indulging in desired levels of consumption and

reproduction results in the misery of an environmentally degraded and overpopulated planet.

The Second Noble Truth, with its emphasis on desire as the cause of suffering, is the key to a Buddhist environmental ethic. But before we can develop the implications of the Second Noble Truth for environmental ethics, it is necessary to clarify the meaning of the term "desire," since that term is widely misunderstood, with the result that Buddhism is often caricatured as a pessimistic, world-denying religion. The English word "desire" is the translation usually chosen for the Pali *tanha* and the Sanskrit *trishna*, but the connotations of the term "desire" are not strong enough to carry the meaning of Second Noble Truth. Most English-speaking people regard desire as inevitable and only a problem if it gets out of hand. But, in Buddhist psychology, *trishna* is always out of hand, inevitably out of control. Therefore, I believe more accurate connotative translations of *trishna* would be "addiction" or "compulsion," which more adequately convey its insatiable demands and counterproductivity. "Grasping," "attachment," "clinging," "craving," and "fixation" are also possible and more accurate translations, and the way the term "greed" is now used when discussing some multinational businesses also could translate *trishna*. All of these terms suggest that the object of desire is actually more powerful, more in control, than the desiring subject, which is precisely why *trishna* causes *duhkha*—misery.

Trishna is not about having lightly held plans or about preferring an adequate diet to malnourishment, as many people think when they try to refute Buddhism by saying that life without attachment is impossible. *Trishna* is about the extra weight we bring to our plans and preferences when they so control us that any change throws us into uncontrollable, heedless emotional turmoil. That is how *trishna* causes *duhkha*. *Trishna* is also about the mistaken view that getting something—wealth or a male child, for example—will bring happiness and satisfaction. Because of this view, such goals are pursued compulsively and, therefore, suffering results. Thus, it is clear that from a Buddhist point of view, *trishna* is at the root of both excessive consumption and overpopulation. Neither would occur if people did not think that more wealth or more children would satisfy an existential itch that is in reality cooled only by equanimity. "I want . . ." are the two words that fuel the suffering of excessive consumption and overpopulation.

Because it is so counterintuitive in our culture to suggest that attachment is the cause of human miseries, let us perform a mental exercise I often use with my students. Buddhists, contrary to popular Western stereotypes, regard happiness as favorably as do any other people. The First Noble Truth is not about preferring misery to happiness but about noting that conventional ways of pursuing happiness produce sorrow instead. Most people think that happiness results from getting what we crave, whereas Buddhists would say that happiness happens when *trishna* is renounced. Thus, craving and happiness are incompatible. Some reflection on one's last experience of unrelieved, intense longing will quickly confirm that it was not a pleasant experience. One endures the longing because of the pleasure that comes when cravings are satisfied. But the satisfaction is short-lived and is quickly replaced by yet another longing. The satisfaction of our cravings is virtually impossible because of the insatiable, addictive nature of *trishna*, which always wants more. Since craving and happiness are incompatible, which one should be renounced?

The good news of Buddhism is that the mental attitude of grasping and fixation is not the only alternative. "I want . . ." can be replaced with simply noting what is. The enlightened alternative to *trishna* is detachment— equanimity and even-mindedness beyond the opposites of hope and fear, pleasure and pain. It is the unconditional joy that cannot be produced by the satisfaction of cravings, but arises spontaneously when we truly experience unfabricated mind. Equanimity has nothing to do with getting what we want and everything to do with developing contentment with things as they are. It is the hard-won ability to be at least somewhat even-minded whether one gets one's heart's desire or is denied it. It is the hard-won ability to put space around every experience, to realize without feeling cheated that nothing lasts forever, and to be at least somewhat cheerful no matter what is happening. Therefore, fundamentally, *trishna* and equanimity are states of mind; they have little to do with what we have or do not have. According to Buddhism, external factors, whether other people or material objects, are not the source of joy or suffering; rather, *attitudes* toward people and things determine whether we experience joy or suffering. Both rich and poor can be ridden by *trishna*, and both can cultivate equanimity, though extreme poverty is not especially conducive to developing it. Those in poverty are often too consumed with survival to develop equanimity and enlightenment—strong arguments to work toward a small population living well rather than a large population living in dire circumstances or the current extreme inequities between rich and poor.[4]

On the other hand, greed is normal in people who live conventional lives, which is why it seems so counterintuitive to suggest that longings, such as those for more wealth or more children, are the cause of suffering. According to Buddhism, greed is normal in conventional people because of a pervasive and deep-seated erroneous view of the self. Craving for *more*, whether children or things, is rooted in ignorance. Ignorance of what? Classically, craving is rooted in ignorance and denial of our fundamental nature, which is the lack of a permanent individual self—*anatman*. But *anatman* is simply another name for interdependence. Because we are interdependent with everything else in the matrix of existence, we do not exist in the way we conventionally believe that we do—as self-existing, self-contained bundles of wants and needs that end with our skin or, if we feel generous, with our immediate families. That imagined independent self which greedily consumes and reproduces itself is a fiction. It has never really existed, and so giving up on it is not a loss but a homecoming. This is the aspect of Buddhism that has been so inspiring to deep ecologists, who have claimed that Asian worldviews are more conducive to ecological vision than Western emphases on the unique, independently existing, eternal individual.

Furthermore, when Buddhists discuss *trishna* as the cause of suffering, all compulsions are equally problematic because craving is incompatible with equanimity. Therefore, on grounds other than interdependence, one cannot delink population from consumption, or either from the environment. Frequently outsiders will ask whether it is not permissible to have "good" longings. The negative answer to this question is especially important in this context because it puts desire for too many things and desire for too many children on exactly the same footing. Both are equally problematic and destructive. The environmental crisis is not solved by arguing about whether overpopulation or excessive consumption is more serious but by "both-and" linkages between them.

These contemplations on individual longing in an interdependent world are rather steep, but they have many virtues in promoting a more radical way of linking consumption, reproduction, and the environment. The most important is that, while in terms of absolute truth individuals do not exist as independent entities, in terms of relative truth, a profound reorientation of consciousness to that fact, individual by individual, is necessary if the root causes of excessive consumption and reproduction are to be overcome. While I certainly favor governmental, economic, and social programs and policies that discourage excessive consumption and reproduction, I also think that by themselves such interventions at the macro level will be insufficient. Nor does Buddhism have a great deal to say about such policies. But, in addition to such policies, individual people need to realize and experience that their happiness does not require or depend on *more* of anything, and Buddhist practices have a great deal to offer in promoting such personal transformation. So long as limits, whether to consumption or fertility, are regarded as a dreary duty imposed from above and a personal loss, people will resent and try to evade them.

But if one experiences such limits not as personal loss but as normal, natural, and pleasant in an interdependent matrix, then they are not a problem. In terms of behaviors in which I personally take pride that aid environmental viability—it is no problem to be childless, a point I often make to young people pressured by family and society to have children against their better judgment. People talk of zero population growth or of China's one-child policy as if they were extreme, but, given the counter-productivity of recent population growth, a declining population and many childless people are more in order. So many things and people in our world need nurturing that one hardly needs to have biological offspring to find something worthy of nurturing.

It is no problem to drive a fifteen-year-old car, the second I have ever owned (I would prefer not to need one), and it is no problem to share my spacious, highly valued personal sanctuary of a hundred-plus-year-old house with others (for modest rent). I even share my cats with my house-mate—and I prefer cats to most other creatures and things. I do these things not out of economic necessity (I could easily afford a much newer car and not to share my home) but because they are reasonable, sane ways to tread more lightly on the environment. This combination of not regarding limits as a problem and not cultivating exclusive personal possessiveness concerning what one values is important for long-term environmental viability. Buddhist practices certainly are helpful in internalizing such attitudes, in converting them from externally imposed duty to self-existing environmentally friendly behaviors.

Such contemplations also protect against one of the most difficult and depressing aspects of trying to live somewhat modestly—the fear that so many people are not limiting their consumption and their fertility that one's own actions make no difference. But if living with limits is pleasure rather than duty, joining the feeding frenzy of a society oriented toward personal greed and family immortality is not tempting or appealing. My housemate wants a hot tub in the back yard; I could afford one, but I think they are wasteful, self-indulgent, and certainly not good for the environment. Recently at my cabin, a guest suggested that washing dishes without running water is too much trouble and that we should use paper plates instead. His justification—so many people are doing it that our abstinence makes no difference—is more logical, and probably more realistic, than my assumption that washing dishes is the right action in this case. But the appeal of such convenience does not lure me because I already feel I should stop using paper towels in favor of cloth rags and toilet paper in favor of an Indian-style water cup. The point is not that these small efforts on my part will make much difference to the big picture—that is not the issue or the motivation for my behaviors and I do not think about the results of my actions. Rather, Asian notions of worrying about right action rather than the outcome of those actions have been with me so long that I am content with the actions, not needing their success or failure as my motivator. The important point is that wanting to engage in more convenient, more wasteful practices does not occur, and so I am not being heroic. What Buddhism can offer to an environmental ethic is practices that help individuals value right action rather than consequences.

This discussion of Buddhist practice must also note, however, that contemplative practices have been emphasized in this chapter. Most Buddhists would not regard contemplative practices as sufficient by themselves to produce the personal transformations discussed above. They still partake somewhat of view or belief, and most Buddhists would say it is not possible to think ourselves into deep personal transformation. Such contemplative exercises need to be founded upon meditative disciplines in which one learns to be with the entirety of experience without acceptance or rejection, without manipulation, without praise or blame, with openness and equanimity. Such meditative exercises, part of Buddhist oral tradition, are the basis for internalizing these contemplative practices until they become second nature. In addition, they are energizing and calming at the same time, thus providing staying power and cheerfulness for the long run, rather than the burnout and bitterness so characteristic of zealots.

⌇ Does It Work? Practical Results to Buddhist Practice

A frequent complaint against religion in general and Buddhism in particular is that the profound ethical insights of the tradition have little practical impact on the world. In popular stereotypes, Buddhism in particular, with its emphasis on silent, motionless meditation practices, is accused of being otherworldly. But this widespread evaluation is, in my view, based on a serious misunderstanding of Buddhist ethics regarding social action. Buddhism generally teaches that the first moral agenda is to develop clarity and equanimity oneself, before trying to intervene in or influence society at large. Thus, Buddhism's emphasis on practices promoting individual transformation is not antisocial or otherworldly in any way, but instead is aimed at avoiding the self-righteous excesses so common in religions that promote activism for all. According to Buddhist understandings of moral development, the meditative and contemplative practices discussed above result in the development of genuine compassion, said to be the only basis for a helpful program of social action. In addition, as I have already argued, I do not believe the changes we need to make to survive as a species and as societies will occur *without* the inner personal transformations discussed above. Practices promoting such internal transformation are Buddhism's specialty and the piece often missing from other programs for ecological survival.

Furthermore, stereotypes aside, the Buddhist record of personal transformation leading to social benefit is impressive. It must be remembered that Buddhism has been the dominant religion in very few societies; those societies, such as those of Tibet and Southeast Asia, are not especially overpopulated and have not been markedly aggressive since their conversion to Buddhism. Two of the most respected and effective recent winners of the Nobel Peace Prize, the Dalai Lama and Aung San Suu Kyi, are Buddhists and base their social activism directly on Buddhist principles and their meditative discipline. The Dalai Lama has publicly advocated both population regulation and environmental protection as vital to the survival and well-being of the planet. These are not isolated examples. Twentieth-century Buddhism has developed a global movement called Engaged Buddhism,[5] which some see as the Buddhist equivalent of liberation theology. Nor is the historical record devoid of examples of effective personal transformation leading to Buddhist social action. A well-known example is that of Emperor Ashoka of ancient India, famous for becoming a pacifist after his conversion to Buddhism.[6] One could also cite the fact that the Tibetans, who were militarily very sophisticated and successful before their conversion to Buddhism[7] completely lost interest in military affairs after they became Buddhists.[8] And in East Asia, though Buddhism was used to train soldiers in military discipline, it has also been credited with bringing new practices of compassion and charity to those societies.[9]

As already noted, thus far contemporary Buddhist ethical thought has not brought together the interrelated issues of population, consumption, and the environment; but certain conclusions regarding appropriate actions follow inevitably from understanding the view of interdependence and following the practice of replacing compulsion with equanimity. Within a finite matrix, it is not possible to have both all the material goods and all the fertility that people living conventionally want. Some choices must be made. We could continue the current obscene distribution patterns, with a few people consuming most of the earth's resources and the majority of people pushing the margins of existence. If consumer goods are the ultimate concern, we could have a world in which most people have their personal automobile—though only with a significantly reduced population if breathing oxygen continues to be necessary for humans. If fertility and reproduction are the ultimate concerns, we could reproduce until the entire earth is as crowded and impoverished as today's most crowded places, though I think the traditional controllers of population—

violence, epidemic, and famine—would intervene well before such an apocalypse could occur. (How much less suffering is involved in limiting human population through fertility regulation rather than through war, disease, and starvation!) Or we could chart a middle course, balancing consumption and reproduction in ways that result in a world in which there are few enough people consuming moderately enough that all can be adequately cared for materially, emotionally, and spiritually. Without doubt, Buddhism, with its longstanding advocacy of a middle path that avoids extremes would favor that latter course and lend its views and practices to supporting such action.

I will conclude this chapter exploring the ways in which some traditional Buddhist ethical teachings might be applied to issues of population, consumption, and the environment, especially given the current inequities in resource distribution and rates of reproduction. I will work with Buddhist teachings specifically devoted to providing guidelines for compassionate action—the *paramitas* ("transcendent virtues" in one common translation) discussed as part of the bodhisattva path in Mahayana Buddhism. After some proficiency in understanding interdependence and the Four Noble Truths, these teachings become relevant to the Buddhist practitioner, at least as some forms of Buddhism understand the Buddhist path of ethical development. Once one has some clarity about how counterproductive *trishna* is in an interdependent matrix, one may have some idea about how to help in a world consumed by *trishna*.

A rich literature of contemplation and commentary revolves around *paramita* practice, and I will draw on some of this literature. I will also link my discussion of *paramita* practice with some Western ethical concepts relevant to issues of population and consumption, namely, the language of rights and responsibilities. For Western Buddhists in particular, such linkages and cross-cultural conceptual translations are important, both for our understanding of Buddhism and for making Buddhist contributions to our Western cultural milieu. That such efforts are sometimes disparagingly compared to the early period of Chinese Buddhism, when "matching concepts" between Chinese and Buddhist worldviews was practiced by many,[10] does not lessen the relevance and appropriateness of this method.

In this context, it is helpful to focus on the first two of the six *paramitas*, generosity and discipline. Generosity is highly valued in Buddhism as a whole. Wealth, in and of itself, is not inappropriate for a Buddhist, but wealth should be circulated to promote widespread ethical and spiritual well-being, rather than hoarded. Generosity is thus evaluated as the primary virtue of the bodhisattva, without which the other *paramitas* cannot develop or will develop improperly. On the other hand, generosity by itself is meaningless and may well be counterproductive. It needs to be balanced and informed by the *paramita* immediately following generosity—discipline. (In Buddhist thought, not just the members of a list but their order on the list are important clues.) If it is not so balanced and informed, generosity may well lead to what my teacher called "idiot compassion"—giving people things that are not helpful to them because one lacks discipline and *prajna* (discriminating awareness wisdom) in being generous. Instead, he often said, the *paramita* of discipline involves uttering "the giant NO," when the situation called for it. One could even talk of the gift of the "giant NO." (It should be pointed out that ideally *paramita* practice is based on enough understanding of interdependence—emptiness or *sunyata* in Mahayana language—that the practice is nondualistic. Therefore, the question of giver and receiver of generosity or discipline does not arise. There is simply one spontaneous field of action.)

I suggest that it might be helpful to link this discussion of generosity and discipline to Western language about rights and responsibilities. Regarding such language, I agree with the widespread observation that it is a product of the European Enlightenment and individualism and does not fit easily into most Asian systems of thought, including Mahayana discussions of the *paramita*s. This lack of fit is due to the fact that language of rights and responsibilities is extremely dualistic, based on assumptions of independently existing individuals who have rights and responsibilities vis-à-vis each other. I would also argue that in much contemporary Western discourse, rights and responsibilities have become dangerously delinked from one another. Claims for multiple rights abound, but very few wish to discuss the corresponding responsibilities, which often lends a tone of childish demand to claims about rights.

Nevertheless, despite lack of a perfect fit between the *paramita*s of generosity and discipline and Western concepts of rights and responsibilities, some comparisons may be instructive. The example of the way generosity and discipline are linked in Mahayana thought may well prove a useful model for how to link rights and responsibilities in Western discussions. One could see generosity as roughly analogous to rights and discipline as analogous to responsibility. Those in need have rights to the generosity of those with more wealth but, to merit continued generosity, they have responsibilities to be disciplined in their own lives. Likewise, those with relative wealth have a responsibility to be generous with their consumables, but they also have both a right and a responsibility to exercise discipline in giving and to avoid "idiot compassion." Because generosity and discipline so balance and inform each other, the sharp line between rights and responsibilities is diminished. Those with wealth have something beyond responsibility to share it; sharing is a spontaneous discipline beyond rights and responsibility. Likewise, discipline undercuts the question of rights and responsibilities; whatever rights one may think one has, discipline is more integral to self-esteem and well-being. When discipline is well established, responsible and generous action is spontaneous and joyful, rather than onerous.

The way in which generosity and discipline balance and inform each other suggests how to balance and link rights and responsibilities in Western discussions of population, consumption, and the environment. One frequently hears claims of rights to an adequate standard of living, as well as rights to reproduce as much as an individual chooses. But corresponding discussions of the effects of unlimited exercise of these "rights" on the ecosystem or the quality of life, corresponding discussions of the need for responsibility when exercising these rights are not always heard. The net effect is that these two rights are on a collision course with each other. Rather than discussing such rights as if they could be independent of each other, it is important to realize that the more seriously we take the claim of a right to a universal minimum standard of living, the more critical universal fertility regulation becomes. Only if we don't really think it is possible to divide the world's resources equitably can we afford to be casual about universal fertility regulation. And the more unrestricted fertility the earth experiences, the more difficult it will become ever to achieve equitable distribution. Conversely, if unregulated wasteful consumption continues unabated, inequities of wealth and poverty can only grow; then the poor, whose only resource is their children, cannot possibly do without enough of them to put minimal food on the table and to provide minimal old-age care. The more that destructive patterns of growth and consumption increase, the more difficult it becomes to avoid excessive population growth. Only if it is thought that the wealthy can somehow insulate themselves from the negative environmental consequences of such growth can we afford to be casual about the need to forbid excessive and wasteful consumption. Like generosity and discipline, rights exist only in interdependence with responsibilities. Those who refuse to meet their responsibilities lose their rights, which is why involuntary fertility regulation and involuntary limits to consumption are not always inappropriate. No one's rights to their consumables or their fertility are so absolute that they include destroying or damaging the environment in which we all live.

While writing this chapter, I returned to my childhood home, once again noting with sadness the negative effects of more people than ever before consuming at greater levels than ever before. The spring, the outhouse, and the woods to provide firewood are still there and all are still used, but traffic noise from long-distance eighteen-wheelers hauling con-

sumables to and fro often interrupts the silence unpleasantly. My cabin is now on the first open land from town, and a nearby lake, wild and unsettled in my childhood, is now surrounded by houses as crowded together as if they were in a city. Year by year increasing population increases the pressure to subdivide and sell my land; before I die higher taxes that result from these population pressures may force me to sell. One can still see more stars in the black sky than in a city, but those to the north are whited out by light pollution from the nearest town. Now I comment on dragonflies, butterflies, and fireflies because they are not as common as they once were.

To trade in this sacred, pristine environment to support more people consuming at unprecedented levels seems a poor bargain. I can see no way in which all this "more"—more people, more stuff—has improved the quality of life, except perhaps that I can now buy Chinese spices at the local grocery store! But surely we can figure out ways to increase quality without increasing quantity, and if not, I'd rather do without Chinese spices than without the spacious, untrammeled environment. More is not better, whether it is more people or more consumables, "Growth," the god we worship, is a false idol, needing to be replaced by "no growth," if not by "negative growth." "Growth" and "more" represent the unbridled reign of trishna, not appreciation and reverence for the interdependent matrix of the environment in which we live and upon which we depend unconditionally. But to be consumed by trishna is not human nature, not our inevitable lot or inescapable original sin. With enough meditation and contemplation of interdependence, trishna will give way to equanimity. Would that trishna would give way to contentment and equanimity—speedily and in our time!

Finding Renunciation and Balance in Western Buddhist Practice: Work, Family, Community, and Friendship

THIS CHAPTER INVOLVES a contemporary contemplative commentary on classical Buddhist issues and concerns. One of the most basic perennial Buddhist questions concerns what kind of lifestyle actually promotes "enlightenment." While for many of us, enlightenment may seem to be something we can't define adequately, I think most of us hope to become more sane, gentle, grounded, helpful people through our involvement with Buddhist practice. For me, that constitutes the beginnings of an enlightened quality in my life, and fuller experiences of enlightenment will have to grow out of those qualities. But what lifestyles actually promote those qualities of gentleness and sanity? If the question of appropriate lifestyle is resolved, then we need to question what attitudes are to be cultivated as we go about our lives, since observing the external formalities associated with a specific lifestyle is not guaranteed to result in gentleness and sanity.

In early Buddhism, the answer was obvious: renunciation of the conventional lifestyle of career and reproduction in favor of a monastic lifestyle that bypasses both was thought to be more conducive to enlightenment for most people because it was more conducive to an attitude of detachment. But for some forms of Buddhism, especially those belonging to later developments in Buddhism lumped together as "Mahayana Buddhism," the distinction between monastics and laypeople is not so clearcut. The *attitude* of renunciation is thought to be more important than any particular lifestyle and not necessarily linked with any specific lifestyle. Nevertheless, except for Pure Land Buddhism and, to a lesser extent, other Japanese forms of Buddhism, most forms of Mahayana Buddhism still continue to honor monastics over householders in some way.

Therefore, for me, doing my practices in the Tibetan tradition, in which there is a clear distinction between monastics and householders, and in which monastics are highly valued, this distinction is perhaps more decisive than it is for other Western Buddhists, whose training is in one of the less monastic Japanese forms of Buddhism. On the other hand, Tibetan Buddhism also honors nonmonastic lifestyles that encourage intensive Buddhist practice, which means that the monastic–lay distinction is not as decisive as in early Buddhism, which equated serious Buddhist practice with the monastic lifestyle.

Obviously, in a certain sense, for most Western Buddhists, the question of choice of lifestyle has already been made. In terms of the formal, traditional distinction between monastic and lay Buddhists, most Western Buddhists are lay practitioners, in that we have not taken vows that imply celibacy and renunciation of family and occupation. That affiliation as lay Buddhist practitioners, however, does not have the same simplicity and finality for us American lay Buddhists as it does for most classical Asian patterns of Buddhism, nor does it limit us to the same peripheral role of supporting monastics as it does in most forms of Asian Buddhism. Most of us see ourselves as trying to engage in full-fledged Buddhist practice as laypeople who also have some involvement in family and some responsibility for livelihood—an ideal that would have seemed preposterous in many forms of Asian Buddhism. Therefore, for us, questions of the interface between "enlightenment" and work, family, community, and friendship are nowhere nearly so clear-cut as they probably were for many lay Buddhists. We are in many ways without map or model, trying to find our way and to discover workable paths.

◌ Renunciation and Community: The Basic Tools

In my path-seeking in this chapter, I want to use two torchlights from traditional Buddhism to light my way and guide my contemplations.[1] One of them comes from the lineage supplication chant of my tradition, the Karma Kagyu sect of Tibetan Vajrayana Buddhism.[2] It consists of a single line from that chant: "renunciation is the foot of meditation." This line, of course, brings up an obvious question: What is renunciation? My other source of inspiration is the life story of the Buddha, read in a *midrashic*[3] style. In my *midrash*, I will counterpoise the Buddha's renunciation of conventional family and livelihood with his founding of a countercultural community that replaced them, asking what message we lay meditators can read from these choices. In these two traditional beacons, I think we may find some clues about how to deal with community, friendship, family, and work in the context of Western Buddhism and as lay practitioners who fully engage the traditional Buddhist discipline usually taken on only by monastics.

In order to work with these two guide lights, I will need to flesh out two definitions and then develop two theses. Obviously, the term "renunciation" needs to be discussed at some length, since the traditional formal renunciation of family and livelihood is not what is meant by renunciation in the lifestyle of the lay practitioner. Nevertheless, the more I am involved in Buddhism, the more clearly I see that renunciation is indeed foundational to Buddhist outlook and practice and the more I am drawn to its mood. Perhaps the fact that my refuge name[4] includes the word "renunciation" has added some intensity to my contemplations of renunciation in the context of lay meditation. People should be forewarned, however, that in Vajrayana tradition renunciation may not look like many peoples' image of renunciation as asceticism. Second, I need to discuss what I mean by "community" and by "friendship." I contend that in the lifestyle of the lay meditator, they are "the matrix of enlightenment," by which I mean that they are at least as essential to developing sanity and gentleness as are study and practice, which are traditionally stressed as the matrix of enlightenment. I have dealt extensively with this thesis in previous works, especially in my book *Buddhism after Patriarchy*, in which I devoted a major portion of my last chapter to developing this point.

Building upon these definitions, in this contemplation I will explore two theses that interlock and intertwine throughout this chapter. It is my contention that in contemporary America, including American Buddhism, people spend far too much time and energy on work and family and far too little time and energy on friendship and community for a sane lifestyle ever to develop. Second, it is my contention that proper limitation of work and family is essential to a viable American lay Buddhism and that, without such limitation, lay Buddhism simply dribbles off into conventional worldly, distracted, nonaware living. Such proper limitations of work and family are among the most essential meanings of renunciation for the lifestyle of the lay Buddhist meditator.

"Renunciation is the foot of meditation." To assert that renunciation is foundational to spiritual life is not an easy or attractive message to proclaim today. Renunciation is decidedly unpopular in American culture, and, when the topic of renunciation is broached, the kind of religious asceticism associated with some aspects of Christianity justifiably comes in for its share of criticism, from feminists among others. It has become commonplace to point out how some ascetical styles of renunciation, emphasizing anti-body, anti-sexual, and otherworldly attitudes, have promoted guilt, repression, and sexism. For obvious reasons, many Buddhists would prefer to distance themselves from such culturally familiar versions of renunciation.

Nevertheless, the longer I am involved with Buddhism, the more clearly I experience that Buddhist practice is fundamentally about renunciation. The lineage chant, with its proclamation that without renunciation there is no Buddhist practice, is not outdated. The fact that renunciation was central to the life story of the Buddha and to the life of the early community is not a superficial, culturally discardable incidental to the main story line. The critical question, however, concerns what is the renunciation that is the foot of meditation? I do not believe that the *content* or *form* of renunciation remains constant in all Buddhist contexts. Rather, it is the *mind-set* of renunciation that cannot be discarded in Buddhist practice. Not only can it not be discarded; renunciation is central to Buddhist discipline and vision at all stages of the Buddhist path.

The form that renunciation took in early Buddhism—that is, celibacy and homelessness—was not an end in itself. It was the *method* used to promote a certain psychological and spiritual transformation, the experience of "cooling," the experience of the freedom, detachment, and tranquillity known in shorthand as "enlightenment." To experience that state of being, certain things that go against the grain of ego, against the conventional hopes and dreams that are so deep-seated in ordinary humans, are required. We have to give up, to surrender, to recognize that we will not have our way in the world of impermanence. This is what is meant by the renunciation that is the foot of meditation. That is where renunciation fits into the Buddhist path. At the most basic level, what must be renounced are the hopes and dreams for permanence, ease, and security that drive conventional lifestyles. Renunciation is a matter of finding the right tools to promote that transformation, not of an ascetical lifestyle.

That kind of renunciation is ongoing, moment-by-moment renunciation, beginning with the first moment of agreeing in meditation practice to do the technique we have been given and to renounce our habitual wildness of mind, our conventional tendency to let our minds go as they please into whatever fantasy or fixation seizes us at any given time. What happens then? In a recent retreat, I was overwhelmed by the clarity of the demand to renounce triviality, superficiality, glibness, distractibility, and smugness. To renounce superficiality is to see deeply into things as they are, always central to Buddhism. In classic Buddhist language, with proper renunciation, one no longer mistakes the relative for the absolute, which is clearly being done when petty goals and issues dominate one's con-

sciousness and dispel detachment and tranquillity. Or, to put it more col-
loquially, if one properly, fully renounces, one no longer mistakes the
molehill for the mountain.

Clearly, no lifestyle can guarantee renunciation of fixation and triviality,
which is why some forms of Buddhism are less insistent that monasticism
is necessary for renunciation. As American lay Buddhists, we participate in
those less-monastic forms of Buddhism without giving up our zest for
renunciation. What does the renunciation that is the foot of meditation
have to do with community, friendship, family, and work? The Buddha, we
will remember, clearly renounced family and work and set up an alternative community to take their place. Lay Buddhist practitioners do not
renounce work and family in the same formal definitive way, but try to
regard them as a realm of practice, as an extension of the meditation cush-
ion and the meditation hall. That is to say, work and family become the
arena for meditation in action. On the other hand, since we practice not
only for the accumulation of merit but also for the accumulation of wisdom,[5] renunciation is integral to our practice. We cannot simply do what
we want to do anyway and call it "meditation in action."[6] It will not be
"meditation in action" without the proper attitudinal foundation of renunciation, which is perhaps the greatest threat to the integrity and genuine-
ness of nonmonastic forms of renunciation.

I would contend that there are definite limits to the practice of taking
work and family as arenas for meditation in action, to the amount of work
and family one can take on without simply falling into merely conventional distraction and attachment. Getting too immersed in work or family will definitely preclude the mind of detachment and renunciation that
is central to the Buddhist vision and to Buddhist suggestions about how to
solve the unsatisfactoriness of conventional existence. If I could suggest a
subtle distinction of connotation, I would contend that while in Mahayana vision one does not necessarily need to renounce the householder
lifestyle to achieve genuine renunciation, one definitely does need to
renounce *domesticity*. The ideal of settling into a comfortable predictable
existence characterized by nesting and self-perpetuation is not compatible
with renunciation. Rather, vision must replace conventionality and comfort seeking. Therefore, there is a definite quality of being on the razor's
edge when one attempts to bring work or family into full-fledged Buddhist
practice. Such a method of Buddhist practice requires proper renunciation,
in the form of *properly limiting* work and family.

Community and friendship, on the other hand, are the "matrix of
enlightenment," I contend. Buddhist tradition itself affirms that, in this
nontheistic path, the companionship and feedback of our fellow travelers

are so basic and so central that they are called a "refuge," one of the very few that we have.[7] Though renunciation is an important theme in the life of the Buddha and of the early community, he established a *community* for his renunciants; he did not send them off *individually* to pursue enlightenment. This model is not to be ignored or taken lightly. In earlier work, I have emphasized the meaning of the fact that the *sangha* is, in fact, the third of the Three Refuges. But I also suggest that this fact has been overlooked and its significance ignored in Buddhism, as the *sangha* comes in a poor third to the Buddha and the dharma as a priority for Buddhists and Buddhism.[8]

It is critical, however, that "community" be understood as the *sangha* or community that is the third of the Three Jewels, not as a club or ingroup. Equally important, by community I do not mean merely a collection of individuals having the same institutional affiliation nor a group of people indifferent to one another but focused on some common purpose. If domesticity and nesting are inappropriate ways to integrate family and work into the lifestyle of lay Buddhist mediators, they are equally inappropriate understandings of the task of human community in Buddhist vision. The purpose of *sangha*, as one of the Three Refuges, is to midwife enlightenment by providing feedback and companionship on the path, not to provide the security of a group ego or a safe social environment. By *sangha*, I mean a group of people who, in their pursuit of the common purpose of enlightenment, are acutely attentive to the need for friendship, for psychological comfort and emotional nurturing as part of the spiritual journey, and who, therefore, care for and take care of one another, without falling into unhealthy codependence.

An important extension or deepening of the definition of *sangha* or community as a matrix of enlightenment includes, in my view, special friendships of spiritual or dharmic partnership. To be discussed more fully in a future essay, "dharmic consortship" refers to nondomestic, often nonreproductive pairing whose major purpose is to promote the spiritual development of both partners. Modeled on some materials found in Tibetan Buddhism,[9] dharmic consortship is even less recognized and less well understood than is the reality of *sangha* as the matrix of enlightenment.

In pre-feminist Buddhism, awareness that *sangha* as a community of caring friends is an element essential to the matrix of enlightenment has been minimal. It will take feminist consciousness in Buddhism, I suggest, fully to appreciate the profundity of community as "matrix of enlightenment." This is because, under patriarchal gender constructions, women are far more likely than are men to notice the absolutely critical importance of friendships to spiritual well-being. In fact, in my view it is no exaggeration to suggest that friendship and community are as fundamental to spiritual well-being as are study of basic Buddhist teachings and the practice of meditation, which are so emphasized in Buddhist tradition. That is why the Buddha organized his followers into a community and declared community to be the third of the Three Refuges. This awareness needs to be integrated into Buddhism far more consciously, more deliberately, and more fully than has ever been done in the past. I also believe that this message is sorely needed in Western Buddhism, in which the Western myth of individualism, especially its American version of the lonesome cowboy hero, seems to justify the highly individualistic interpretation of Buddhism typical of many Western Buddhists.

∼ Renunciation, Work, and Family in the Practice of Lay Meditators

Lay Buddhist practitioners need to work out our pursuit of career and our practice of family life within the context of these core Buddhist values of renunciation and community. These classic Buddhist concerns, especially as seen through the lens of feminist interpretation, will provide some checks and balances for determining an appropriate level of involvement in work and family for lay Buddhist meditators. Having asserted that, in general, American Buddhists invest too much time and energy in work and family and too little in friendship and community, let us explore renunciation and community as values against which to measure how much is too much work or family in a sane and grounded Buddhist lay meditator's lifestyle.

It is not difficult to make the case that the typical American lifestyle is far too workaholic, at least among the educated and professional types most likely to be attracted to and involved in lay Buddhist practice. The time demands of most professional and business careers are becoming ever more out of control, with little discussion of how to reverse the trend. The impact of such demands on both family life and community, to say nothing of their impact on the requirements for serious Buddhist meditation practice, is devastating. Certainly the feminist vision and demand that women participate in the satisfactions of meaningful work did not seek a situation in which everyone, including both partners in an ongoing relationship, work sixty-hour weeks, to the detriment of community life, which now no one has time to organize or participate in, and to the detriment of friendships, which are often the major casualty of a workaholic lifestyle. Rather, part of the feminist agenda was to share the burdens of earning a livelihood, so that both partners could experience the satisfaction of meaningful work while neither would be burdened with unreasonable and counterproductive demands to spend all or most of one's energies on work. This feminist vision has not been realized—a serious problem for both women and men, particularly if they are also serious lay Buddhist practitioners heavily involved in the time-consuming disciplines of study and meditation practice. In *Buddhism after Patriarchy*, I suggested that properly limiting one's livelihood and avoiding workaholism are important contemporary interpretations of "Right Livelihood," the fifth component of the Eightfold Noble Path, Buddhism's Fourth Noble Truth.

However, that too much energy and time go into family, especially in comparison to the time and energy that are put into community may not be so intuitively obvious. Many people feel that families and family time are being neglected, not overindulged, in an age of dual-career families. And if the contest is between excessive demands from the fast-track workplace and the needs of family life, I definitely would agree. But I am concerned about an imbalance between energy being devoted to *community* and energy being devoted to *family*, not about an imbalance between energy devoted to *work* and energy devoted to *family*. I am suggesting that community, friendships, and dharmic partnerships are unlikely to be given the priority, energy, and involvement that would be appropriate for Buddhist lay meditators because people choose or feel compelled to give that energy to family instead, especially to family as a reproductive unit. Furthermore, I am suggesting that this imbalance is a problem for Buddhist lay meditators because community is more likely to foster sanity and tranquillity than is family. The conventional family is often conflict-ridden and riddled with suffering and frustration, not because of ill will or problems that can be fixed but because of the inherent nature of family life.

Because of the potential unpopularity of my message, let me make some qualifications clear. First of all, my skepticism is not directed at "family" in an extended sense, which is somewhat akin to what I mean by "community," but primarily at the nuclear family cut off from the community, isolated unto itself and fostering expectations of great emotional fulfillment and even spiritual meaning within its narrow confines. Furthermore, I do not claim that family life, even in its more narrow definition, cannot be an arena of Buddhist practice and a manifestation of sacred outlook. I only claim that conventional approaches to and expectations for family life are inappropriate in a Buddhist context because proper and necessary limits are not observed, or, to put the matter in Buddhist terms, the Middle Way is not observed. The result is that conventional family life is not a matrix of sanity, tranquillity, happiness, or fulfillment, but rather of frustration, suffering, and full-scale, unabashed *samsara,* particularly in the case of intergenerational relationships. The expectations are too high, the attachments too great, and the needs too overwhelming for any other result. As the most basic Buddhist teachings affirm, such needs and attachments cannot produce anything but suffering. And, as early Buddhism analyzed, family life easily produces intense needs and attachments.

Family life is *inherently* difficult, in my view, because we are introduced to the inevitable limitations, frustrations, sorrow, and unsatisfactoriness of *samsara* in our families. Some of the outburst of anger that we as children feel against our parents and what they did to us is, I think, nothing more than frustration with the inevitable limits of human life, its finitude and unsatisfactoriness, which, as parents, they were compelled to teach us. (This is not meant to deny that there is real abuse above and beyond the inevitabilities of *samsara.*) From the other side, I often watch parents frantically trying all the latest tricks of parenting, as if by being good enough parents, they could protect their children from ever encountering *samsara.* This initial encounter with *samsara* occurs in a context in which attachment and ego are very likely to be enhanced rather than diminished. Even meditators have a difficult time achieving any detachment vis-à-vis their own families, whether their parents or their children. Is it any wonder that family life so often involves so much struggle and frustration, so little tranquillity or sanity?

Nor do I think that such assessments of family relationships are recent or confined to the supposedly degenerate West. Some contemporary Western Buddhist teachers and practitioners claim that the needs of Western meditators are quite different from those of Asian Buddhists because the Asians come from healthy family environments, whereas many Western Buddhists do not and therefore need therapy in addition to meditation. While I do not dispute that many Western families are dysfunctional and that, therefore, in some cases, therapy may be useful for some meditators, I disagree that Asian Buddhists come from healthier family environments. First and foremost, Asian Buddhists grow up in intensely patriarchal family environments, which simply cannot be sane and psychologically healthy environments. Nor do I believe that the flood of literature detailing family woes, from incest to psychological abuse, that are so obvious in our time and place actually represents a new level or experience of *samsara.* I simply think that, for various reasons, we are more willing to acknowledge that particular variety of *samsara* now than in the past.

The sad part, however, is not that family life is often so difficult. Why should we expect anything else, if we understand Buddhist teachings? The sad part is that people try so desperately to deny these realities and to replace them with the nonexistent mythically happy family. They neglect their communities, sending more energy into family, trying to fix its relationships, to achieve tranquillity and happiness. Sometimes I liken it to sending good money after bad, when there are better investments readily available. However, when one concedes the reality of inevitable unsatisfactoriness in family relationships, some of the bitterness of that reality is diminished, just as when one concedes the First Noble Truth of suffering, there is immediate relief. Simply recognizing the likely limits of satisfaction and sanity in family relationships frees one not to expect or pursue more and encourages one to devote appropriate energy to other dimensions of life, such as community and work. Paradoxically, relaxing one's grip on the satisfactions sought in family life may well improve family relations. Focusing one's attention outward into the community and loosening the bonds of the nuclear family, ironically, probably make family life more satisfying than any other medicine.

Practicing renunciation regarding family as a lay Buddhist meditator means, first and foremost, realism of expectations regarding family life, which promotes more appropriate balance in the energy devoted to family and to community. But unless certain practical limits are honored, such balance is difficult to achieve, no matter how clear one's understanding and intentions may be.

Of primary importance among practical guidelines to renunciation is the need to limit reproduction, for many reasons, not the least of which is simply that one's time and energy are also and desperately needed for other concerns. As Mahayana Buddhists, our primary commandment is not "Be fruitful and multiply," but "Save all sentient beings." There is no dearth of sentient beings already needing our concern and care, and our commandment is to work with sentient beings, not especially to produce more. It should be obvious why, from a Buddhist point of view, only children who can be well cared for should be conceived. With so much misery already present in the world, we should not add to it by producing children that cannot be properly cared for, both physically and psychologically. There is no particular Buddhist rationale for having one's own biological children at all, and one should not feel pressured into parenthood by conventional demands. Unless one is particularly gifted and apt at parenting, it may be more appropriate and compassionate to forgo the experience.

In particular, Buddhists should be wary of reproduction that is due to lack of mindfulness or reproduction motivated by ego. Apart from birth control failure, it is difficult to reconcile accidental conceptions with long-term training in mindfulness practice. More serious, reproduction as an extension or aspect of one's ego is extremely inappropriate for lay Buddhist meditators. To reproduce oneself and to perpetuate the family lineage are extremely common conventional reasons to reproduce; one sees such motivations frequently. Another version of the same motivation occurs when people try to use reproduction to fill a void in their own lives or to find something to do with their lives.

When reproduction is an aspect or extension of ego, the child is in fact conceived to fill some obsessive fixation or need on the part of the parents, which is rather hard on the child. Such motivations for reproduction lead to styles of parenting that involve undue and unhealthy enmeshment in families. Detached parenting is impossible; the parents are too personally invested in who their children become or how they turn out. In other words, the parents' egos are excessively wrapped up in their children, which, of course, puts tremendous pressure on children. In many scenarios, which I fear are not all that rare, the parents, in effect, try to live the children's lives for them or become excessively emotionally dependent on their children. Such psychological incest is, in fact, almost as devastating as its physical counterpart. And it is unavoidable unless parents limit their investment in family properly, balancing that investment with investment in community, work, and spiritual discipline.

The tragedy is that such emotional incest, such undue family enmeshment was and is probably thought inevitable and appropriate in conventional samsaric logic, including the logic by which many Asian families operate. I believe that one of the areas where Buddhists could have the most to contribute to sane family patterns is in thinking through detached parenting, in bringing the Buddhist understanding of the virtues of detachment and renunciation to the arena of parenting and family life. And obviously, this vital addition to Buddhist understanding will come from lay Buddhists rather than monastics.

Therefore, I would urge Buddhist leaders and communities not to romanticize and idealize nuclear families but to investigate more thoroughly the limits, both quantitatively or qualitatively, that are appropriate for lay Buddhist meditators for whom reproduction and nuclear families are viable lifestyle choices. Even more important, Buddhist leaders and communities should investigate and encourage other modes of bonding and of structuring primary relationships within the community. Lay meditators for whom nuclear families are not appropriate lifestyle choices should be supported rather than discouraged. For at least some American Buddhist communities, including my own Vajradhatu community, taking these suggestions seriously would mean far less pressure to form nuclear families and to reproduce, and far more attention to alternatives.

◇ Community as Priority:
Some Concluding Suggestions

Taking time and energy for friendships and community often seems to be the lowest priority, to be fitted in after work and family needs are satisfied, *if* any time is left. Currently, my own local Buddhist community has almost ceased a meaningful level of community activity because too many members feel that they can attend or participate in only a few community programs per year after they have discharged their work and family responsibilities. I would argue that the priorities should be reversed among lay Buddhist meditators, if the vision of lay life as an expression of meditation in action is to have any validity. Giving community higher priority is important because community is a central part of the matrix of enlightenment, but the priority given to community is completely out of balance with the energy that goes into work and family in much current American Buddhist practice. The lack of sufficient community, of genuine friendship, psychological comfort, and emotional nurturing within one's Buddhist *sangha* is one of the most pressing and vital issues facing contemporary American Buddhists. In fact, I would claim that, along with developing forms of hierarchy and authority that acknowledge achievement without becoming oppressive, developing a theory and praxis of community as the matrix of enlightenment is *the* agenda for Western lay Buddhist meditators.

But how can such an enormous agenda even be contemplated, especially given the highly alienated and individualized context of American culture in which such developments would have to occur? The most important requirement is simply the *recognition* that community is so basic to Buddhist life. In some ways, this is a radically new insight for Buddhists, and in other ways it is not, given that *sangha* is the third of Three Jewels. Not only did the Buddha declare the *sangha* to be the third jewel; he and the Buddhist community throughout history have devoted considerable attention to detailed suggestions for how to make the *monastic* community work. In the monastic context, it was recognized both that community is important to the spiritual development and discipline of the monastics and that community does not happen without detailed attention to what is required if a group of individuals are to foster one another's practice as a spiritual community. But such insights regarding communities of lay meditators do not seem to have occurred or to be part of the Buddhist tradition, probably because that institutional form is relatively underdeveloped in Buddhism.

What in fact is required is something comparable to the monastic *vinaya*, or rules of discipline, for lay meditators, which detail what is required if the *sangha* of lay meditators is to function as a genuine third refuge, matrix of practice, and matrix of enlightenment. If we concede that it is indeed important for lay Buddhist communities to function in such a manner, what can we say about guidelines for such Buddhist communities?

Perhaps only a single guideline will suffice. Proper balance between the energies devoted to community and relationship, on the one hand, and the energy devoted to family and work, on the other hand, is sorely needed. Nurturing and comforting other people, one's *sangha* members, should be a very high priority in a functioning and functional *sangha*. Instead, one often finds that many people are so absorbed in their nuclear families and their jobs that they claim they do not have the time or energy to be a friend, to comfort and nurture *sangha* members. From my own experiences, I will offer several examples of what seems to me to be a severe lack of such balance. Unfortunately, based on observations, I do not think my experiences are isolated and infrequent.

Several years ago, while I was grieving the death of my partner, most of my friends abandoned me. Since I have no family, they were my only source of comfort, but they all kept their distance. I cried in near despair that unless one had one's meathooks into someone as a family member, no one cares or comforts. It struck me then as highly inappropriate that in a Buddhist context, one had to have that level of legal, formal attachment to someone to receive attention and comfort. Now, some years later, after having learned as much from that grieving as from anything else I have ever experienced, I still feel that such abandonment was inappropriate. In a Buddhist environment, of all places, one should not have to have possessive legal or blood ties with people to receive appropriate humane and human concern and attention. In a functioning community human bonds and humane emotional support would not be dependent on legal or biological ties. People would not so overvalue such legal or biological ties and so undervalue friendship that friends always get the leftovers of attention and love.

People often invoke their favorite rationale for ignoring friends and community in much less extreme circumstances than grief or loss. Many act as if it is appropriate for anyone, anywhere, anytime to say, "I'm too busy," "My job is too demanding," or "I'm tied up with family," with the expectation that ties of friendship can go unattended and community responsibilities can be shunted off onto other "less busy" people. Asking such people what are their priorities or giving feedback that priorities are skewed often arouses hostility in them. The neglected friend or community is expected to accept such priorities without question and without complaint. Recently a long-term valued friend suddenly came up with this rationale, week after week, for not maintaining our usual level of interaction. He expected me to understand that, of course, spending time with me was a low priority compared to work demands and also expected me not to mind being neglected, even not to interpret his actions as neglect. When I responded that I could not but regard it as neglect and as giving our friendship low priority because we always find time for the things that are really important, my feedback only brought more defensiveness and alienation. Finally, I became frustrated enough to make a wish for him: "May your life experiences teach you the value of friends."

To rectify this situation, in which community is undervalued but absolutely essential to detached, sane well-being, I believe certain steps will be required. In my view, we need to take on the discipline of being a *sangha* member in the same formal and serious way that we take on the disciplines of meditation practice and of study of classic Buddhist texts and doctrines. The discipline of being a community member needs to be regarded with the same seriousness that is accorded to meditation and study and to be equally at the center of Buddhist methods of working with our lives. When one goes for refuge to the Buddha and the dharma, the first two of the Three Refuges, one expects, indeed vows, to take seriously the example of the Buddha's meditation practice and to use his dharma teachings as guideposts to one's life. In the same way, when one goes for refuge to *sangha*, it should be understood as a *vow* to do what needs to be done to foster community, including the boring and backbreaking work required to maintain a schedule of programs and maintain a center. That third refuge should also be understood as a vow to attempt to provide appropriate and necessary feedback and comfort to one's fellow travelers. For that to occur, of course, there first need to be specific and definite practices one can do to foster one's ability to be a *sangha* member, just as there are definite and specific methods of meditation and study. To say the least, developing such practices and such priorities has been rather neglected outside the monastic *sangha*. This may be one of the important historical tasks for American Buddhists, who need to think very seriously about how to develop such techniques and practices so that the lay meditators' *sangha* is as genuinely a matrix of enlightenment as is the monastic *sangha*. To do so, we need to discover and develop techniques of group process and individual contemplation that enhance peoples' sensitivity to others and our ability to listen, to befriend, and to nurture, as well as our ability to defuse our own projections and aggressions, rather than turning them loose. We need to develop these skills and abilities to be able to focus on the priority of community as the matrix of enlightenment.

CHAPTER 9

Buddhist Values for
Overcoming Pro-natalism
and Consumerism

T HIS CHAPTER WILL BRING traditional Buddhist values into conversation with the interlocked issues of the environment, resource utilization, and population growth, with an emphasis on overcoming pro-natalism based on religious ideology. Since Buddhism always suggests that we need to deal with things as they are, not with fantasies, it is appropriate to begin with some brief consideration of how the ecosystem, consumption, and population actually interact. When relating these three concerns to one another, one can imagine three alternatives: a sufficiently small population living well on a stable, self-renewing resource base; an excessive population living in degraded conditions on an insufficient resource base; or the present pyramid of a few people living well and large numbers of people barely surviving. Obviously, only the first option contains merit. How people could value reproduction so much to prefer the second option to the first is incomprehensible, and the current pyramid of privilege is morally obscene.

It should also be clear that population is the only fully negotiable element in this complex. In other words, when we look at the three factors under discussion—the environment, population, and consumption—there are two non-negotiables and one negotiable. Fundamentally, it is not negotiable that the human species must live within the boundaries and limits of the biosphere. However it is done, there is no other choice because there is no life apart from the biosphere. Morally, it is not negotiable that there be an equitable distribution of resources among the world's people. While an equitable distribution of resources would mandate much less consumerism in part of the world, there are very non-negotiable limits below which humans should not be expected to live for the sake of unlimited reproduction and population growth. These two non-negotiables mean that population size is the negotiable factor in the equation. It is hard to question that a human population small enough so that everyone can enjoy a decent standard of living without ruining the environment is necessary and desirable. We cannot increase the size of the earth and can only increase its productivity to a limited extent, but we, as a species, can control population. All that it requires is the realization that many other pursuits are at least as sacred and as satisfying as reproduction.

Religions commonly criticize excessive consumption but commonly encourage excessive reproduction. Therefore, though I will note the Buddhist values that encourage moderate consumption, I will emphasize the Buddhist values that encourage moderation and responsibility regarding reproduction, which are considerable. I emphasize these elements in Buddhism precisely because there has been so little discussion of religious arguments that favor restraining human fertility. The example of a major, long-standing world religion whose adherents lead satisfying lives without an overwhelming emphasis on individual procreation certainly is worth investigating.

Buddhism can in no way be construed or interpreted as pro-natalist in its basic values and orientations. The two religious ideas that are commonly invoked by most religions to justify pro-natalist practices are not part of basic Buddhism. Buddhism does not require its members to reproduce as a religious duty. Nor do most forms of Buddhism regard sexuality negatively, as an evil to be avoided unless linked with reproduction, though all forms of Buddhism include an implicit standard of sexual ethics. Therefore, fertility control through contraception as well as abstinence is completely acceptable. The practices regarding fertility and reproduction that would flow from fundamental Buddhist values favor reproduction as a mature and deliberate choice rather than an accident or a duty. Because of the unique ways that Buddhism values human life, only children who can be well cared for physically, emotionally, and spiritually should be conceived. Few Buddhists would disagree with the guideline that one should have few children, so that all of them can be well cared for without exhausting the emotional, material, and spiritual resources of their parents, their community, and their planet.

By contrast, pro-natalism as an ideology is rampant on the planet; those who gently suggest that unlimited reproduction is not an individual right and could well be destructive are derided. Suggest that there is a causal relationship between excessive reproduction and poverty and watch the fallout! Pro-natalist ideology includes at least three major ideas, all of which are subject to question. Pro-natalists always regard a birth as a positive occasion, under any circumstances, even the most extreme. To suggest that reproduction under many circumstances is irresponsible and merits censure rather than support makes one unpopular with pro-natalists. Furthermore, pro-natalists claim that it is necessary to reproduce to be an adequate human being; those who choose to remain childless are scorned and suffer many social and economic liabilities. Finally, pro-natalists regard reproduction as a private right not subject to public policy, even though they usually insist that the results of their reproduction are a public, even a global responsibility. The tragedy of pro-natalism is that excessive populations could be cut quite quickly by voluntary means, but lacking those, probably will be cut by involuntary means involving great suffering—disease, violence, and starvation. Therefore, it is critical to counter the mindless and rampant pro-natalist religious doctrines, socialization, peer pressures, tax policies, sentiments, and values that senselessly assault one at every turn.

Before beginning to discuss Buddhist teachings as a resource for developing an ethic of moderation concerning both reproduction and consumption, it is important to pause to acknowledge two controversial issues. They cannot be debated in this context, even though my conclusions regarding them will be apparent in my discussion of Buddhist ethics, the environment, consumption, and reproduction.

Because the Buddhist concept of all-pervasive interdependence makes sense, I see no way that individual rights can extend to the point that an individual exercising his or her supposed rights can be allowed to threaten the supportive matrix of life—a point that has been reached regarding both consumerism and pro-natalism. Despite personal wealth or values that may drive a person to inappropriate levels of consumption or reproduction, it is hard to argue that people have individual rights to exercise those levels of consumption or reproduction without regard to their impact on the biosphere. The rhetoric of individual rights and freedoms certainly has cogency against an overly communal and authoritarian social system. But today that rhetoric and stance threaten to overwhelm the need for restraint and moderation to protect and preserve communities and species.

Furthermore, especially in the need to counter pro-natalist ideologies and policies, we have reached a point beyond relativism. In the human community, we have learned too late and too slowly the virtues of relativism whenever it is feasible. We have been too eager to condemn others for having a worldview different from our own. Relativism regarding worldview is virtuous because diversity of worldviews is a valuable resource. On the other hand, relativism regarding basic ethical standards leads to intolerable results. Are we really willing to say of a culture in which women are treated like property or children are exploited that

"that's just their culture?" There would be no possibility of an international human rights movement if people really believed that ethical standards are completely relative and arbitrary. And both consumption and reproduction are ethical issues of the highest order, since their conduct gravely affects everyone's life. We can no longer afford to let individuals who believe that they should reproduce many children do so, just as we no longer condone slavery, the exploitation of children, or treating women as chattel. Certain long-standing and deeply held cultural and religious values are at stake in the claim that pro-natalism is an intolerable and inappropriate ethical stance given current conditions. Some religions need to adjust their recommendations regarding fertility to the realities brought about by modern medicine, which has greatly reduced the death rate but not the birth rate, resulting in a dangerous growth in populations, all of which want to consume at higher standards than have ever been known previously.

∼ The Middle Path: Buddhist Guidelines for Valuing Human Birth

One of the most basic teachings of Buddhism concerns interdependence, already discussed in an earlier chapter. As already explained, this teaching is the basis upon which all further comments on consumption and reproduction must be made, since interdependence is the bottom line which cannot be defied. Rather than being isolated and independent entities, Buddhism sees all beings as interconnected with one another in a great web of interdependence. All-pervasive interdependence is part of the Buddhist understanding of the law of cause and effect, which governs all events in our world. Nothing happens apart from or contrary to cause and effect according to Buddhism, which does not allow for accidents or divine intervention. Furthermore, since Buddhism understands cause and effect as interdependence, actions unleashed by one being have effects and repercussions throughout the entire cosmos.

Therefore, decisions regarding fertility or consumption are not merely private decisions irrelevant to the larger world. Any baby born anywhere on the planet affects the entire interdependent world, as does any consumption of resources. It cannot be argued that either private wealth or low standards of material consumption negate this baby's impact on the universal web of interdependence. Nor can it be argued that private desires for children outweigh the need to take into account the impact of such children on the interdependent cosmos, since the laws of cause and effect are not suspended in any case. Similarly, consumption of resources anywhere has repercussions throughout the entire planetary system. Often consumption of luxuries in one part of the world is directly related to poverty and suffering in other parts of the world. Thus, the vision of universal and all-pervasive interdependence, which is so basic to Buddhism, requires moderation in all activities, especially reproduction and consumption, because of their impact on the rest of the universe. When the Buddhist understanding of interdependence is linked with the scientific understanding of the planet as finite lifeboat, it becomes clear that Buddhism regards appropriate, humane, and fair fertility control and equitable distribution of consumables as requirements. It is equally clear that Buddhism would regard ecologically unsound practices regarding reproduction or consumption as selfish, privately motivated disregard for the finite, interdependent cosmos.

The vision of cosmic interdependence presents the big picture regarding reproduction and consumption. This vision becomes more detailed when we look more specifically at the human realm within the interdependent cosmos. On the one hand, Buddhism values tremendously the good fortune of human rebirth, and, on the other hand, Buddhism sees all sentient beings as fundamentally similar in their basic urge to avoid pain and to experience well-being. Thus, birth as a human is both highly valued and seen as birth into a vast web of interdependence in which what relates beings to each other is much more fundamental than what divides them into species. So two phrases—"precious human body" and "mother sentient beings"—need always to be kept together when discussing Buddhist views about the human place in the interdependent cosmos. The preciousness of human birth is in no way due to human rights over other forms of life, for a human being *was* and could again be other forms of life—though Buddhist practice is also thought to promote continued rebirth in the human realm. Additionally, all beings are linked in this vast universal web of interdependence and emptiness from which nothing is exempt. This web is so intimately a web of relationship and shared experience that the traditional exuberant metaphor declares that all beings have at some time been our mothers and we theirs. Therefore, rather than feeling superior or feeling that we humans have rights over other forms of life, it is said over and over that because we know how much we don't want to be harmed or to suffer, and since all beings are our relatives, as much as possible, we should not harm them or cause them pain.

As is commonly known, traditional Buddhism does believe in rebirth and claims that rebirth is not necessarily always as a human being but depends on merit and knowledge from previous lives. Among possible rebirths the human rebirth is considered by far the most fortunate and favorable, favored even over rebirth in the more pleasurable divine realms.

That belief alone might seem to encourage unlimited reproduction. But when one understands *why* human birth is so highly regarded, it becomes clear that excessive human reproduction destroys the very conditions that make human rebirth so valued. Rebirth as a human being is valued because human beings, more than any other sentient beings, have the capacity for the spiritual development that eventually brings the fulfillment and perfection of enlightenment. Though all beings have the inherent innate potential for such realization, its achievement is fostered by certain causes and conditions and impeded by others. Therefore, the delight in human rebirth is due to the human capacity for cultural and spiritual creativity leading to enlightenment, a capacity more readily realized if sufficient resources are available. *Mere* birth in a human body is not the cause for rejoicing over "precious human birth," since human birth is a necessary but not a sufficient condition for the potential inherent in humanness to come to fruition. It is very helpful, even necessary, for that body to be in the proper environment, to have the proper nurturing, physically, emotionally, and spiritually. This is the fundamental reason why a situation of few people well taken care of is preferable to many people struggling to survive.

The conditions that make human life desirable and worthwhile are summed up in one of the core Buddhist values—that of the Middle Way or the Middle Path. This middle path is also discussed as right effort, not too much, not too little, not too tight, not too loose. To make the most appropriate use of the opportunity represented by the "precious human birth," a person needs to walk the Middle Way, and *to be able* to walk the Middle Way. To avoid extremes in all matters is one of the core values of Buddhism, learned by the Buddha before his enlightenment experience and a necessary precondition to it. First he learned that a life of luxury is meaningless, but then he had to learn that a life of poverty also leads nowhere. The Buddha concluded that in order to become fully human, one needs to live in moderation, avoiding the extremes of too much indulgence and too much poverty or self-denial.

The guideline of the Middle Way emphasizes that too much wealth or ease can be counterproductive spiritually, since it tends to promote complacency, satisfaction, and grasping for further wealth—all attitudes that are not helpful spiritually. Thus the concept of the Middle Way provides a cogent criticism and corrective for current patterns of rampant consumerism and overconsumption. However, the concept of the Middle Way also makes the fundamental point that there are minimum material and psychological standards necessary for meaningful human life. Buddhism has never idealized poverty and suffering or regarded them as spiritual advantages. Those in dire poverty or grave danger and distress do not have the time or inclination to be able to nurture themselves into enlighten-ment, into actually benefitting fully from their human rebirth, which is quite unfortunate. Buddhism celebrates moderation, but it does not cele-brate poverty because it sees poverty as unlikely to motivate people to achieve enlightenment—or even to allow them enough breathing time to do so.

Therefore, Buddhists have long recognized that before Buddhist teach-ings can be effective, there must first be a foundation of material well-being and psychological security. Buddhism has always recognized that one cannot practice meditation or contemplation on an empty stomach or create an uplifted and enlightening environment in the midst of degrada-tion, deprivation, or fear. Buddhists have known for a long time that deep spiritual or contemplative practice—which is seen as leading to the great-est joy and fulfillment possible to humans—is usually taken up *after* rather than *before* achieving a certain basic level of material comfort. Before that, people really do think that once they have enough material things, they won't suffer. One has to attain a minimal level of satisfaction of basic physical and psychological desires before one begins to realize that desire and its attendant sufferings are much more subtle. At a point *after* basic needs have been met, when people begin to experience that desire and suffering are not so easily quelled, the basic message of Buddhism begins to make sense.

This point dovetails quite nicely with the point made by many who advocate that curbing excessive population growth is much more possible if people have an adequate standard of living. It is by now a well-known generalization that one of the most effective ways to cut population growth is to improve people's economic lives, that people who have some material wealth can see the cogency of limiting their fertility, whereas people who are already in deeply degraded circumstances do not. Buddhist thought consistently advocates investigating cause and effect, since the entire interdependent world is governed by cause and effect. Overpopula-tion does not just happen; it is the result of causes, one of which is experi-encing too much poverty, which makes it impossible to walk the Middle Way between too much luxury and too much poverty.

However, it is equally clear that too much reproduction would over-whelm all attempts to curb poverty because a finite earth has limited resources. Thus we return to the need to recognize the interdependence of excessive consumption, overpopulation, and poverty. If one of these key elements is left out, as is done by religious and cultural systems that have no guidelines that limit human reproduction, then an interdependent cos-mos will be severely stressed. Again, it is important to point out that all religions and most cultures do have ethical guidelines limiting consumption. Often they are not kept, but the guidelines exist. But few religions advocate limiting human fertility. Most encourage or require their members to reproduce, without providing any guidance about limits and without any recognition that there could be too many people. Therefore, the example of religious systems that can be invoked to provide religious reasons to limit fertility are critically important.

The vision of interdependence combined with the advice to walk the Middle Way in all pursuits certainly provides such guidance. Taken together, these concepts of interdependence, of the value of human birth into appropriate circumstances, and of the Middle Way provide some sensible and obvious guidelines regarding fertility control and consumption. Regarding consumption, it is critical to see that the call for the Middle Path points in two directions. Clearly, excessive consumption violates the Middle Path. *But so does too much deprivation.* The advice to walk the Middle Path is *not* a demand to undergo whatever hardships would be required to provide equal distribution of resources to whatever population results from unrestricted exercise of so-called reproductive rights. It is advice to limit *both* fertility and consumption, which are interdependent, so as too make possible a lifestyle conducive to enlightenment for all beings. Certainly too much fertility for earth to sustain its offspring and for communities to provide adequate physical and emotional nurturing would be a contradiction of the Middle Way. It is crucial that human population not grow beyond the capacity of a family, a community, or the earth to provide a life within the Middle Way to all its members.

Simply providing sheer survival is not enough, and arguments that the earth could support many more people are not cogent because *quality* of life is far more significant than mere *quantity of bodies.* In addition to minimally adequate nutrition, sufficient space to avoid the overcrowding that leads to aggression and violence is important. Availability of the technological, cultural, and spiritual treasures that make life truly human is also basic. Therefore, globally, communally, and individually, it is important to limit fertility so that all children actually born can have adequate material and psychological care. Not to do so would be wanton disregard for the spiritual well-being of those born into a human body. Neither the poverty nor the emotional exhaustion that results from trying to raise too many children is helpful to anyone—least of all to the children resulting from unlimited or excessive fertility. In Buddhist terms, this basic fact far outweighs private wishes for "as many children as I want" or pro-natalist societal and religious norms and pressures.

These guidelines strike me as impeccable advice on how to negotiate problems of population pressure and resource utilization, though, clearly, reasonable and kind people could agree on the guideline and disagree on its implementation. Obviously, the Middle Way does not mean the mindless consumption of the first world, but neither does it mean the mindless pro-natalism of some religions, some patriarchal cultures, and some segments of the first world. And it does, in my view, include some technological basics that really enhance the quality of life—flower gardens, pets, computers, good stereo systems, international travel, electricity, refrigeration, cultural diversity, and humanistic education—things that cannot be provided to unlimited populations without extreme environmental degradation. Since many things in life are more sacred and more satisfying than reproduction, it would seem ludicrous to give up such cultural treasures in order to have large populations that lack those treasures.

◁ What's Worth Nurturing?
Transmitting the "Enlightened Gene"

Many religions, including major Asian traditions with which Buddhism has coexisted, command perpetuation of one's family lineage as a religious obligation. For a Buddhist to have any children at all is not a religious requirement. In the Buddhist vision, one does not need to reproduce bio-logically to fulfill the acme of one's responsibilities to the interdependent web of mother sentient beings or to realize the most exalted possibilities of human life. In fact, though in their traditional form the arguments ele-vate celibacy over the householder lifestyle rather than childlessness over biological reproduction, a great deal of Buddhist tradition suggests that biological reproduction may interfere with helping the world or realizing one's highest potential. Since Buddhists are like other human beings, it is important and interesting to explore what inspires them to embrace reli-gious ideas that do not require reproduction, and also to investigate Bud-dhist discussions of appropriate reproduction.

The command to perpetuate the family lineage is quite strong in some traditions and fuels pro-natalist behaviors. Usually this command exists within a complex of ideas and practices that include the judgment that one is unfilial and seriously remiss in one's religious obligations if one does not have a male heir, that everyone must marry and reproduce, and that women should have few or no options or vocations beyond maternity. Tra-ditions which insist that one must reproduce biologically to fulfill one's obligations rarely, if ever, also include the corollary command not to repro-duce excessively, which could bring the preferred behaviors back from an extreme into some variant of the Middle Way. In fact, often such traditions discourage any attempts to limit fertility, and people who want to do so are made to feel unworthy if they limit reproduction, even if they already have produced an heir to the family lineage. Buddhism, which sees such

absolute concern with perpetuating the family lineage as merely an extension of ego, of the self-centeredness that causes all suffering, has never
enjoined its adherents to do so. And Buddhism has come in for major crit-
icisms from Asian neighbors for not requiring biological reproduction of
its members.

The Asian criticism of Buddhists for being selfish in not requiring reproduction strikes Buddhist sensibilities as very odd. The Buddhists' reply
would be twofold. First, to contribute that which is most valuable to the
interdependent web of mother sentient beings is in no way at all dependent on biological reproduction. Furthermore, biological reproduction is
often driven by very self-centered and selfish motivations. Let us examine
both of these ideas closely, because I think they are both important
resources in countering the self-righteous moralism of much pro-natalist
thinking.

These conclusions regarding reproduction are not negative limits
demanded of unwilling subjects. Rather, from the Buddhist point of view,
they are rooted in deep knowledge of what people ultimately want, of what
satisfies our deepest longings. Buddhists would say that the simultaneous
pursuit of wisdom and compassion, to the point of enlightenment and
even beyond, is what satisfies our deepest longings because it speaks to our
fundamental human nature. Buddhists, contrary to much popular thinking, both Asian and Western, do not live their preferred lifestyle of moderation, meditation, and contemplation out of a self-centered motivation
seeking to avoid pain. Buddhists do not reject family lineage as an ultimate
value to seek individual fulfillment instead. Buddhists claim that we can
never find fulfillment through reproducing or, equally important, through
economic production and consumption, no matter how popular these pursuits may be, or how rigorously religious or social traditions may demand
them. Instead, we need to realize our spiritual potential. Finding life's purpose in either consumption or reproduction simply strengthens what Buddhists call "ego," the deeply rooted human tendency to be self-centered in
ways that ultimately cause all our suffering.

Rather, Buddhists see perpetuating family lineage as trivial compared
with cultivating and perpetuating our universal human heritage and
birthright—the tranquillity and joy of enlightenment. Rather than seeking
self-perpetuation through biological reproduction, Buddhists are encouraged to arouse *bodhicitta,* the basic warmth and compassion inherent in
all beings. Then, to use a traditional Buddhist metaphor, having recognized that we are pregnant with Buddha nature (*tathagatagarbha*), we vow
to develop on the bodhisattva's path of compassion pursuing *universal* liberation instead of private fulfillment. Rather than a personal loss, this
choice is regarded as joyfully finding one's identity and purpose in a maze

of purposeless wandering and self-perpetuation. "Today my life has become worthwhile" reads the liturgy for taking the bodhisattva vow, the vow that is so central to Mahayana Buddhism. Upon taking this vow, one is congratulated for having entered the family and lineage of enlightenment.

Given that *bodhicitta* (awakened heart, the basis for a bodhisattva's compassion) is regarded as the basic inheritance and potential of all sentient beings, including all humans, rousing and nurturing *bodhicitta* in oneself and encouraging its development in sentient beings *is* fostering family lineage in its most profound sense, beyond the narrow boundaries of genetic family, tribe, nation, or even species. The way in which such values actually foster perpetuation of our most valuable traits is pointed out by an idiosyncratic modern translation of the term *bodhicitta*. My teacher sometimes translated *bodhicitta* as "enlightened gene," a translation that emphasizes *bodhicitta* both as one's inherited most basic trait and as one's heritage to the "mother sentient beings." Who could worry about transmitting family genes when one can awaken, foster, and transmit the gene of enlightenment?

By contrast, the motivations to biological reproduction are often quite narrow and unenlightened. Many religious traditions have criticized material consumption as spiritually counterproductive. Few traditions have seen that biological reproduction can be equally self-centered and ultimately unsatisfactory, or that excessive reproduction stems from the same psychological and spiritual poverty as does excessive consumption. Buddhism, however, can easily demonstrate that biological reproduction is often driven by self-centered motivations, particularly by a desire for self-perpetuation or for the expansion of one's group. And self-centered desire always results in suffering, according to the most basic teachings of Buddhism. To expose the negative underbelly of emotionality and greed motivating much reproduction, to name it accurately, and to stop perpetuating false idealizations of the drive to biological reproduction are more than overdue. Such idealization is part of the pro-natalist stance that drives even many people for whom parenthood is not a viable vocation into reproduction. Regarding all reproduction as beneficial was always illusory, even in times of stable and ecologically viable population density; to continue to encourage or require everyone to reproduce their family lineage under current conditions is irresponsible.

Driven by a desire for self-perpetuation, parents often try to produce carbon copies of themselves, rather than children who are allowed to find their own unique life-ways in the world. The suffering caused by such motivation to reproduction is frequently unnoticed and perpetuates itself from generation to generation. As someone reared by parents who *wanted* a child—but a child who would replace them and reproduce their values and lifestyle, which I have not done—I am quite well acquainted with the emotional violence done to children who are conceived out of their parents' attachment, to fill their parents' agendas. Buddhist literature is filled with such stories.

Frequently, personal neediness is the emotion fueling the desire to reproduce. Certainly the mental state of some people who want to reproduce is far from the calmness and tranquillity recommended by Buddhism. I am deeply suspicious of people who need and long to reproduce biologically—suspicious of their psychological balance and of the purity of their motives. In my experience, most of my yuppie friends think that population control is a vital issue—for some other segment of the population—but that their drive to reproduce as much as they want to is unassailable. The level of hostility and defensiveness that wells up upon the suggestion that maybe they are motivated by desire for self-perpetuation rather than by bodhisattva practice, convinces me that, indeed, my suspicions are correct. My suspicions are deepened even further when such people endure extreme expense and go to extreme measures to conceive their biological child instead of adopting one of the many needy children already present in the world.

Finally, many people simply are overwhelmed by religious, family, or tribal pressures to reproduce and don't even make a personal decision regarding reproduction. Instead they are driven by collective ego, which is not essentially different from individual ego. Like all forms of ego, collective ego also results in suffering.

Implicit in this call to recognize the negative underbelly of motivations to reproduction is the call to value and validate alternative, nonreproductive lifestyles, including lesbian and gay lifestyles. One of the most powerful psychological weapons of pro-natalism is intolerance of diversity in lifestyles and denigration of those who are unconventional. People who are childless should be valued as people who can contribute immensely to the perpetuation of the lineage of enlightenment, rather than ostracized and criticized. As a woman who always realized that in order to contribute my talents to the mother sentient beings, I would probably need to remain childless, I am certainly familiar with the prejudice against women who are childless by choice. It begins with badgering from parents or in-laws about how much they want their family lineages perpetuated and how cheated they feel. It continues with continual feedback that one is self-indulgent to pursue one's vocation and will come to regret that supposed self-centeredness eventually. Then there is the loneliness that results from friends who are too busy with their nuclear families to be proper friends. And, finally, most especially, there are the self-centered, self-indulgent middle-aged men whose goal in relationships, approved by many, is to have second families with young women. Patriarchal pro-natalism is deeply prone to such prejudices.

Needless to say, of course, reproduction can be an appropriate agenda in Buddhist practice, and much contemporary Buddhist feminist thought is exploring the parameters of reproduction as a Buddhist issue and practice. In my view, for reproduction to be a valid *Buddhist* choice and alternative lifestyle, it must be motivated by *Buddhist* principles of egolessness, detachment, compassion and bodhisattva practice, not by social and religious demands, conventional norms and habits, compulsive desires, biological clocks, or an ego-based desire to perpetuate oneself. I also believe that such detached and compassionate motivations for parenthood are fully possible, though not anywhere nearly as common as is parenthood.

Enlightened wisdom sees the interdependence of all beings and forgoes the fiction of private choices that don't impinge on the rest of the matrix of life. Enlightened compassion cherishes all beings, not merely one's family, tribe, nation, or species, as worthy of one's care and concern. The great mass of suffering in the world would be dramatically decreased if the detached pursuit of the Middle Way more commonly guided the choices people make regarding both consumption and reproduction. According to Buddhist vision, *bodhicitta* is our inalienable enlightened gene, both our inheritance from and our heritage to the mother sentient beings. Therefore, what makes life fulfilling is developing compassion and being useful—not self-perpetuation, whether through individual egotism or biological perpetuation of family, tribe, or nation. In case it is not yet completely clear, this compassion is regarded not as something one has a duty to develop but as one's inheritance, the discovery of which makes life worthwhile and joyful.

Pro-natalism as religious requirement or obligation has nothing to do with this membership in the lineage of enlightenment. Freed of pro-natalist prejudice and valued for their contributions to the lineage of enlightenment, not their biological reproduction, human beings who have sufficient talent and detachment to become parents could do so freely, out of motivation more pure than compulsion, duty, or self-perpetuation. And those who make other, equally important contributions to the mother sentient beings would be celebrated and valued equally.

⌇ Sexuality and Communication: A Few Comments on Vajrayana Buddhism

A commandment to perpetuate the family lineage, combined with criticism of people who limit or forgo biological reproduction, is only one of the major *religious* sources of pro-natalism. The other is at least equally insidious. Anti-sexual religious rhetoric is quite common in religions, including some layers of Buddhism. Frequently, sexual activity is claimed to be problematic, evil, or detrimental to one's spirituality. Guilt, fear, or mistrust of sexual experience stemming from religious rhetoric and rules leads to several equations or symbolic linkages, all of which foster the agenda of pro-natalism, among other negative effects. Regarding sexual experience as forbidden fruit in no way fosters mindful and responsible sexuality.

The first of the major equations that grow out of religious fear of sexuality is the identity between sexuality and reproduction that is so strong in some religious traditions. Some religions espouse the view that the major, if not the only valid purpose of sexuality is reproduction. Sexual activity not open to reproduction is said to produce negative moral and spiritual consequences for people who engage in it. Therefore, the potential link between sexual activity and reproduction cannot and should not be questioned or blocked. Nonreproductive sexual activities, such as masturbation, homoerotic activity, or heterosexual practices that could not result in pregnancy are discouraged or condemned. The *effect* of such views, however, often aids the pro-natalist agenda. Encouraging people to feel negatively about their sexuality does not seem to curb sexual activity significantly. But because people have been trained to link sexual activity with reproduction, or even forbidden to take steps to disassociate them, their sexual activity results in a high rate of fertility, which, combined with the current lower death rates, contributes greatly to excessive population growth.

Breaking the moral equation between sexual activity and reproduction is a most crucial task, since so long as nonreproductive sexuality is discouraged or condemned, high birth rates are likely to continue. That equation is easily broken by reasking the fundamental question of the function of sexuality in human society. It seems quite clear, when we compare human patterns of sexual behavior with those of most other animal species, that the primary purpose of sexuality in human society is communication and bonding. Unlike most other species, sexual activity between humans can, and frequently does, occur when pregnancy could not result because a woman, though sexually active, is not fertile. These nonreproductive sexual experiences are crucial to bonding and communication between human couples and thus to human society. In addition, sexuality, properly understood and experienced, is one of the most powerful methods of human communication. Reproduction is, in fact, far less crucial and is far less frequently the outcome of sexual activity. Thus, it is quite inappropriate to rule that sexual contact must be potentially open to

pregnancy if sexual activity is not to involve moral and spiritual defile-
ment. Instead, mindful sexuality, involving the use of birth control unless
appropriate and responsible pregnancy is intended, should be the sexual
morality encouraged by all religions.

The view that sexuality should be inextricably linked with reproduction
is closely tied with several other equations that are equally pro-natalist in
their implications. When sex cannot be dissociated from fertility and
when females have no valid and valued identity or cultural role other than
motherhood, most women will become mothers. Therefore, a symbolic
and literal identity between femaleness and motherhood is taken for
granted. For example, not many years ago, everyone assumed that a female
deity would inevitably be a "mother-goddess." I remember well that such
platitudes were commonplace when I began my graduate study in the history of religions. However, the assumption that *all* females—even divine
females—would be mothers proves to be incredibly naive and culture-
bound. When mythology and symbolism of the divine feminine are investigated free of prevailing cultural stereotypes about the purpose of females,
it is discovered that divine females are many things in addition to, often
instead of, being mothers. They are consorts, protectors, teachers, bringers
of culture, patrons of the arts, sponsors of wealth, and so on. Nor in
mythology is their involvement in other cultural activities dependent on
their being nonsexual. In mythology, one meets many divine females who
are quite active sexually but who are not mothers or whose fertility is not
stressed. Clearly, such religious symbolism and mythology of sexually
active but nonreproductive females would not promote pro-natalism.
Therefore, a final caution is necessary. Great care must be taken in symbolic reconstructions of motherhood in contemporary feminist theology,
lest the symbols again reinforce the stereotype that to be a woman is to be
a mother, literally.

The third equation links nurturing with motherhood, an exceedingly
popular stereotype in both traditional religion and popular culture and
psychology. The negative and limiting effects of this equation are various,
not the least of which is the way in which this equation plays into the pro-
natalist agenda. If nurturing is so narrowly defined, then those who want
to nurture will see no option but to become parents. The equation
between nurturing and motherhood also fosters the prejudice against non-
reproducers already discussed, since it is easy to claim that they are selfish and non-nurturing. However, the most serious deficiency of this
equation lies in the way that it limits our understanding of nurturing. If
nurturing is associated so closely with motherhood, then other forms of
caretaking are not recognized as nurturing and are not greatly encouraged,
especially in men. The assumption that nurturing is the specialization,

even the monopoly of mothers, and therefore is confined to women, is one of the most dangerous legacies of patriarchal stereotyping. Because of the strength of this stereotype, it is often assumed that feminist women, who will not submit to patriarchal stereotypes, would not be nurturing. But obviously, the feminist critique is not a critique of nurturing; it is a critique of the ways in which men are excused from nurturing and women are restricted to, and then punished for, nurturing within the prison of patriarchal gender roles. Feminism is not about restricting nurturing even further or discouraging it but about recognizing the diversity of its forms and expecting it from all members of society. Since nurturing is valuable and essential to human survival, it is critical that our ideas about what it means to nurture extend beyond the image of physical motherhood to activities such as teaching, healing, caring for the earth, engaging in social action. It is equally important that all humans, including all men, be defined as nurturers and taught nurturing skills, rather than confining this activity to physical mothers.

Because some of the grounds for fear, mistrust, and guilt surrounding sexuality are in religion, a *religious,* rather than merely secular or psychological, alternative view of sexuality would be significant to this discussion of religious ethics, population, consumption, and the environment. A religious evaluation of sexuality as sacred symbol and experience, helpful rather than detrimental to spiritual development, would certainly inject relevant considerations into this forum. Vajrayana Buddhism, the last form of Indian Buddhism to develop, which is today significant in Tibet and becoming more significant in the West, includes just such a resource. Needless to say, it is crucial that discussions of Vajrayana Buddhism be disassociated from some popular titillating accounts of "Tantric sex" that actually stem from fear and guilt about sexuality.

Symbolism and practice of sacred sexuality, such as that found in Tibetan Vajrayana Buddhism, are radically unfamiliar to many religious traditions, including those most familiar to Western audiences. In Vajrayana Buddhism, the familiar paired virtues wisdom and compassion are personified as female and male. Not only are they personified; they are painted and sculpted in sexual embrace, usually called the *yab-yum* icon. This icon is then used as the basis for contemplative and meditative practices, including visualizing oneself as the pair joined in embrace. After many years of working with this icon personally, I am quite intensely captivated by the liberating power and joy of this symbol. Rather than being a private and somewhat embarrassing, perhaps guilt-ridden indulgence, sexuality is openly portrayed as symbol of the most profound religious truths and as contemplative exercise for developing one's innate enlightenment.

One of the most profound implications of the *yab-yum* icon is the fact that the primary human relationship used to symbolize ultimate reality is that of equal consorts, of male and female as joyous, fully cooperative partners. This contrasts sharply with the tendency to limit religious symbolism to parent–child relationships, whether of Father and Son, or of Madonna and Child, which is so common in other traditions. It also contrasts strongly with the abhorrence of divine sexuality that has been such a problem in those same traditions. One cannot help speculating that this open celebration of sexuality as a sacred and profoundly communicative and transformative experience between divine partners would significantly defuse pro-natalism based on a belief that sex without the possibility of procreation is wrong.

In the realm of human relations rather than religious symbols, insofar as the two can be separated, this symbolism has led, in Vajrayana Buddhism, to the possibility of spiritual or dharmic consortship between women and men. (The question of whether non-heterosexual relationships are also possible is more difficult to answer.) Such relationships are not conventional domestic arrangements or romantic projections and longings, but are about collegiality and mutual support on the path of spiritual discipline. Sexuality seems to be an element within, but not the basis of, such relationships. Though relatively esoteric, such relationships were and still are recognized and valued in late north Indian Vajrayana Buddhism, as well as in Tibetan Buddhism. Western Buddhists are just beginning to discover or recover this resource, this possibility of consortship as collegial relationship between fellow seekers of the way and as mode of understanding and communicating with the profound "otherness" of the phenomenal world. To value, valorize, and celebrate such relationships would profoundly undercut pro-natalist biases regarding the place of sexuality in human life, as well as contribute greatly to the creation of sane, caring, egalitarian models of relationship between women and men.

CHAPTER 10

Children, Children's Rights, and Family Well-being in Buddhist Perspective

IHAD NEVER REFLECTED SYSTEMATICALLY on childhood in Buddhist perspective until stimulated to do so by a request to participate in a multi-faith conference on the United Nations Convention on the Rights of Children. Nor had representatives of other religions taking part in this event. This fact reveals that traditional religions have not thought very much about childhood, in and of itself. Many of them expect their followers to produce children as a religious duty, have legislated how those children should be dealt with, and have prescribed ways of ensuring that those children become replacements for their parents. But none of these concerns quite constitutes dealing with *childhood* itself from a religious point of view, nor does it constitute dealing with the rights of children as children, without reference to their status as future adult carriers of the religion into which they are born. Buddhism is no exception to these generalizations. Therefore, functioning as a Buddhist constructive theologian, I will reflect on how Buddhism might address topics such as children's rights and the religious dimensions of childhood and family life. Of course, my conclusions as a Buddhist about Buddhist perspectives on children's rights will also be colored by other things important to my worldview, such as feminism and my own particular experiences as a child.

Furthermore, my reflections will be somewhat determined by the view of childhood and children's rights expressed in the United Nations Convention on the Rights of Children, since our collective deals with childhood not in the abstract but in connection with that specific document. The United Nations Convention on the Rights of Children has been summarized as addressing four major topics: survival, protection, participation, and promotion. Insofar as they are relevant, I will frame my discussion of the links between Buddhism and the United Nations Convention on the Rights of Children around these four topics, especially protection and participation.

~ Childhood in Buddhist Perspective: Theoretical Considerations

My first reaction to being asked to think about the religious dimensions of childhood was that many of my contemplations were quite familiar. I noted that many of the same themes and conclusions occurred to me when I thought about Buddhism and the rights of children as had occurred to me as I thought about Buddhism in connection with issues of pro-natalism and consumerism. On that topic, I had concluded that the Buddhist ideal is to reproduce few enough children so that all can be cared for well. That I reached similar conclusions in this presentation is not at all surprising, since the first right and need of a child is to come into a world in which she can be wanted and welcomed because there is room for her and sufficient resources, physical, emotional, and spiritual, for her to live well, not merely to survive minimally.

However, in thinking specifically about Buddhist views of childhood and children, a major conclusion seems self-evident. In its classic forms, Buddhism does not especially focus on children or on the family, either doctrinally or institutionally. It is not a child-centered or a family-centered religion. This is because its deepest goals are not the worldly continuities so sought after and valued by some religions but the transformation of conventional attitudes into enlightened mind. As discussed more fully in other chapters, according to Buddhism, we need to see clearly into the deepest nature of reality as ceaseless impermanence, interdependence, and emptiness, becoming familiar and comfortable with that reality and developing detachment, because that alone brings freedom, tranquillity, and compassion. This insight, experienced so deeply that it transforms one's very core, is far more valued than is maintaining cultural and familial continuities or economic success. Therefore, transforming grasping and fixation into detachment and tranquillity is far more central to the Buddhist vision of the ideal life than are reproduction and economic activity.

Because Buddhism values enlightenment far more than wealth or fertility, its core practices are dedicated to the pursuit of enlightenment rather than to goals such as reproduction, maintaining the family line, promoting the local culture, or economic success. Family life is not necessary to fulfilled human living. Unlike some popular religious viewpoints that regard the physical reproduction of children as essential for future well-being, for Buddhism the future of the religion lies in its ability to speak effectively to our suffering and to our longing for freedom, tranquillity, and gentleness, pursued through various spiritual disciplines. Because physical reproduction and family life do not especially alleviate or even address these concerns and needs, they are not the major focus of Buddhism. Indeed, from the Buddhist point of view, physical reproduction and family life, if pursued with a conventional mind-set of attachment and desire, intensify rather than diminish suffering. (This is not to deny that popular practices oriented to gaining fertility and wealth are found in all forms of Buddhism. It is only to place the doctrinal heart of Buddhism correctly on enlightenment.)

Nevertheless, physical reproduction, the continuity of one's family or culture, and economic activities can be appropriate activities for a Buddhist whose main practice is seeking enlightenment. It is crucial to understand that enlightened mind and enlightened activity are not *incompatible* with family life and raising children, or with the economic pursuit of right livelihood. The primary question is the mind-set with which one acts, not the actions themselves. For Buddhism, there is no simple, black-and-white dichotomy between "worldly" activities and "spiritual" practice. The central dichotomy is between conventional attitudes and ways of living that involve grasping, fixation, or attachment, and an enlightened attitude of detachment and tranquillity, *rather than* between "worldly" and "spiritual" activities. Either could be done with either mental attitude, and it is the attitude with which activities are done, not the activities themselves, that makes all the difference.

I emphasize this point because enlightenment has too often been popularly presented in the West as an "otherworldly" or world-denying goal that disallows conventional family life or economic pursuits. Thus, my conclusion that Buddhism is not especially child or family oriented is easily subject to the erroneous conclusion that Buddhism is, therefore, anti-family. That assessment is not accurate, since it relies much too heavily on Western either-or thinking and a duality between this disvalued, mundane, transient world and the next transcendent, changeless realm of superior value. As a long-term Buddhist practitioner and scholar, I find it utterly foreign when I hear Buddhism described as an "otherworldly religion."

Since developing enlightened attitudes is so basic to Buddhism, its central space is the meditation hall, not the fields, the hearth, the sacramental table, the sacrificial altar, or the bazaar. People fare best in the meditation hall as adult individuals, which is why Buddhism is not especially oriented toward or focused on families and children, however important these concerns are to some Buddhists. Meditation halls, with their silence and aloneness, even in the midst of a crowd, are not especially "child friendly," as many Western Buddhists discover in their attempts to raise Buddhist children in Western societies. Certainly if one thinks of the contrast between a Passover seder, with its ritual inclusion of even the youngest child, or a Christmas eve service focusing on the baby Jesus and the typical Buddhist meditation hall, the point that Buddhism is not child-centered is forcefully made. Children can be useful participants in the fields or the bazaar, at the sacramental table or the sacrificial altar, and, consequently, can feel at home there. The meditation hall is usually not interesting to people until they become adults, facing the sorrow and complexity of life as a human being in *samsara*, the infinite ocean of birth and death fueled by karma, the inexorable law of cause and effect.

Furthermore, unlike Christianity, Hinduism, or various pre-Christian religions that focused on the birth and rebirth of the seasonal deity, there are no child heroes in Buddhism, and the cult of the divine child is unknown. The child Siddartha is neither divine nor enlightened when he is born, and his birth, in and of itself, is not salvific. It is true that the story of the birth of Siddartha is well known and Buddha's birthday is celebrated as an important holiday in some Buddhist countries. But there is little focus on the *childness* of the future Buddha, in contrast especially to the stories of Krishna, the divine child, and even in contrast to the baby Jesus, who, unlike the newborn future Buddha, does not engage in acts that are usually impossible for babies (speech and locomotion). In fact, regarding Siddartha's life prior to the momentous occasion on which he sat under the Bodhi tree, there is at least as much focus on his previous lives, even those in animal form, as on his childhood in this human life. The child Siddartha is no more the focus of religious attention than are children in general in Buddhism.

It should come as no surprise, then, that the state of childhood itself is not regarded as a special state. Children are neither especially endowed with innocence and goodness beyond what adults possess, nor are children in an unredeemed or depraved state of nature different in quality from that of adults who have been initiated or processed in some way. They are not waiting for some ritual, such as baptism or circumcision, to be performed on them to transform them into human beings, members of a culture, beings capable of a state of grace. They are simply children—pre-adults going through the karmic process of moving from childhood, with its physical, mental, and spiritual conditions, into adulthood, at which point one is physically, mentally, and spiritually capable of practicing meditation to pursue enlightenment.

Having thus indicated that Buddhism does not have definitions and doctrines of childhood as part of its classic repertoire of teachings, let me now apply core Buddhist values to the somewhat modern concept of childhood as a special condition. Two things should be emphasized about how Buddhists might answer the question, What is a child? The first is that all children, like all sentient beings, are endowed with Buddha nature (*tathagatagarbha*), or inherent indwelling enlightenment, which only needs to be realized or awakened. The second is that children enter the world not with a blank slate, as is thought by some Western psychologies, but with a history, with endowments and propensities that, while they are not viewed as rigidly deterministic, do predispose children in unique and specific ways. These two conclusions about children seem, in some ways to point in opposite directions. On the one hand, all children are the same and are equal in being endowed with Buddha nature; on the other hand, each child is the result of a unique combination of causes and conditions, which means that children are neither the same nor equally endowed with specific talents. Yet both statements are valid and important.

It is easier to explain how and why children are unique and individual. Classical beliefs concerning karma and rebirth mean that every child who is born already has a long history. In fact, the cycle of birth leading to death leading to rebirth is said to be endless, so that any and every baby has a karmic history stretching back into beginningless time. Thus, a child is born inheriting not only its parents' genetic materials and, to a lesser extent, its parents' culture with whatever strengths and weaknesses come from those sources; it is also born with its own self-created potentials, the result of its various efforts in past lives. These "karmic" inheritances from past lives are probably more important than genetics in determining a child's character and endowments, in traditional understandings. Furthermore, traditional understandings would suggest that the union of parents and child is, in fact, the result of previous associations on the part of each, not merely the biological result of the meeting of egg and sperm.

To what extent modern people can literally believe in rebirth is an open question; many Asian Buddhists take it for granted, while many Western Buddhists take rebirth more metaphorically. However, the traditional teachings make a very salient and relevant point. Children are not cut from the same mold, the same cookie cutter, but have unique and different talents and abilities. Any attempt to raise and educate children which understands equality as treating all children as if they were equally endowed with the same talents does a serious disservice to both the children and to the larger society. Thus, some aspects of Buddhist thinking lead us to focus on individuality and uniqueness in a way that is almost Western when we try to understand what a child is in Buddhist perspective.

However, the unique combination of causes and conditions that results in a specific child is only part of what makes a child who she is. That child,

like all other beings, is endowed with Buddha nature, which in some interpretations is also called "basic goodness." This component of the child is
not unique and individual but universal and identical in all beings, though
the ability to become aware of it is more developed in some beings, such
as human beings, than in other beings, such as animals. The inherent presence of Buddha nature explains why children do not need to be made into
humans by ritual means and why they are not considered depraved or ani-
malistic without cultural interventions. Buddha nature or basic goodness
is conferred by neither human nor divine beings, nor by ritual. For most
people, spiritual practices and teachings prove to be extremely helpful in
making a person more aware of Buddha nature, but awareness only uncov-
ers what is there; it does not cause or create that inherent seed of enlightenment (*tathagatagarbha*).

These two perspectives can now be brought together. A child is born
with both personal idiosyncratic potentials, based on its karma as well as
its genetics, and with Buddha nature, which is the same for all beings.
Childhood is simply the karmic life stage in which most of these potentials are still latent, and growing up is a process of karmic development in
which they unfold. (It is crucial to remember that karma simply means
"cause and effect," not predestination in the Western sense, so that a curious five-year-old is the karmic result of a well-cared-for infant, and ado-
lescence is the karmic result of childhood, and so on.)

Because the bottom line for every being is Buddha nature, and since spiritual discipline is the most effective way to awaken that potential, the
most succinct definition of a child is that a child is a future meditator, no
matter what its personal, idiosyncratic inheritances may be. Thus, in
ranking the personal, idiosyncratic traits of a child against the common
and universal trait of Buddha nature, the latter is more basic and central.
This does not mean that the former can be ignored; on the contrary, Buddhist tradition has recognized that, in their present lives, it could be doing
violence to some individuals to try to force them to awaken their Buddha
nature through spiritual discipline.

In defining childhood as the prelude to adulthood, I want to stress two
interlocking points. First, regarding the child's karma, the notion of karma
has often been used to excuse grave social injustice, as in the explanations:
"it's your karma to be poor, to be oppressed," and the like, or "because you
are a girl, your bad karma makes you a second-class human being." Since,
according to Buddhist thought, everything is due to karma, oppression is
indeed due to karma, to processes of cause and effect. But the *effect* of present oppression is more cogently explained as due to a *cause* located in present oppressive structures than to misdeeds in a past life on the part of an
oppressed child. This interpretation of karma runs counter to an Asian

tradition of using the concept of karma to encourage people to accept very difficult circumstances as appropriate and just. Second, given *tathagata-garbha*, a child is not only a future meditator, but also a future Buddha. A child is *not* the possession of its parents or its culture, a point that is also driven home by the belief that a child comes into the world with a unique karmic past that pushes it in certain future directions. Thus, from both sides, Buddhist understandings of what a child is drive home the point that reproducing one's family ego or the cultural ego is not the reason to be a child or to have a child. This point can hardly be overemphasized, since desire to reproduce one's ego, one's family line, or one's culture so often is the motivation for physiological reproduction. Such motivations lead to regarding the child as the possession of its parents or its culture, obligated to reproduce them in its own life, while disregarding the child's Buddha nature and its unique karmic heritage. These are declared to be irrelevant, especially if they lead the child away from its family and culture of origin.

～ Taking Care of Children: Buddhism and the United Nations Convention on the Rights of Children

Traditionally, Buddhism does not lay down detailed regulations for any aspect of lay life, but only gives the guidelines of basic precepts, the most important of which is non-harming. Therefore, childrearing practices, as is the case for most other aspects of lay Buddhist life, simply follow the norms of the culture in which lay Buddhists are living and practicing Buddhism. Most often, it seems that Buddhist children simply absorbed Buddhism by growing up in a culture that was deeply influenced by Buddhism. Additionally, in traditional Buddhist countries, monasteries often served as important educational institutions, at least for boys. In some cases, monasteries also served as orphanages, where parents could deposit children when they had too many.

For Western Buddhists, things are not so simple, and there is considerable discussion both about how to raise Buddhist children in a non-Buddhist environment and about whether and how childcare can be a dimension of Buddhist meditation practices. Combining serious Buddhist meditation practice with the householder lifestyle, including childrearing, especially in conjunction with the input of feminist theory and practice, will revolutionize some aspects of traditional Buddhism.

However, I will not focus on Buddhist childrearing practices, whether traditional or Western, in my discussion of the United Nations Convention on the Rights of Children. Instead, I wish to return to the Buddhist understanding of childhood and children suggested above and ask what a child needs, given a Buddhist understanding of children. Every guideline I suggest as important to serving children's rights and needs will derive from my interpretation of a child as a potential future meditator, endowed with both idiosyncratic karmic potential and Buddha nature. My primary question will be what attitudes and practices regarding children allow individual children to unfold into adults who realize both aspects of their potential and what attitudes and practices regarding children are detrimental to that unfolding. This is the context in which I will discuss the United Nations Convention on the Rights of Children, noting both ways in which the Convention and Buddhism seem to agree and some ways in which the Convention may not go far enough to protect the needs and rights of children.

I suggest that a successful childhood, a childhood that nurtures rather than undercuts the endowments of a child, is most likely if certain basic conditions can be met. Furthermore, all children merit a successful childhood. It should not be argued that some children's karma has merited them a difficult childhood. All children should be cared for adequately, materially, emotionally, and spiritually. For a successful childhood to be possible, I suggest that three problems must be avoided at all costs. The first is more children than can be cared for adequately, or *overpopulation*, whether locally or globally. The second is *poverty*, or insufficient resources for everyone in the population, whether adults or children, to be able to nurture their Buddha nature through a lifestyle appropriate to each individual. The third is an attitude of *possessiveness* regarding children, whether on the part of their family or their culture. When this attitude is present, as it often is, children are pressured into repeating the patterns of their parents or their culture regardless of their own karmic potential.

Upon close inspection, the United Nations Convention appears to address itself mainly to the third concern and to do so in considerable detail. The convention could be interpreted as a document that affords children significant protection against overly possessive parents and cultures. It does not especially endorse those who regard their children as beings whose primary responsibility is to perpetuate their parents or their culture. However, overpopulation and poverty are not directly recognized as conditions detrimental to the rights and needs of children. Insofar as they are dealt with at all, it is only in connection with promoting certain needs of children that can be provided only when communities have an appropriate balance between numbers of children and resources available to care for them.

The first, most basic guideline regarding the rights and needs of children is stark and simple. The most basic requirement for the proper unfolding of childhood is a balance between the number of children and the material, emotional, and spiritual resources of their community and family. This is the point at which Buddhist concerns for children intersect with Buddhist ideas about population control. Because each child is both a future Buddha and a karmically unique individual, it is unreasonable and irresponsible physically to produce such beings without being able or willing to care for them properly. In discussing proper care, it is important to note that sheer, minimal physical survival is not the only issue. The time and energy required to properly nurture a child emotionally, intellectually, and spiritually are more important. It is obvious that overcrowded homes, schools, and societies, and a planet with dwindling resources and burgeoning populations, do not provide an ideal environment for such developments. For these reasons, I think few Buddhists would disagree with the guideline that there should be few enough children that all can be well cared for without intolerable burden to the families, their communities, and the planet. It must also be noted that the United Nations Convention on the Rights of Children does not mention this most basic protection needed by children.

Poverty is a major deterrent to spiritual well-being, contrary to some popular ideas. As discussed in the previous chapter, Buddhism has always proposed the Middle Way between extremes as its most essential guideline, recognizing that grinding poverty is just as counterproductive to human well-being as are mindless wealth and consumption. For adults, too much poverty means too little time for spiritual cultivation. For children, it often means too much labor too early and not enough time or resources for education. The obvious link between poverty and excessive reproduction should be noted in this context. If we trace the lines of cause and effect back one more step, what often drives excessive reproduction is the fixated need to have children, usually male children, to continue one's family. Again, the Convention does not explicitly deal with adequate standards of living as a right and need of children, though many of the rights that it extends to children are possible only if populations and economic resources are in balance with each other.

The third guideline concerning the rights and needs of children in Buddhist perspective could easily generate controversy, even in Buddhist contexts. It will be discussed at some length, since I regard it as fundamental both to Buddhism and to the Convention. It has been suggested repeatedly that a Buddhist perspective on children would emphasize their unique karmic heritages and potentials. The conventional and common attitude, quite at odds with this perspective, is to regard children as extensions or possessions of their parents or culture. From a Buddhist point of view, it should be obvious that it is important to try to limit the temptation to regard children primarily as carriers of the familial or cultural ego whose function is to extend and reproduce that group's ego. This extremely wide-spread expectation of families and cultures is the largely unrecognized downside of conventional notions about the religious importance of family life and of conventional parenting practices. Throughout human history, uncounted millions of children have undoubtedly been sacrificed on this altar of familial and cultural demands that children continue the patterns laid down by the group into which they were born. That parents routinely expect to be able to program their children's lives in this fashion is well demonstrated by numerous stories in Buddhist literature in which parents (presumably Buddhists) in Buddhist societies discouraged or prohibited their sons and daughters from becoming monks and nuns, from taking up a religious vocation instead of the family business.

I read the United Nations Convention on the Rights of the Child as extending the modern concept of individual rights to children, who are here seen as individuals who inherently possess individual rights. Thus, we are dealing with two concepts that are modern rather than traditional. The first is the concept of individual rights, which is often seen as a Western outlook that may or may not fit well with other ways of understanding the relationship between the individual and her surrounding matrix of society and the phenomenal world. The second is the extension of that concept to children, who are often viewed or treated as rightless minors, even in societies that value individual rights for adults.

A full discussion of Buddhist perspectives on the concept of individual rights would take us too far afield at this point and would add little to a discussion of Buddhist perspectives on religious dimensions of childhood and family life. Clearly, as has already been discussed in my comments on children as unique individuals, the concept of individual rights is not utterly foreign to Buddhism, which does posit individual enlightenment as the first, though not the only goal of religious life. The caveat, from the Buddhist point of view, is that it is ridiculous to talk of individuals as independent of their matrix, as so often happens in some modern discussions of individual rights. According to the most basic Buddhist teaching of *pratityasamutpada*, or interdependence, individuals have no inherent or independent existence as such, but only exist in interdependence with all other beings. Therefore, any discussion of individual "rights" must be grounded in the basic fact that no supposed right can overcome or override interdependence. Any exercise of supposed rights that damages or harms others in the interdependent matrix is not really exercise of a "right," but harmful conduct, a violation of the first and most basic precept of Buddhist ethics.

On the other hand, traditional Buddhist teachings are easily reconciled with that stream of individual-rights rhetoric which stresses that no individual is a tool or an instrument of another. This view is, in my opinion, far more at the heart of individual-rights theory than the exaggerated hyper-individualism that is sometimes associated with the notion of individual rights in some Western capitalist contexts. Thus, a person—to use the conventional designation—is not a tool or instrument of another but a unique being with its own karmic connections within the matrix of interdependence. This formulation strikes me as a middle path between claiming potentially irresponsible and cruel autonomy for the individual, as so often happens in Western contexts, and claiming that the individual owes all his or her allegiance and effort to the family or the culture, as so often happens in traditional contexts.

However, as already noted, even in societies that are adamant about individual rights for adults, individual rights are not always extended to children. As essentially rightless minors, in both traditional and modern societies, children are usually treated as extensions of their family or culture, under the protection and control of their families and cultures but not existing independently of them. Parents and communities, including religious communities, are often extremely protective of their "right" (is this one of their rights as an individual?) to raise their children as they see fit and as they prefer, without supposed interference from a larger society, which might influence the child into alternative values. Thus, the job, the assigned task of children, is to grow up to reproduce the patterns of their parents and their culture. Their job is also to fulfill the expectations and needs of their parents and culture, often without regard for whether those expectations and needs match with the child's interests and inclinations. Since so many who value individual rights regard it as their right to mold and possess their children as extensions of themselves, the concept of children's rights is potentially explosive, even in modern societies. In fact, I do not think that so-called modern and so-called traditional societies are significantly different on this point.

The United Nations Convention of the Rights of the Child contains several articles that would significantly limit the family's or the culture's ability to exercise some traditional rights and controls over children. Articles 13 and 14 specifically accord to children the right to freedom of expression, and to freedom of thought, conscience, and religion. That I possessed such rights would certainly have been news to my parents and to the religion into which I was born, which is one reason why I suggest that children's rights are no more commonplace in the modern West than in traditional societies. Other noteworthy ways in which this convention limits parents' controls over their children are found in article 24, which seeks to abolish traditional practices that are detrimental to children's health (though these practices are not named or defined), and in article 29, which proclaims that children shall be educated to appreciate the equality of the sexes—certainly not something foremost in most educational programs, whether in the modern West or in traditional societies. The document consistently refers to the best interests of the *child* as the principle to be used in deciding contested issues. I take it that such language elevates the best interests of the child over the interests of the parents or the culture, in cases where these conflict.

Finally, the convention seems to protect as a children's right, the child's right *to be a child*, which would protect it from being forced to take on adult responsibilities prematurely. Thus, article 28 regards education as something children have by right; article 31 protects their rest, leisure, and play, as appropriate to children's age; and article 32 protects children from economic exploitation and work that is hazardous or interferes with their education. Articles 19 and 34 protect children from sexual exploitation, a provision of extreme importance in situations in which girls are married off at an early age. These principles again could be construed as elevating the child's best interests over those of the parents or as affording the child protection from its parents or culture, since in many contexts, taking care of parents and helping them in their work is considered to override children's needs for play or education.

Thus, I interpret this convention as providing, at least in some measure, two things that are essential to children. One is the need for children to be able to be children rather than premature adults. Some children's rights are really children's needs, and the convention might more appropriately use such language on occasion. One such need is most certainly the need for children not to be forced into adult economic or emotional roles prematurely. The convention does not explicitly mention children's need to be freed from adult emotional roles, but such a need is almost as important as being free of inappropriate economic responsibilities or sexual demands, which are protected by the convention. Adult emotional roles are forced on children in two ways that only seem to be opposites of each other. Sometimes a child is forced to become the confidant and emotional caretaker of an unhappy parent. At other times the unhappy parent virtually ignores the child while indulging his or her own emotional needs, thus also forcing the child into the adult emotional roles of fending for herself psychologically. The other right, tentatively but not resoundingly provided by the convention, is protection for children from their families and cultures. Such phrasing may sound extreme, but as an educator, I often encounter young adults whose families and religions were extremely possessive of them, who discouraged them from any independence of mind or spirit, and who regarded these children, who are now my students, primarily as extensions of themselves. It is primarily in the modern West that the ability and tendency of parents to wound and maim their children psychologically in both these ways has been noted, but I do not believe that these tendencies are limited to the modern West. I am particularly sensitive to such parental excesses because I was subject both to premature adult emotional roles as a child and to the demand that I fulfill my parent's needs and expectations rather my own dreams.

Clearly, negotiating a path that takes account of both these needs or rights of children is difficult. When children are protected as *children* rather than forced into adult roles, it is tempting also to want to mold them, to direct and form their development, which all parents and all cultures must do to some extent. But it is difficult to remember that such molding is subject to limits, that children, though interdependent with their parents and their culture, are not merely extensions and possessions of their parents and cultures, but beings with their own karmic links with the interdependent matrix—links that may carry them far from their families and cultures of origin.

On the other hand, the convention also makes much of promoting the child's right to maintain connections with its culture and language of origin, especially in cases of minorities, refugees, or orphans. For example, while intercountry adoption is allowed in article 21, article 20 states a preference that children remain in the ethnic, cultural, linguistic, and religious background of their birth. Thus, while the convention sometimes seems to recognize that children may well need to be protected from their families and cultures, it also safeguards families' and cultures' interests in children by assuming that continued involvement of families or cultures in their children's lives is always the preferred option, unless contravened by extreme circumstances.

In my view, the United Nations Convention makes more of preserving the child's culture of birth than is appropriate and more than I believe is warranted from the point of view of Buddhist values. According to Buddhism, just as a child is not its parents' possession, so it is not the possession of its culture. Buddhism regards culture as quite relative, having little, if anything, to do with spiritual well-being. In part, this is because Buddhism as a religion wears its links with culture very lightly and readily, even deliberately, sheds them when it crosses cultural frontiers. Furthermore, cultural identity can easily be a form of ego, in the Buddhist sense of ego as an unnecessary and undesirable burden; therefore, culture can easily be overvalued. If there is a choice between a child being well cared for physically, emotionally, and spiritually as the result of a cross-cultural or cross-racial adoption or remaining in its culture of birth under negative circumstances, I believe Buddhist values would encourage the former choice. Thus, in my view, Buddhism would not oppose but would, in fact, encourage cross-cultural and cross-racial adoptions, especially given current population pressures and problems. However, these comments on the relative unimportance of culture should not in any way be construed as endorsing policies of forced assimilation of small cultures by large cultures. They only suggest that if the child's culture of birth cannot care for it adequately, and others can, culture is not so overridingly important that the child's well-being should be sacrificed to save its original cultural identity.

In terms of protecting children from their parents and cultures, I also would contend that the convention is not sufficiently explicit regarding children's rights to defy their culture's gender roles. While the convention encourages educating children in the equality of the sexes, it does not protect those who do not conform to conventional gender roles, which are the biggest and most frequently overlooked impediment to children's ability to unfold their karmic potential in adulthood and to become adult meditators. The United Nations Convention also largely ignores the negative impact traditional gender roles have on children and on family well-being. As the author of *Buddhism after Patriarchy*, I am more than well aware of how detrimental the conventional female gender role has been to the physical, emotional, and spiritual well-being of girls. For example, in some Buddhist societies, girls were and are routinely routed away from the monastic lifestyle that is so prestigious when taken up by a boy. Less well noted is that the conventional training of boys for aggression and warfare is no more productive of human decency than is the training of females for submissiveness and docility. In short, since the rise of patriarchy, human beings have trapped countless millions of girls and boys into conventional gender roles that produce limited, stunted human beings. Only a few women and men have overcome this conditioning. Any attempt to take seriously the rights of children and the religious meaning of childhood as preparation for a useful and fulfilling adult life would have to look much more seriously into the ways in which conventional gender roles are anti-human for both men and women.

The United Nations Convention is lacking in that it does not emphasize fostering talent as a high priority among children's rights. In the United Nations Convention, the handicapped receive their special due, but the gifted are ignored and overlooked. This reflects the way in which gifted people are looked down upon in many children's subcultures, as well as in adult cultures. To make matters worse, many educational programs and policies dumb down the curriculum, try to even out achievements, and in general try to ignore the fact that children are not equally endowed with the same talents. Buddhism's recognition that children enter the world not with a blank slate but with a karmic history would argue against such educational policies. Indeed, in addition to serving as orphanages, in some Buddhist cultures, especially Tibetan Buddhism, monasteries also served as training centers for the unusually gifted children, recognized as *tulkus*[1] and given special training from an early age. Though there are many problems with the system, especially its exclusion of girls, the basic idea of giving special treatment to especially talented children is sorely needed today. A society that defines equality as equality of achievement, rather than equality of opportunity, and therefore does not foster talent, is violating something important to its own well-being, as well as to the well-being of gifted children.

As a concluding summary, it must be emphasized that Buddhism has not historically manifested itself as a religion focused on children and the family, especially in contrast to other religions, such as Hinduism or Confucianism. Its most influential sacred texts do not contain a theology of childhood. And Buddhism, going against the grain in so many ways, does not easily lend itself to ethical positions regarding children and childhood that many would consider to be self-evident. Most importantly, any view of childhood consistent with basic Buddhist values must recognize that children are fundamentally sentient beings endowed with Buddha nature and their own karmic potential; only secondarily are they carriers and perpetuators of the family or cultural lineage. From this basic and somewhat unconventional insight flow all the other comments and recommendations on Buddhist perspectives on the religious meanings of childhood.

CHAPTER 11

Impermanence, Nowness, and Non-judgment: Appreciating Finitude and Death

B UDDHISM HAS A REPUTATION among religions for going "against the grain," for analyses of the human situation that completely contradict the usual conventions and norms of religions. On no point are such religious surprises more striking than with Buddhism's teachings on impermanence and its corollary—finitude. I have long appreciated that what other religions mourn as the finitude of the human condition, which their faithful hope to transcend eventually, Buddhists acknowledge as impermanence, regarding it simply as the way things are, without praise or blame. This link between finitude and impermanence, as well as the differences between Western assessments of finitude and Buddhist assessments of impermanence have long intrigued me. And I have long felt that the most profound teachings of Buddhism circle around the Buddhist naming of reality and human experience as all-pervasive impermanence.

In this chapter, I will narrate how personal experiences with grieving made transparent to me the wisdom and comfort inherent in Buddhism's matter-of-fact, nonchalant statement that to be human is to be impermanent and finite. These experiences have transformed my life and made existential the teachings of Buddhism as has nothing else. But the wisdom that comes with accommodating finitude and impermanence is not limited to dealing with personal loss; once the reality of finitude and impermanence becomes clear, existentially as well as theoretically, the destructive effects of the ways in which some religious teachings and practices war against these realities becomes ever more obvious. At the end of this chapter, I will briefly discuss how dis-ease with finitude and impermanence fuels wasteful attempts to defy and defeat death, and how this dis-ease is implicated in wanton and careless disregard for the finite matrix of life that is our planet and its ecology.

∽ Impermanence, Nowness, and Non-judgment: Leaning into Grief

For me, the topics of finitude and death are most immediate in my experiences with grief. I probably have more experience of grieving the loss by death of loved and valued immediate collegial consorts than most people my age. The single most life-giving experience I have ever had was a genuinely mutual relationship of collegial consortship, but that experience was framed by two experiences of intense grief over loss by death of a lover or consort. Both of these experiences of loss were literally life-shaping and life-changing. One of them brought me into Buddhist practice and the other matured my practice in ways that go well beyond what I had learned from thousands of hours of formal meditation. I have never learned as much from anything else as I have from these three experiences. It is not hard to understand that a "positive" experience, such as a relationship of mutuality and appreciation with a consort, would result in learning and growth. What is more counterintuitive is that the anguish of grieving, which no one would ever choose, could be so productive. I want to explore why this is so by suggesting that through leaning into grief I learned that finitude is impermanence, and that fighting impermanence only brings suffering, while dancing with impermanence launches one into the immediacy of nowness, beyond judgments about good or bad. But these rather theoretical statements need to be fleshed out in story, for understanding and expression flow out of experience, rather than the other way around.

As already narrated in an earlier chapter, in September 1973, I was walking across the parking lot toward my office on the kind of almost unbearably beautiful fall day that makes living so far north so pleasurable, thinking about how to teach the Four Noble Truths, which I didn't think I understood very well, in my upcoming Buddhism class. I was also quite miserable, for I had spent the previous year living with the grief and trauma of discovering that the young philosopher with whom I was in love had a terminal brain tumor. I had just moved to Eau Claire after my first teaching appointment, truly a "job from hell," and, though I knew no one in Eau Claire, it was already apparent to me that I was far too radical religiously to find much collegiality at the University of Wisconsin, Eau Claire. I had spend the previous weekend visiting my friend for what I knew would be the last time. So there I was, experiencing at one and the same time both intense misery at my own situation and intense appreciation for the beauty in which I was immersed. Clearly, by conventional standards, one of these experiences was "desirable" and the other was "undesirable," but their co-emergence rather than their contrast impressed itself upon me. Something suddenly snapped in my mind and I said to myself in wonder, "The Four Noble Truths are true!" This experience was not superficial or short-lived, for it motivated me to seek out Buddhist meditation disciplines and sent my life onto a course that previously I had never deemed possible or appealing.

But what had I noticed that had eluded me before? Certainly not the First Noble Truth, that life lived conventionally is pervaded by suffering, for I had been more aware of my misery than I cared to be for quite some time, without any sudden insight as to the truth of the Four Noble Truths. Rather, the Second Noble Truth, that suffering derives from desire, and its connection with the First Noble Truth impressed itself upon me. I realized that my own desperate longing for things to be different was actually what made what seemed to be "inside" my mind so painful in contrast to what seemed to be "outside" my mind. This connection between suffering and one's own mental state is much more basic to Buddhism than acknowledging suffering but attributing it solely to external factors. The clarity of this insight brought some of the immediate relief to my anguish that the Third Noble Truth—the truth of the cessation of suffering—promises. Altogether, this experience convinced me that if the more philosophical teachings of Buddhism were true, then I should also heed Buddhism's practical advice, as conveyed in the Fourth Noble Truth regarding the path of moral development, meditation practice, and the seeking of wisdom. Classic Buddhist texts suggest that the Four Noble Truths are not realized sequentially but simultaneously; for me, clearly, the experience that turned me toward Buddhist practice was an insight into the coherence of the vision provided by the Four Noble Truths, not a piecemeal deduction from one assertion to the next.

After this surprising fruit of grief, I had to wait a long time to experience again the creativity and renewal that come with a consort relationship of mutuality and collegiality, since I would not settle for long for the living death of a relationship based on conventional gender roles. Discussing why such a relationship is so vital for women's intellectual and spiritual creativity is not the topic of this chapter; that will be discussed instead in a future paper on the links between eros and intellectual or spiritual creativity in women. Nevertheless, my beliefs in the potential of such relationships were confirmed by my experience of such a relationship.

After a few years, however, I was again dealing with the loss by death of a consort with whom I had had a mutual and collegial relationship—this time within the context of a relationship that had, in fact, been much more complete. The level of anguish was sometimes profoundly unbearable. But after more than fifteen years of Buddhist meditation, I was also much more familiar with the practice of neither leading nor following my thoughts and other mental activities.[1] When I worked with my mental processes as I had been trained to do in meditation, I discovered an overwhelming urge to indulge my memories of a lovely past and my fears of a lonely future. I discovered that what I wanted to believe was grief was simply a habitual pattern of discursive thought—fantasies and projections run wild. When I simply stayed in the immediate moment, something very different happened—pure feeling that was neither this nor that, neither grief nor happiness. And no matter how intense such feelings might be, they were bearable. They did not leak out into an intense desire to do something to change what I was feeling because it was too unbearable. That only happened when I was, in fact, not in the present but in the past and what I had lost or in the future and what I wouldn't have. Nevertheless, the temptation to indulge in memory or in dread was constant. So I learned to do better than I had ever done in thousands of hours of formal meditation practice the essential meditative technique of dropping thoughts, without judging them, and returning to nowness—the nowness of winter sunlight, of incense smoke, of cat's fur, of Gregorian chant. . . . Whatever the content of immediate nowness, the experience always had the same quality as that second of sunlight on the fall-colored trees in the parking lot on my way to my Buddhism class.

Because I had countless opportunities to practice returning to nowness, gradually the process became more self-existing in the fabric of my spirit. The results were quite astonishing. It became clear to me and to many of my friends that I was, in fact, in better shape psychologically and spiritually than I had ever been previously, including during the happy and creative years of collegial consortship. I frequently told people that, while I had benefited immensely from finally having a mutual relationship, I had learned as much from having to deal with losing it as I had from having it.

Why should that have happened? I certainly don't want to draw ridiculous conclusions from my experiences, such as that suffering is good for us and so we should not seek to alleviate it, or that some theistic entity is pulling strings to bless us in disguise. Rather, the whole key to understanding how such processes could occur is in the Buddhist insight into all-pervasive impermanence, the fulcrum of all Buddhist teaching, and the closely allied teaching that fighting impermanence is the root cause of suffering.

> The basic teaching of Buddhism is the teaching of transiency, or change. That
> everything changes is the basic truth for each existence. No one can deny this
> truth, and all the teaching of Buddhism is condensed within it. This is the
> teaching for all of us. Wherever we go, this teaching is true.[2]

Impermanence is something so basic that we all can easily concede it
intellectually. It is so obvious. Nevertheless, emotionally it is the most
difficult teaching of all to integrate into one's being, which is why it is the
fulcrum point of all Buddhist teaching. From the Buddhist point of view,
whole religions are built mainly on the denial of impermanence, which is
understandable, given how difficult impermanence is to accept emotionally, though unfortunate, given how important acceptance of impermanence is to spiritual freedom. One could accurately state that Buddhist
meditation is nothing more than a discipline that brings home again and
again, ceaselessly, how impermanent everything is.

From an intellectual point of view, such teaching may seem to be cold
comfort, but experientially, the results of really getting this teaching are
astounding. Really accommodating impermanence, not merely as an
intellectual doctrine but emotionally as the most intimate fabric of our
being, is nothing less than the cessation of suffering, the nirvana that so
mystifies so many. To continue quoting Suzuki Roshi,

> This teaching is also understood as the teaching of selflessness. Because each
> existence is in constant change, there is no abiding self. In fact, the self-nature
> of each existence is nothing but change, the self-nature of all existence. . . .
> This is also called the teaching of Nirvana. When we realize the everlasting
> truth of "everything changes" and find our composure in it, we find ourselves
> in Nirvana.[3]

Since nirvana is always evaluated by Buddhists as a transformative and
valuable experience, it is clear that experiencing impermanence fully brings
freedom and joy rather than sadness and grief, which is how most people
evaluate impermanence when they analyze these issues intellectually.

Finding our composure in impermanence can also be discussed as the
experience of staying in the present, of experiencing *now* rather than past
or future. As is so commonly said by Buddhists, since everything is always
changing, *now* is all we really have or are. Therefore, it could also be said
that nirvana, or the cessation of suffering, is a matter of riding the razor's
edge of nowness. Most people, in fact, probably would evaluate moments
of nowness very positively. The vividness, intensity, and joy that come
with being fully present to one's life and one's experiences are intensely
appealing. The problem is that it is very difficult to realize that nowness
and impermanence are two names for the same thing, one of which people

want and the other of which they don't want, conventionally. Suzuki Roshi continues his commentary: "Without accepting the fact that everything changes, we cannot find perfect composure."[4] Thus, all the positive states that we strive to cultivate, such as equanimity, joy, vividness, appreciation, and a sense of humor are, in fact, dependent on our ability to find our composure in impermanence. They cannot be experienced in any consistent way so long as we believe in and strive for permanence. It would be very nice to experience nowness without impermanence, but that does not seem possible. How can the exact razor of nowness be anything other than completely fleeting and impermanent? How can there be something else that lasts forever? The trick is simply to give up on achieving something other than impermanence and to "find our composure in it," which are both the point and the result of Buddhist spiritual discipline.

Real experience of impermanence and nowness also involves non-judgment. When one is immediately focused in present experience, what is central is the experience itself, not some judgment about it. Judgment follows after rather than being one with experience and is less definitive than experience itself. Usually, indulging in judgment about an experience is a clue that one is not finding composure in impermanence, but has strayed from nowness into past and future, hope and fear. In fact, judgmentalism usually interferes with the vividness of experience itself, distancing one from its immediacy and raw power. This is why value judgments and determinations that something is absolutely good or bad are relatively unimportant to Buddhists. (Relative judgments, subject to change and not tightly held, are much more appropriate.)

Finally, we can come full circle. Clearly, in many cases, suffering arises from the judgment or the view that I shouldn't have to experience this or that I don't want to experience this, rather than being inherent in the experience itself. In most cases, what one doesn't want to experience is simply impermanence. One is rebelling against impermanence, which brings grief rather than the permanence or the changes that one thinks one wants and needs. As Suzuki Roshi continues, after stating that only by accepting impermanence can we find composure,

> But unfortunately, although it is true, it is difficult for us to accept it. Because we cannot accept the truth of transiency, we suffer. So the cause of our suffering is the non-acceptance of this truth. The teaching of the cause of suffering and the teaching that everything changes are two sides of one coin.[5]

All these points are very clear in the autobiographical comments made earlier in this paper. The link between experiencing suffering and fighting impermanence is completely clear. What may still be less obvious is how these grief-filled experiences gave way to something else. But when I really gave in to impermanence and experienced the present, repeatedly, more than a hundred thousand times,[6] something else happened. I began to find composure in impermanence and needed less to try to be someone else experiencing something else. I needed the judgment that I couldn't or didn't want this experience less and less. Eventually, I found a way to enjoy my life in spite of grief and loneliness. However, let me make one point absolutely clear. I am *not* talking about not experiencing feelings, such as grief or anger or longing or disappointment, the usual misinterpretation of equanimity. I am talking about the *impermanence* of feelings, *all* feelings, no matter their content. Wallowing in feelings, seeking to prolong them, accepting some and rejecting others—these are what promote suffering and what one no longer does when one finds some composure in impermanence. But *experiencing* feelings, the sheer, raw power of feeling, is unavoidable. When one stays with the immediate, impermanent, fleeting, evanescent, ever-changing feelings, they are *much more vivid and intense*, precisely the opposite of the dullness of feelings judged, analyzed, and clung to or pushed away.

To say that I found a way to enjoy my life as I became more proficient at staying in the present is not to say that things have gone smoothly. Many experiences have been quite frustrating, most especially seeking a collegial consort with whom mutuality is possible in a world in which even accomplished men usually practice a patriarchal politics of mate selection, preferring less accomplished women to more accomplished women. Nevertheless, I have been unconditionally cheerful for too long now to have manufactured that cheerfulness. I get frustrated, but I don't dwell on frustration as much as I used to. Instead, I notice my frustration and drop fixation on it—at least much of the time. I am more efficient and productive, rarely wasting time thinking about how busy I am or despairing that I can't get everything done.

Furthermore, I take as a deliberate practice not only leaning into every experience as much as possible while dwelling on none but also contemplating, on a daily basis, my own impending and inevitable death. Such contemplations are a venerable and famous technique in the Buddhist repertoire of formal meditation exercises, going all the way back to the charnel ground meditations recommended in early Buddhism. But, though I have done such formal practices, the spontaneous contemplations that I now do, based on my own coming to terms with impermanence through grieving, have more pith and poignancy for me. Interestingly, I find my own death more regrettable now that I enjoy life more than I did when I fought impermanence all the time. But the regret is not a complaint; it is part of the appreciation of nowness that comes with accommodating impermanence.

∽ *Stop the World! Some Examples of Dissatisfaction with Impermanence*

I began this essay by suggesting that what Buddhism understands as finitude and impermanence, which simply names things as they are without praise or blame, other religions often regard as a problem that the faithful hope to transcend eventually. It is now time to turn to this contrasting belief system. It is well known that changeability and limitation are widely regarded as flaws, especially in the stream of Western religious thought that was most influenced by Greek thought. In classical expressions of theistic religions, the deity is perfect precisely because deity does not participate in flawed mutability and limitation. Ordinary human life is problematic, simply because the natural human condition involves uncompromising finitude and unceasing changeability leading to death. But the hope and the promise of many religions are that this "flawed" human condition can be transformed into a condition of permanence and infinite life by the proper relationship with some transcendent reality. This generic portrait of conventional religion is so familiar that many people, including most of my students, do not imagine that there could be any religious alternatives, which is why Buddhism often seems so odd, so against the grain, when it is first encountered.

At the most extreme, these alternatives present two radically different interpretations of the same basic experience. In any case, an embodied human being experiences ceaseless change and limitation throughout the life cycle and death follows. The Buddhist interpretation, which I have discussed elsewhere as "freedom within the world,"[7] is that finitude and impermanence are inevitable but that that does not have to be a problem. Another classical interpretation of these same facts of life, prominent in many streams of Western theistic religions, regards these facts as an immense problem, for which humans are to blame. (This is the most frequent interpretation of the myth of Adam, Eve, and the serpent in the Garden of Eden.) As many feminist scholars have pointed out, a common solution to this intolerable problem is to reject finitude, to abhor and fear it, as well as any reminders of finitude, such as the mortal body, the ever-changing realms of nature, and women, who seem, according to this analysis, to be more bodily and more natural.[8] In this same interpretation of bodily life, the classic proposed solution is salvation from impermanence and finitude, not by way of finding composure in impermanence, but by

way of eventual abolition of impermanence effected by a deity who is infinite and eternal and who rescues some from the curse of finitude and
impermanence. Even in a postmodern culture, in which belief in a transcendent deity has been severely eroded, denial of impermanence still per-
sists, and other saviors, such as medical technology, function to allow
denial of the reality of impermanence, finitude, and death.

Such wholesale rebellion against impermanence and finitude has many
negative consequences that are rarely linked with their true cause—denial
of impermanence and finitude. For example, once one accommodates
impermanence, the enormous resources spent at the extremities of the life
cycle become morally unacceptable. How can over a million dollars be
spent on one premature infant in an overpopulated world in which millions of other basically healthy children lack even the most basic medical
care, such as routine vaccinations? How can we tolerate the percentage of
our total health care costs that goes into the last few days of forced living
for dying people who are not fortunate enough to die quickly, before the
medical establishment can get them hooked up to tubes? It is clear that
denial of impermanence drives most of the extraordinary measures that
have become routine medical practice. Only the attitude that death is an
insult to be avoided at all costs, rather than an unproblematic part of life,
could fuel such practices. It seems that in the post-religious Western
world, we have given up the otherworldliness and transcendence of classical religious beliefs, but not the hatred of the impermanence of this
embodied earthly life that went with them.

After death, common funeral practices continue the denial of death, as
has often been pointed out by cultural commentators. Professionals have
taken over dealing with the body, so that friends and family do not confront the reality of a cold, stiff corpse. Formaldehyde is shot through the
body to preserve it from the decay that is natural, making it like a pickled
laboratory sample. Makeup disguises the pallor of death. Fancy, expensive
coffins continue the waste and denial. Finally, the body is encased in a concrete box, prohibiting it from mingling with the earth that is its source,
robbing the earth of its trace minerals forever. Thus, even in death, permanence is sought as much as possible.

Perhaps because Buddhist attitudes toward death are so different, so
matter-of-fact, Buddhists have become experts in dealing with death in
many cultures to which the Buddhist religion has traveled.[9] Here in the
United States, Buddhist practices surrounding dying and death are far different from the common cultural norm. Dying is viewed as an unavoidable
process that offers great opportunities for the dying person and her family
and friends to deepen their understanding of impermanence and to develop
greater detachment and equanimity. Death itself is one of the main expe-

riences that are conducive to enlightenment if the dying person is detached and mindful. But there is no reason for useless medical extremes, particularly if they dull the mind and cloud awareness. After death, as before, the body is not given over to impersonal experts but is prepared for cremation by family and friends, who meditate with the body non-stop until cremation. There is no embalming and no makeup or other cosmetic measures.

Outsiders sometimes recoil from these descriptions, but I have found the practices to be anything but gruesome. Instead, they are grounding and energizing, and one feels gratitude toward the dying/dead person for all the lessons they are imparting, even in such extreme circumstances. It seems so matter-of-fact and so sane for the dead person to be in his bedroom or shrineroom, surrounded by shrine objects and meditators. Chanting around the body while waiting for the crematorium to heat up is a final service and watching the body burn is a final teaching imparted by the dead person. The whole experience is very ordinary, very matter-of-fact, grounding, and energizing at the same time.

Turning from the intimate concern of death practices that do not attempt to evade impermanence to the very large concern of the survival of our environment, we find a similar dis-ease with finitude and impermanence and preference for nonearthly transcendence at the heart of the matter. Beginning with Lynn White, many commentators have sought in Western religious attitudes the root of the Western world's disregard for this finite earth that we know and on which we depend unconditionally.[10] While White's proposed explanation, locating the roots of environmental devastation in the permission to dominate the earth given in the creation story in Genesis has merit, I would claim that this permission is embedded in a deeper set of values. In Western theistic religions, the transcendent creator of the world alone is of supreme worth; the world, seen as a dependent creation, is robbed of the sacredness many religions would attribute to it. Therefore, humans are to thank and honor the transcendent creator, not the earth on which they live.

The same feminist theologians who have articulated so clearly the dualistic, otherworldly worldview of much classical Western religion have pointed out that the classic, otherworldly worldview goes hand in hand with rejection of our world of ceaseless change and finite capabilities as our true home, to be treasured and cared for. Instead we are taught to long for a transcendent realm, which, unlike this earth, is immutable and eternal (and in which we also become immutable and eternal). In that process, this earth becomes something of a throwaway, to be used and then discarded for a superior alternative. No wonder people can plunder and pollute the earth with abandon; because it is finite and ever-changing, it is of limited value, to be replaced eventually by an infinite, unchanging realm. The fragile, finite, ever-changing earth is not good enough as it is; it is tamed, cleared, damned, mined, and fertilized until it becomes toxic. It is regarded as a temporary dwelling place, of instrumental value only, and not quite up to par, certainly not by contrast with its imagined opposite, the realm of otherworldly transcendence.

By contrast, feminist theologians concerned with the environment have suggested that our only solution is to embrace and affirm finitude. In a provocative essay Carol Christ links reverence for life with an acceptance of finitude and death. She claims that rejecting finitude and death for transcendence and immortality is at odds with reverence for the only life we know—a life that is very finite and ends in death. She makes clear the connection between embracing finitude rather than transcendence and reverence for life.

> If we experience our connection to the finite and changing earth deeply, then we must find the thought of its destruction or mutilation intolerable. When we know this finite earth as our true home and accept our own inevitable death, then we must know as well that spirituality is the celebration of our immersion in all that is and is changing.[11]

In a similar vein, Rosemary Ruether suggests that classical Christianity has misnamed finitude as sin, in the process encouraging humans to think that finitude and mortal life can be overcome through otherworldly salvation. She explains how this belief system fosters environmental degradation.

> The evaluation of mortal life as evil and the fruit of sin has lent itself to an earth-fleeing ethic and spirituality, which has undoubtedly contributed centrally to the neglect of the earth, to the denial of commonality with plants and animals, and to the despising of the work of sustaining the day-to-day processes of finite but renewable life. By evaluating such finite but renewable life as sin and death, by comparison with "immortal" life, we have reversed the realities of life and death. Death as deliverance from mortality is preferred to the only real life available to us.[12]

∾ Conclusion

"When we realize the everlasting truth of 'everything changes' and find our composure in it, we find ourselves in Nirvana."[13] Everything always changes and everything is finite, including ourselves. But that basic fact has been assessed very differently by Buddhism and by classical Western religions. In this essay I have tried to indicate how the shock of dealing with impermanence in the form of death of loved consorts taught me to discover "the everlasting truth of 'everything changes'" and to find my own composure in that truth. I have also suggested that discussion of many current issues could benefit from a healthy dose of the wisdom that everything always changes and is finite, and I have highlighted terminal care and dying, as well as concern for the viability of our supporting environment as two concerns that would be handled differently if impermanence and finitude were taken more seriously. Clearly, I would suggest that Buddhist teachings regarding impermanence and finitude have great merit and wisdom.

It strikes me that one of the points at which classical Buddhism and classical Christianity most differ from each other is in their evaluation of impermanence. It also strikes me that this is one of the points at which what I understand as the mainstream of Christian tradition could learn the most from the mainstream of Buddhist tradition. I am not suggesting that Buddhism is free from tendencies to promise or threaten some kind of permanence, especially in certain strands of popular Buddhism. Nor am I suggesting that all versions of Christianity are so oriented to eternalism. Most especially, it is important to recognize that Buddhist and Christian people both grasp and cling to permanence, trying to make things last, or to push away the impermanence that is not wanted. That is the nature of samsaric or conventional human psychology. But a major difference is striking: Classical Buddhist thought does not encourage or promote such longing for permanence, whereas some classical Christian thought, deriving from the Hellenistic version of Christianity, seems to encourage people to believe that they can overcome impermanence. And the results of trying to overcome impermanence are devastating for everyone.

PART 3

Buddhist Perspectives
in Feminist Theology

Introduction: What Is Buddhist Theology?

THE PHRASE "BUDDHIST THEOLOGY" would strike some as an oxymoron, given that Buddhism is a nontheistic religion. Clearly, the term is new, one of the many innovations involved in the transition of Buddhism to the West. Theology is uniquely important in Western religions, and "Buddhist theology" is at this point a hybrid Western enterprise. It consists of the self-conscious reflections of recent Western converts to Buddhism who also have professional training and interest in the construction of religious thought. We Buddhist theologians are not content merely to repeat what we have learned about Buddhism, but wish to use the wisdom and compassion we have learned from our study and practice of Buddhism to construct religious thought that speaks to contemporary issues and problems. The chapters in this section all comment, from a Buddhist perspective, on issues important to Western feminist theology. And no issues have been more central than the transcendence and the exclusively male imagery so prevalent in Western constructs of deity and so problematic to feminists working within the Western traditions. These Buddhist alternatives to a transcendent exclusively male deity could be called "Buddhist feminist theology."

But why name the construction of Buddhist thought in its new Western homeland "theology" in the absence of "theos" or "deity," as that term has traditionally been understood by Western religions? Buddhism posits no eternal, immutable, self-existent, independent creator—not even in Vajrayana Buddhism, which talks quite freely of "deities"—a common translation of the Tibetan term *yidam*, which is of considerable importance in most of the chapters of this section.

The basic reason for using this term is convenience. "Theology" is well known and at least reasonably well understood by the audiences to which we write and speak as people who think and write professionally about religion. This is important to someone such as myself, since I do not address myself only to other Buddhists or to Buddhalogists. Furthermore, I do not believe that contemporary theology is any longer always about a personal anthropomorphic creator deity in the classical sense. Theologians of Jewish and Christian persuasion write and talk about an ultimate reality that is not always the classical anthropomorphic deity, and I think it is quite well known that Buddhist theologians would not be writing about such a deity. Thus, we Buddhist theologians are using the term "theology" in ways that are similar to the ways that some of our Western colleagues also use the term. Finally, the term "theology" has a distinct advantage, in my view. The term clearly connotes that we are thinking *within* the confines of a specific tradition, not as free agents, and we place ourselves under the authority of that tradition. Of course, this does not mean that we accept the received tradition lock, stock, and barrel without suggesting contemporary interpretations of that received tradition. That is why we are "theologians," not merely historians or philologists. But, nevertheless, I work *within* the broad confines of the Buddhist system. For these reasons, I definitely would not want to call my work "philosophy," because I believe that the difference between philosophy and theology is not whether one thinks speculatively about the nature of ultimate reality but whether one considers oneself to be working within a given system and under its authority, or whether one considers oneself to be a free agent under no authority. Therefore, I actually regard the phrase "Buddhist philosophy" to be more of an oxymoron than "Buddhist theology," though I suspect many will disagree with me on that issue.

Is there a more appropriate term for doing contemplative, speculative Buddhist thought? Is there a way to find or coin a more traditional Buddhist term? Clearly, if we look at traditional Buddhism, what we are doing as Buddhist theologians is studying and commenting on the dharma, a time-honored practice in Buddhism. But what could one call the discipline and the practice of studying and commenting on the dharma and coming up with dharmic solutions to twentieth-century issues? Are we doing "dharmalogy"? Such a neologism is awkward and ugly-sounding. But, technically, it is more accurate than either "theology" or "Buddhalogy." Neologisms have the disadvantage of being unfamiliar, needing constant explanation. And they often don't catch on, which renders them useless. On the other hand "androcentrism" was also a neologism when we began to use it twenty-five years ago, but, because of the great need for such a term in the language, it has caught on quite well and has become standard English. As more Western, English-speaking people come to study and comment on the dharma, there will be more need for a word to name what we do. Perhaps "dharmalogy" would catch on.

Or perhaps we should avoid the Western tendency to turn every kind of study into an "ology" and avoid any term with that ending. As the more user-friendly term "god-talk" is replacing the term "theology" in some contexts, perhaps we could say that we do "dharma-discourse," a suggestion that I think may have some merit. We make suggestions as to the contemporary interpretations and applications of the classic formulations of *buddhadharma,* and I think the term "dharma-discourse" could come to mean precisely that.

Unfortunately, there is also a serious problem connected with this term. There is as yet no term for someone who engages in god-talk, other than "theologian." If we were to call our activity "dharma-discourse" what would we call ourselves? The traditional term would be "dharma teacher," the term I am called when I present my comments in a Buddhist context to a Buddhist audience. But the term is less appropriate in the wider public arena, which does not presume that we share the same outlook or are one another's teachers. Nor does the term leave much room for the suggestive, speculative, and provisional nature of many of the ideas we Buddhist theologians are presenting. Our comments, in hindsight, may not turn out to very appropriate and may not be included among the ever-increasing canon of genuine dharma. In my opinion, the term "dharma teacher" should be reserved for traditional teaching contexts and the assumptions that go with those contexts; it should not be used of the kinds of work done by public theologians. Given all that confusion and complexity, it may be best simply to opt for the oxymoronic but culturally appropriate (for Western Buddhists) term "Buddhist theology." To me, that compromise seems unproblematic, but I would be delighted with a better solution to this naming problem.

Whatever such Buddhist constructions eventually are called, the five chapters in this section represent some of my work as a Buddhist feminist theologian commenting on issues that have been important to feminist theology. These suggestions point in two directions. On the one hand, as a longtime feminist who was a feminist before I became a Buddhist theologian, I bring feminist critique and reconstruction to Buddhism, especially in the last chapter of this book. But, on the other hand, because Buddhism is my religion of choice—as a woman and a feminist—I want to contribute some of the profound comfort and intelligence I have found in Buddhist thought and practice to feminist discourse concerning some of the most painful issues women have faced in their religious lives.

The first of these chapters takes a somewhat different approach to questions of immanence and transcendence than is common in feminist theology. I suggest that in a non-theistic context, immanence and transcendence are not primarily about deity but about our own lives and our own visions. While immanence has been lauded in feminist circles, I suggest that transcendence is an important psychological experience for a religious consciousness socialized in patriarchy.

The final four chapters together represent the progression of my thinking about the important topic of the so-called "feminine principle" in Vajrayana Buddhism. As a very early critic of male monotheism who wrote important early contributions to the topic of female god-language,[1] I approached the topic of a "feminine principle"[2] in Vajrayana Buddhism with both relief and skepticism. I was relieved that *yidam*s, the nontheistic deities of Vajrayana Buddhism, were routinely portrayed in both sexes, thus relieving me of the burden of exclusively masculine deities. But I was also skeptical that their traditional portrayal would be free of androcentrism. Over my many years of meditation practice with both female and male *yidam*s and continued contemplation of them, this skepticism has both been allayed and proven to be partially correct, as these four chapters, taken together, will demonstrate.

The chapter "Some Buddhist Perspectives on the Goddess," while not the first to be written, is presented first because it presents an overview of the issues and some information on the topic of Buddhist "goddesses." The next chapter, on the feminine principle in Tibetan Vajrayana Buddhism, was the first article I wrote on the topic of feminine imagery in Buddhism and its implications for feminist theology. First written in 1982 soon after I had received the initiations required to do the meditation practices of Vajrayogini, an important female *yidam*, this chapter describes my initial immersion into a symbolic universe and set of meditation disciplines that few Western feminists have experienced. By 1984, I had completed the formal requirements of Vajrayogini practice and wanted to describe much more fully to my Western feminist colleagues some of what I had experienced. "'I Will Never Forget to Visualize That Vajrayogini Is My Body and Mind'" was presented at a dramatic panel on women's experiences of initiation at the 1985 annual meeting of the American Academy of Religion. By 1994, I had also formally completed a set of practices involving Cakrasamvara, an important male *yidam* visualized in union with Vajrayogini, and felt that some of my skepticism regarding whether or not these traditional practices were androcentric had been laid to rest in a way that only immersion in the meditation practices could accomplish. But questions and concerns remained. How I have continued to reflect on them is discussed in the final chapter "Life-giving Images in Tibetan Vajrayana Buddhism."

Immanence and Transcendence in Women's Religious Experience and Expression: A Nontheistic Perspective

I N SOME FEMINIST CIRCLES, it is commonly claimed that theologies of transcendence are masculine and that women are more likely to be attracted to a theology of immanence. The traditional Western emphasis on divine transcendence is claimed to be inadequate, especially for women. Additionally, the concept of a transcendent deity is said to lead to disregard for our earthly home of the environment around us and to foster otherworldly, anti-body alienation. Advocates of this view go on to claim that if women had participated in the naming of reality, such an excessive emphasis on transcendence would never have occurred and we would have much healthier and saner lifestyles and attitudes. In naming patriarchy as the demon to be overcome, many have included divine transcendence in that demonic presence, and have sought to create a theology of the immanent goddess instead, claiming that she and her devotees could never give rise to the kind of excesses that are so characteristic of patriarchal transcendence.

As a Buddhist feminist, I have affirmed that a more "immanent" interpretation of Buddhism, "Buddhism as freedom within the world" is more appropriate than a more "transcendent" interpretation of Buddhism as "freedom from the world." I have also declared that the ultimate purpose of Buddhist spiritual discipline is the "immanent" goal of equanimity and sanity, rather than the "transcendent" goal of achieving supranormal states of consciousness or freedom from rebirth.[1] Thus, superficially it might seem that my work also demonstrates the generalization that women prefer theologies of immanence to theologies of transcendence, but I believe that the situation is considerably more complex than the simple claim that men prefer transcendence while women prefer immanence.

Initially, the issues and definitions seem simple and straightforward: "immanence" seems to refer to a particular concept about Ultimate Reality or Deity, and about how Ultimate Reality is related to humans. Then the major question would be whether and why women seem to prefer a theology that locates Ultimate Reality "within" rather than "beyond." But when I revisit some of the questions about immanence, transcendence, and spiritual discipline that have haunted me for some time, the issues become more tangled. The question of what people experience when they call something "transcendent" is crucial, for transcendence has a venerable history and wide appeal. I found it worth remembering my own pre-feminist religious experiences, which used the only religious language then available—a language of transcendence. That language seemed quite appealing and inspiring at that time. In addition, I still find that language appropriate, for I titled my most painful wrestlings with questions of "immanence," "transcendence," and spiritual discipline in *Buddhism after Patriarchy* "Spiritual Discipline: Vision and *Transcendence* in Remaking the World." I am not retracting that title, but rather seek to explicate how transcendence fits into feminist religious life as I defuse the thesis that men prefer transcendence while women prefer immanence.

◦ Do Women Always Choose Theologies of Immanence?

My answer to this question is fueled by my distaste for any thesis that posits inherent or necessary links between sex and theology or spirituality. Asked to comment on the thesis that "a focus on immanence is inevitably found in women-created religions,"[2] my initial impulse is to seek to falsify the thesis because it seems to link a theological position with women's biology. That women prefer theological immanence may be a statically accurate generalization. However, the claim that women create symbols of immanence *because* of their female biology and that men create symbols of transcendence *because* of their male biology is unpalatable to me. The tendency, popular even in some feminist circles, to attribute emotions and preferences common but not universal in men or women to biological sex rather than to cultural gender is dangerous for women's autonomy. Any form of biological determinism is dangerous for women. Instead, I would claim that if there is a link between women and theologies of immanence, that link is between the female *gender*, as constructed in specific cultural situations, and immanence, *not* between the female *sex* and immanence. Therefore, such links would not be invariable or inherent but would be dependent on cultural variables. In other words, although theology is not dependent on sex, theology is deeply affected by gender. That is to say, gender of necessity affects theology, because culture affects theology and gender constructs are part of culture. But there are no necessary and predictable correlations between theological positions and sex, because biological sex does not determine theological positions. Culture, including gender constructs, and tradition determine theological positions.

To defuse the thesis of a necessary link between women and theologies of immanence, I remind readers of an argument that is sometimes used against the feminist theological call to invent and renew feminine symbolism of the divine. One often hears the argument that goddesses are quite prominent in some patriarchal religions and seem to do nothing to promote women's interests or needs. Thus, there is no inherent link between the presence of goddesses and equitable treatment for women, a generalization that I think is accurate. Furthermore, though Western theologies are transcendent and patriarchal, Hindu theologies are *immanent* and patriarchal. Just as goddesses can be called into the service of patriarchal religion, so can a theology of immanence. So much for any necessary or inherent link between immanence and women's theologies, or theologies that are more beneficial to women than is a theology of divine transcendence.

This does not totally dispense with the issue, however, for I am completely unconvinced by the argument that, since goddesses have been co-opted by patriarchy, therefore, people, including women, don't need the goddess. Though the presence of goddesses does not guarantee equity for women, their absence almost certainly guarantees inequity for women. Likewise, though one cannot link women with theologies of immanence in any biologically determined way, immanence may nevertheless be an attractive concept for contemporary women. In a patriarchal culture that sports a usual theology of transcendence, immanence may be deeply appealing to women—because of their gender, not because of their sex. In the same way, in a patriarchal culture sporting a usual theology of immanence, perhaps transcendence would be more appealing to women. At the end of this essay, I will return to these questions and propose an alternative thesis to explain the seeming correlation between women and theologies of immanence.

∿ *Immanence and Transcendence* as *Religious Experience*

Constructing theology as a Buddhist nontheist encourages one to ask different questions about immanence and transcendence. Usually theologians talk of immanence and transcendence as characteristics of a deity who is assumed to be separate from the phenomenal world and in relationship with it. That deity is either transcendent to the phenomenal world, as in Western monotheisms, or immanent within the phenomenal world, as in the *Bhagavad Gita*, to name only one document of Hindu immanent theology. In other words, "transcendence" and "immanence" are usually thought to modify or describe an ultimate reality that is other to me, even if it is immanent. The meanings of "immanence" and "transcendence" for nontheistic systems, such as Buddhism, are then somehow grafted onto this reference point, because of the predominance of theism in Western culture, though reflection prods one to realize that, as theological concepts, they don't easily fit a nontheistic system.

Therefore, I have become ever less convinced that immanence and transcendence are primarily, in the first order, about deities and increasingly interested in the *religious experiences* behind theological concepts of immanence and transcendence. What are the experiences that may give rise in theistic systems to conceptualizations of deity as transcendent or immanent? To me, given the immense interest of feminist theology in religious experience and its claim that *all* religious beliefs are grounded in experience, this should be *the* major question about immanence and transcendence. I find it curious that questions about the religious experiences behind concepts of divine immanence and divine transcendence have been displaced by the claim that theology and religion created by women will espouse a theology of immanence.

Perhaps this oversight occurs simply because almost all Western discourse on religion, even in academic settings, assumes a somewhat theistic and transcendent stance. Rather than seeing religion as something that emerges from the interior depths of human experience, religion is pictured as something from elsewhere that interrupts human existence. Even in contemporary comparative scholarship on religion, which does not attribute religion to a transcendent divine source, religion is attributed to some "other," interrupting, disrupting experience. Most of the classic historians of religions speak as if humans experience religion primarily as something that comes upon them from elsewhere, as in the work of Rudolf Otto with his "wholly other," G. van der Leeuw with his "kratophanies," even Mircea Eliade and his "hierophanies." (I would also claim that those who regard Eliade's "hierophany" as a covert term for God, the deity of Western monotheism, are completely off the mark.)

As a thought experiment, I invite contemplating what sort of models of religion might emerge in comparative religious scholarship if the master myth of the culture did not posit a transcendent deity. Since I have begun to reflect on nontheistic meanings of "immanence" and "transcendence,"

I have thought that the methods and models of comparative religious scholarship emerging in a culture in which the basic story of where religion came from was the Buddha's enlightenment would be quite different from comparative religious scholarship emerging in a culture in which the basic story is the theophany at Mount Sinai followed by Christ's incarnation, resurrection, and ascension into heaven.

Therefore, suppose that "immanence" and "transcendence" are, in the first order, not words that describe the relationship of the deity with the phenomenal world, but words that describe my own relationship with my world—the world of expectations, hopes, people, phenomenal reality. Either I seek to go beyond my current given world, or I find tremendous depth of meaning and richness within it—which, I find, in my nontheistic symbol system, is exactly how I use these words. Suppose that "immanence" and "transcendence," commonly projected onto a deity, actually are ways to express my relationship, or desired relationship, with my world. How, then, would the terms "immanence" and "transcendence" be used, and what would be their implications for women?

For me, the feelings associated with the word "transcendence," which go back many years, well before my immersion in nontheistic spiritual practices, are *longing* and *vision*. What thrilled me about feelings associated with transcendence as a religious experience was not the concept of a transcendent deity but *my* feelings of exultation and freedom, my transcendence of mundane, stultifying, vapid, trivial pursuits when I clicked into the music, the symbols, the rituals associated with transcendence. They took me quite literally into another world of feeling that was much more satisfying than the petty concerns I was being trained to care about—cleaning, cooking, costuming, repeating creeds. . . . In that world, longing to see clearly and to experience reality was appropriate and satisfying. In that world intelligence and sensitivity are valued as natural and normal.

Thus, transcendence was literally my salvation, though it turned out that the transcendence that mattered was *my* transcendence of a limited world, not the deity's transcendence over the phenomenal world. Religious concepts and rituals about a transcendent deity were merely the method, the medium for me to arouse and experience my own longing and vision, and thus to transcend the narrow limits of my life at that time. What I needed, as an impoverished, culturally deprived person destined for the banalities of the female gender role in mid-America at mid-century was transcendence, not immanence. Nor would I expect that any feminist in a patriarchal system could do without transcendence, in this sense of longing and vision.

Reflecting upon such experiences, I am convinced that the experiential root of concepts of divine transcendence is the experience of vision and longing resulting in the conviction that there's got to be more than this, more than the role I'm being socialized into, more than what people tell me life is about, more than the religious system I'm being handed. For this reason, I would contend that at its root "transcendence" has to do with human religious experience, not with divinity. I would also contend that transcendence as vision and longing is a basic root, if not *the* basic root, of all religious expressions. What the longing produces in terms of religious symbols and concepts, whether theistic or nontheistic religions, whether symbols of divine immanence or transcendence, are, in the final analysis, the effects, not the causes, of such longing.

What then is the basis of immanence, whether as a theological concept about deity or as religious experience? As longing and vision are the experiential base for concepts of transcendence, so, I have come to think, *peace* and *tranquillity* are the experiential basis for the notion of immanence. What we have and what we are is sufficient, throbbing with presence and fullness. Nothing needs to be changed, and the question of whether one is happy or sad makes no sense. Things are as they are and there is no question of anything else. This is not mindless complacency or animal-realm ignorance. It is the deep peace that "passeth all understanding." One is at home.

Though glimmers of such experiences always popped up momentarily, for me any consistency of such equanimity is relatively recent and seems to have required significant suffering and significant life experience. This immanence often expresses itself as deep appreciation of things I was once more inclined to dismiss as "trivial," uninteresting, or superficial—gardening, cooking, the weather, everyday exchanges about how the day went, going for a walk. . . . This appreciation has everything to do with being in the moment, which is so fleeting, with being in the body, which is so impermanent. And immanence or appreciation of this very simple finite experience has everything to do with *being* rather than *doing.*

Therefore, it is possible to recognize the divine or the sacred immediately in everything that moves and does not move. One does not reject this immediate world as divine and sacred to pursue sacredness elsewhere. One does not believe that this world of immediate perceptions and phenomena is too degraded, mundane, or meaningless to be directly sacred. Clearly, such experiences of tranquillity and being at ease affect one's evaluation of the embodied condition, sexuality, mortality, and all our other troubling conditions of finitude and impermanence. One is no longer at war with impermanence and finitude, or their major messengers—sexuality and the body.

Because immanence so clearly affirms this world and embodied experience, some feminists claim that, by contrast, theologies of transcendence inevitably would be otherworldly and anti-body. But, as with the link between the female sex and theologies of immanence, I will seek to falsify the thesis through counterexamples. This equation is due to the power and popularity of the combination of transcendent theology and other-worldly values that reigned in late antiquity in the West, rather than to any inherent link between transcendence and otherworldliness. It is inappropriate to universalize this one example.

Some schools and periods within Buddhism are also somewhat other-worldly and anti-body, despite Buddhism's obvious lack of a transcendent theology. I call these interpretations and varieties of Buddhism "Buddhism as freedom from the world." They are more predominant in pre- and non-Mahayana forms of Buddhism and often are better known to Westerners with a limited understanding of Buddhism. This may explain why so many Westerners, both feminist and nonfeminist, regard Buddhism as an other-worldly religion, an evaluation that now leaves me incredulous because it is so foreign to my experience of Buddhism. On the other hand, the more scholars tell us about the biblical text shorn of the Hellenistic interpretations through which it has been read for so long, the clearer it becomes that earlier biblical religion was not otherworldly or anti-body, despite its strong emphasis on a theology of transcendence.

Apart from counterexamples, however, there is an even more important and cogent reason for rejecting the link between transcendence and other-worldly or anti-body religious attitudes. To long and to have vision do not necessarily imply rejecting the body or rejecting this world in favor of some other immaterial realm. One can long for healing, for community, for wholeness, fleeing from alienation or isolation, but these experiences are more akin to transcendence than to immanence.

Seen in this light, the question of a choice of immanence *or* transcendence is obviously a false dichotomy, whether one is speaking of immanence and transcendence as human experiences or as theological concepts. Clearly, both vision and equanimity, both a sense of longing and a sense of contentment, are necessary in a whole life. Equanimity without vision easily degenerates into complacency or laziness, but longing without peacefulness equally results in rigidity, resentment, and a crusading mentality. In fact, *the* trick of the spiritual life may well be finding and maintaining the *balance* between immanence and transcendence. That balance would not be different for women than for men, though gender socialization might make the *process* of finding the balance different for women than for men in specific cultural or religious settings.

Thus, for contemporary Western women with feminist inclinations, the journey and the balance may well be eventually finding immanence that grows out of a good deal of transcendence, contentment that is preceded by and immersed in a good deal of longing and vision. Such a path would seem to be required for any feminist woman in a patriarchal system. For women, too much immanence too soon would surely lead to stagnation, conformity, complacency, and acquiescence, rather than to peace and tranquillity. Immanence that has not been preceded by transcendence would be rather superficial and dangerous, at least on the part of a woman in a patriarchal system. For example, in my case, now that I have safely transcended the limited world and the limited role that my culture insisted I be content with, I can appreciate gardening, cooking, and taking care of my house. But if I had initially bought into those tasks as my life purpose, I would undoubtedly have missed doing what has made my life worthwhile and useful. I may well even have missed being able to *appreciate* "trivial" things and find contentment in them, rather than merely being *resigned* to my mundane fate. Therefore, at least for our own cultural and religious situation, I definitely do not agree with the thesis that transcendence is not what women need.

∿ Immanence and Transcendence in Feminist Buddhism

The journey of self-discovery and spiritual development prevalent in Buddhism is similar to the journey I have just outlined. For the ordinary practitioner, frustration and suffering are the key experiences at the beginning of the journey. To use the language of this chapter to interpret a typical model, in the life story of the Buddha the journey begins with the insight that there has to be more to life than conventional lifestyles allow. Rejection or *transcendence* of conventionality is followed by a long period of *vision* and *longing*. Finally, breakthrough occurs and he discovers that peace is possible in the present moment, that nothing else is necessary. He rests in immanence.

Nevertheless, there are important differences from Western root myths. According to Mahayana Buddhism, primordial immanence surrounds our longings to transcend, which eventually rest again in that primal immanence. That is to say, according to Buddhist thinking, egolessness, basic goodness, or Buddha nature *are* our basic being. There is no problem, inherently. The reality of inherent goodness is our unalienable birthright. Nevertheless, problems do arise, because of our samsaric, or conventional, inability to see things as they are and to rest in inherent enlightenment. This inability, which is unavoidable for anyone having "the precious human body"[3] is not attributed to perversity or human delinquency. In the long run, there is no logical explanation for this problem, but it is our human situation. As individuals, we become conscious in the midst of our dis-ease with the world of projections, ego, desire, and dissatisfaction to which we have fallen heir. Longing and vision to transcend these conditions are our energy for the journey that brings us home to equanimity. Thus, longing and vision are essential to a mature religious outlook, but they are not the whole story. Our struggles to transcend are only a struggle to be home, the primordial condition. Transcendence and immanence turn out to be interdependent, as I have already suggested they must be in any sophisticated theology. And a theology that does not arrive at some immanence is quite incomplete. This Buddhist overview of the relationship between transcendence and immanence as religious experiences holds true regardless of sex and gender, again throwing into question the easy assumption of an affinity between women and theologies of immanence.

But what of immanence in theologies created by women in our own time in our own cultural context? I will discuss several issues in my own negotiation of the relationship between immanence and transcendence as a Buddhist feminist.

In my work, I have consistently argued in favor of interpreting Buddhism as freedom within the world, rather than as freedom from the world, though I acknowledge that the Buddhist tradition supports both interpretations. Obviously, Buddhism as freedom within the world is more "immanent" than Buddhism as freedom from the world, by any definitions of immanence and transcendence. But, though Buddhism as freedom within the world is more compatible with feminism than would be an interpretation of Buddhism as freedom from the world, I have two reservations. The first is that I believe that if Buddhism were better understood as freedom from the world, one could create a *feminist* Buddhism of world transcendence. Second, I am not sure that my preference for understanding Buddhism as freedom within the world *stems from* my feminism, compatible and mutually helpful as the two value systems may be. Nonfeminist Mahayana Buddhists would also stress that Buddhism involves freedom within the world, since that interpretation is integral to Mahayana Buddhism. Perhaps the most we could say is that I prefer forms of Buddhism that emphasize freedom within the world, rather than freedom from the world, because I am also a feminist who values this-worldly, nonalienated outlooks that do not reject the body and the phenomenal world.

In my work, I have stressed other radically immanent interpretations of Buddhism, but I would claim that they have as much to do with core Buddhist values as with feminism. For example, I stress that, in my view, the point of Buddhist spiritual disciplines is not primarily to prepare for death, though that may also be a result or a side effect of Buddhist meditation. I emphasize that the more important result is to be able to live in the brilliance and vividness of the present moment, and I argue that such an emphasis is cogent because if one knows how to ride the razor's edge of impermanence with equanimity, then one will be able to experience the dying process with equanimity. In other words, spiritual discipline practiced to enable one to live well will surely also prepare one for death, and for rebirth, if there is such a thing. But if one engages in spiritual discipline only or primarily as preparation for death, one may miss one's life in the process. In other words, to regard the purpose of spiritual discipline as preparation for death strikes me as far too otherworldly. (Please note that I am by no means denying the possibility of rebirth; I am simply claiming that we can't know for sure about rebirth. On the other hand, it is completely empirical and obvious that Buddhist practices do work to bring freedom within the world now.)

Such an interpretation goes against the grain of many traditional accounts of Tibetan Buddhism, which has typically included enormous emphasis on death and rebirth.[4] Interestingly, I do not regard this point as one of the more *purely feminist* reconstructions I have suggested. It simply strikes me as common sense. I would argue with fellow Buddhists who disagree with me that they simply have not sufficiently looked into the plain meanings of Mahayana, and especially Vajrayana Buddhist teachings and practices. Instead, they are blinded by Tibetan cultural views, including implicit and total belief in rebirth, which have come west along with the essentials of Vajrayana Buddhism.

Many Buddhists, however, take more exception to my lack of emphasis on death and rebirth than to the more radically feminist claims I make. They have not objected to what I regard as my most radical, controversial, and threatening position—the claim that the verbal dharma (basic Buddhist teachings) currently available to us is incomplete because women have not verbalized the dharma in Buddhist cultures permeated with patriarchal gender roles and stereotypes. I argue that because of the strength of gender roles and stereotypes in Buddhist cultures, women gurus who are not male-identified would not merely amplify the verbal dharma that is already in texts but would add to it in significant ways. Among those ways is my claim that traditionally Buddhism has paid insufficient attention to relationship and community as the matrix for enlightenment, despite the fact that the third of the Three Refuges of this nontheistic religion is the refuge of *sangha,* or the community. I have also suggested that a preponderance of attention has been given the refuges of Buddha as exemplary model and dharma as trustworthy teachings precisely because women, who tend to define well-being in terms of a positive network of relationships, have not been sufficiently represented among those who teach and define the basics of Buddhism. Additionally, I suggest that in a situation in which women had more input into the articulation of Buddhist teachings, there would be the same direct attention to community building as Buddhist practice that is now commonplace regarding meditation and study of the classic teachings and texts.

These claims, however, are ignored by more conventional Buddhists who focus on my suggestion that the purpose of Buddhist practice is to live joyfully with equanimity now, rather than to be ready for death and rebirth. Among my various Buddhist "heresies," the claim that the purpose of Buddhist practice is for life, rather than for death and rebirth, strikes me as minor (and not overtly feminist). So why do more traditional Buddhists, both women and men, focus on my agnosticism regarding rebirth, on my agnosticism toward that particular transcendent concern of conventional Tibetan Buddhism? It strikes me as simplistic to say it has anything to do with sex, nor can I find any correlation with gender.

To return to the focus on transcendence and immanence, these feminist suggestions about teacher, community, and relationship are also "transcendent," in that they express dissatisfaction with the status quo of Buddhism and are a result of longing for things to be different. But these "transcendent" suggestions, arising out of a vision of a radically different way to do things, focus on radically immanent concerns—the everyday issues of relationship and community. But, demonstrating that a complex interweaving of immanence and transcendence is more appropriate for Buddhist feminism than is a simple "either-or" dichotomy and choice, implementing these suggestions would transcend what has been done before in Buddhism.

～ Conclusions

So where does this leave us, finally, in assessing the links between immanence, gender, and sex? I would like to offer the suggestion that the wrong correlation has been picked up in the thesis that "a focus on immanence is inevitably found in woman-created religions." It strikes me that, statistically, the generalization may well be correct, but *not* because of an inherent link between the female sex, or even the female gender, and religious immanence. Rather, the causal link is between outsiders and their predisposition to highlight a dimension of truth that is downplayed or disregarded in the mainstream tradition. This generalized link between women and immanence has been noticed most frequently in connection with Western women who are reworking a Western religious tradition. By virtue of their gender, women are outsiders to the process of symbol creation and theologizing in Western male-dominant culture; furthermore, the dominant symbols and theological constructs of the Western religions emphasize transcendence to a degree that is unusual, even abnormal, in world religions. Outsiders, who have nothing to protect by conforming to the theological tradition, are in a good position to notice what the mainstream has overlooked or deemphasized. Therefore, it seems quite likely to me that Western women, outsiders to their theological system, would emphasize what the system has overlooked, immanence—but because of their gender, not because of their sex. To play with language a bit, we could say that outsiders, who long for an alternative vision, transcend transcendence to arrive at a theology of immanence.

But suppose these circumstances are reversed? Suppose the symbol system is radically immanent in its theology, but women, by virtue of their gender, are still outsiders. Would women then be attracted to transcendent monotheism as a more empowering vision? Could such a situation prevail when transcendent monotheism is the unconventionally new position in a religion or a culture? Could this correlation between outsiders and overlooked, underemphasized religions symbols explain the attraction of transcendent monotheism to at least some women at various points in history? I leave these questions as questions for now. But I do not want to set aside the suggestion that our significant correlation is between outsiders and hidden or de-emphasized truths, rather than between the female sex and immanence.

Likewise, in my own case, as an outsider, both by gender and by culture, to Buddhist systems that often link spiritual proficiency with a happy rebirth, I am in a good position to notice that such a view is not especially consistent with the fundamentally immanent concerns of Buddhism. On the other hand, I have no wish to grind this point into a dogmatic absolute, for that more than anything else would be to renounce immanence for transcendence—a move rightly criticized by many feminists.

In conclusion, I suggest that we should investigate whether outsiders to a theological tradition who become involved in theological discourse have a tendency to notice and emphasize hidden or underemphasized elements of a tradition. Furthermore, I suggest that we drop the hypothesis of an inevitable link between immanence and theologies or religions created by women because its biological determinism is inappropriately essentialist. But even more important is my claim that immanence and transcendence are inevitably intertwined and interdependent with each other, whether in theology or in the spiritual journey. The choice between immanence and transcendence is a false dichotomy. Feminists would do well to recognize that transcendence is an important religious experience and symbol.

CHAPTER 13

Some Buddhist Perspectives
on the Goddess

BUDDHISM IS NOT WELL KNOWN for several reasons to those interested either in Goddess spirituality or in culturally unfamiliar Goddess imagery, mythology, and ritual. First is Buddhism's reputation as simply another version of Asian patriarchal religion, which meshes with the general reluctance of Western feminist theology to deal seriously with non-Western religions. (Even those who delve into premonotheistic resources tend to work mainly with *Western* antiquity.) Second, forms of Buddhism—Mahayana, and especially Vajrayana, or Tantric, Buddhism—that are the most fertile ground for those interested in resources for Goddess spirituality are less well known to Western scholars than are earlier forms of Buddhism, which have almost no feminine (or masculine) imagery of an anthropomorphic ultimate or myth-model. Finally, for those not well versed in Buddhist thought, and even for many who are, Buddhism seems to be characterized by its philosophical abstractness and the rigor of its meditation disciplines but to lack almost completely the symbols, myths, and rituals that would be characteristic of a religion that devotes serious attention to goddesses.

These impressions do not hold up well in the perspective of Buddhist feminist thought or in the experiences of someone with long-term involvement with both Buddhist spiritual disciplines and Goddess theology. In this chapter, I will discuss Buddhist perspectives on "the Goddess" as someone with long-term experience of Buddhism at both the theoretical and the practical levels, but also as someone who addressed the issue of male god-language in the monotheistic context very early in the development of feminist theology[1] and who tried very early in the development of feminist theology to introduce Indian resources into the discussion.[2]

My conclusions will be that Buddhism is exemplary in some of its ways of incorporating feminine imagery and meditation rituals, but that other aspects of traditional Buddhist approaches to the divine feminine are less exemplary and need feminist reconstruction. Because Buddhism is a non-theistic religion, the first issue to be discussed in any commentary on Buddhist perspectives on the Goddess must be the interface between non-theism and Goddess symbolism. Building on the base of Buddhist non-theism, I will discuss late Mahayana Buddhist understandings of Buddhahood and Ultimate Reality contained in *trikaya* (three bodies of Buddhahood) theory, which is the matrix within which Buddhist examples of the "divine female" find their symbolic and mythic existence. I will present two important Buddhist myth-models, Tara and Vajrayogini. I will discuss how *trikaya* theory has traditionally been brought into the human realm, pointing out positive and negative uses of this resource from a feminist point of view. Finally, some feminist reconstructions of inadequate traditional applications of *trikaya* theory will be suggested.

∿ The Resource of Buddhist Nontheism

In my book *Buddhism after Patriarchy: A Feminist History, Analysis, and Reconstruction of Buddhism*, I titled the section in which I dealt with Buddhist nontheism "Count Your Negative Blessings: Battles We Don't Have to Fight." I meant every word of that title. In my judgment, Buddhist nontheism offers feminists two vital resources. The first is the lack of a male Absolute that must be deconstructed before meaningful feminist discourse can occur. The second is the example provided by nontheistic traditions of how one can construct and utilize nonabsolute, nonreified, mythic, symbolic female and male personifications of enlightenment.

It may be helpful first to define briefly what Buddhists mean by non-theism. At the simplest level, nontheism has meant that Buddhism does not posit an Ultimate Other who can create or redeem the phenomenal world, who stands outside the phenomenal world in any way, or who has any kind of dualistic relationship with that world. Lacking the categories of "creation" and "redemption," Buddhism is thoroughly nondualistic. There is no one or nothing to whom to appeal or complain about the state of affairs, no one or nothing who can be blamed for the situation or who can do anything about it except oneself and one's community. (Traditional Buddhists might not include one's community as responsible for the situation; my Buddhist feminist interpretation of the classic Buddhist concept of interdependence [*pratityasamutpada*] leads me to claim that one generates one's situation not solely by one's own karma, but that the whole community helps generate the status quo.)

Defining nontheism as the lack of a Creator or Redeemer is somewhat dependent on the contrast Buddhism presents with more common spiritualities, whether Western or Indian. It is an attempt to define nontheism in theistic terms. At a deeper level, nontheism implies that there is no formula, no practice, nothing that one can borrow and imitate that will launch the seeker into spiritual realization. All the philosophy or meditation in the world will only work to a certain extent to clarify the nature of reality; after that it's completely a matter of insight and intuition. Not only is there no Ultimate Other upon whom one could rely; there isn't even an Ultimate Formula that has captured the essence of truth for us. Fluidity, open-endedness, and nongraspability, always turn out to be the last words in this nondualistic, nontheistic spirituality.

Therefore, Buddhism includes a view of language and truth that is relatively unfamiliar to Western theologians but is quite helpful to those trying to construct or reconstruct Goddess imagery. Put most simply, for Buddhism, "religious doctrines have utility rather than truth; . . . their importance lies in the effects they have upon those who believe in them."[3] According to Mahayana Buddhism, the goal of religious practice is to develop simultaneously and to balance *prajna* and *upaya*. *Prajna* is often translated as "wisdom," but this wisdom is not an accumulated body of truth claims that one believes one can verify empirically or analytically. It is "wisdom" as a skill or an ability, the ability to "think on one's feet," to hone words to fit the context, to take appropriate action in a unique and nonrepeatable situation. *Upaya* is often translated as "method" or "skillful means." "Method" has an impact or promotes certain results. For example, some "methods" are effective in promoting a desirable goal, such as the development of *prajna*. Thus, religious doctrines, as verbal attempts to grasp and communicate intuitive insight, belong to *upaya*, rather than to *prajna*; they are judged by their effectiveness rather than by truth or accuracy. The same principle would apply to mythic and anthropomorphic imagery of Ultimate Reality.

Nontheism, understood both superficially as the absence of a dualistic Supreme Being and nonsuperficially as the recognition that doctrines and images have utility rather than truth, is a wonderful resource for feminist discourse. First, Buddhist feminists do not face the burdens of recognizing the destructiveness of exclusively male-symbolism god-language, reconstructing that imagery, and struggling to convince their religious communities to accept those reconstructions. While it remains completely obvious to me that, from the theistic and monotheistic point of view, male monotheism is patently idolatrous, and while I remain convinced that its idolatry is very easily overcome by feminist reconstruction, I was extremely relieved to leave that particular battle behind when I took up the nontheistic path of Buddhism. At first, I simply regarded the resource of nontheism as freedom from the battle to reconstruct the deity of male monotheism.

However, understanding that religious symbols and doctrines possess utility rather than truth is much more than simple freedom from specific traditional doctrines. When we understand that religious symbols and doctrines are important more for their utility than for their truth, our analysis could move in two directions. On the one hand, to evaluate religious images and doctrines on the basis of their utility enormously fuels the feminist critique of male monotheism. Since it is completely clear that the effect of male god-language has been to reinforce and justify male dominance in society and religion, and since it is equally clear, at least to feminists, that such an effect is completely undesirable, therefore, as *upaya* (and no doctrine is ever more than a method), male monotheism is completely bankrupt. If utility rather than truth were the principle by which monotheists evaluated god-talk, perhaps it would be easier to exorcise the deity who lacks femaleness as part of his transcendence.

On the other hand, seen in its own context, free of polemical implications vis-à-vis theism of any variety, the nontheistic principle that religious symbols and doctrines contain utility rather than truth is radically freeing. The recognition that religious symbols and doctrines never possess truth, but only utility, frees human spirituality immensely, rather than dampening the impulse to construct religious symbols and doctrines. One can freely play with symbols and doctrines, exploring their impact without worrying about the metaphysical status of their referents. Or, more precisely, in terms of Buddhist understandings, there is nothing "behind" these images, since they arise out of Emptiness and dance in that Void. Since no inherent nature or own-being adheres to these mythic and symbolic entities, idolatry can never arise. Idolatry can arise only when one fixates on such a symbol, attributing to it an ultimacy it does not and cannot have. Instead, all images and doctrines are seen as essentially mythic, that is to say, neither true nor false, but sacred. As sacred stories that are neither true nor false, doctrines, images, and symbols should be evaluated on the basis of their utility. Do they promote human wholeness or do they promote alienation and oppression?

Thus, manifold and varied symbols and doctrines could be expected to flourish. This is exactly what eventually happened in nontheistic Buddhism, much to the surprise of those who see nontheism only in its more superficial sense. The vast pantheons of Mahayana and especially of

Tantric Buddhism were created in this fashion and continue to move prac- titioners because of their utility. Mahayana and Tantric Buddhisms include powerful and provocative female representations of enlighten- ment—"goddesses" in popular parlance, but nontheistic goddesses. Their presence is the most surprising and compelling twist in the resource of Buddhist nontheism. One expects to be free of a Supreme Being imaged to be male but not female when one moves from theism to nontheism. But when taking up the path of nontheism, one usually does not expect to meet goddesses who might prove very helpful on one's spiritual journey. Like the sword of *Prajna*,[4] Buddhist nontheism is two-edged. On the one hand, it frees us from having to deconstruct a male absolute before we can begin meaningful discourse. On the other hand, it provides us with mean- ingful but nonreified images of a divine feminine, a myth-model for our own living in the world. As someone who is very wary of spiritualities invented out of present need without deep immersion in traditional resources, these nontheistic Buddhist "goddesses" were an unexpected blessing for me.

∽ Trikaya *Theory, Mythical Buddhas* and *Living Buddhas*

Feminist theology consistently concerns itself with two important ques- tions: What is the relationship between abstract, neuter, non-gynemorphic language about Ultimate Reality, on the one hand, and personal, gynemor- phic images and stories of Ultimate Reality, on the other hand? What is the relationship between either kind of language about Ultimate Reality and human beings?

Buddhism has linked all three levels—the neuter abstract, the personal gynemorphic, and the human—in its concept of the *trikaya*, usually trans- lated as "triple body." Developed relatively late in the history of Buddhist thought, this concept gives theoretical underpinnings to the widespread Mahayana devotion to various popular "celestial" Buddhas and bodhi- sattvas at the same time as it explains the possibility of human spiritual realization. However, this Buddhist concept is relatively obscure, even to many in the Buddhist world, and is almost completely misunderstood in most Western presentations of Buddhism. I remember it being one of the most obscure and incomprehensible of Buddhist concepts when I was attempting to learn Buddhism from the Western academic accounts that were standard in the late sixties and early seventies. In this discussion, I follow an interpretation of *trikaya* prevalent in some varieties of Tibetan Buddhism but not universally followed, even by Mahayana Buddhists.

Misunderstanding begins when *trikaya* is translated "three bodies of the Buddha," a common translation that I have avoided and will continue to avoid. When one hears of "the triple body of the Buddha," one immediately thinks that Siddartha Gautama, the historical Buddha of our world epoch, has somehow taken on two other bodies, and from there the confusions get worse. But Siddartha Gautama, the historical Buddha, is not a deity or an incarnation. The *trikaya* does not begin with him; it ends with him and others who are his equivalents and equals. *Trikaya* is really about three levels or manifestations of Buddhahood, the abstract, the mythic, and the human (*dharmakaya, sambhogakaya,* and *nirmanakaya*). Early Buddhism talked of the abstract and the human levels of Buddhahood and largely limited the human manifestation of Buddhahood to the work of Siddartha Gautama. Mahayana and Tantric Buddhism expanded Buddhahood to include an intermediate mythic manifestation of Buddhahood and also expanded greatly the scope and incidence of human manifestations of Buddhahood.

In Mahayana Buddhism, *dharmakaya,* which I have here translated as the abstract level of Buddhahood, is one of many names for the Ultimate, which cannot, of course, really be named or grasped (which is why it is called by so many names). Sometimes translated as "truth-body," it is the source of Buddha activity in the mythic and phenomenal realms. But that source is not different or separate from Emptiness (*sunyata*) or Suchness (*Tathata*). Little more can be said about that matrix; it is impersonal and neuter, nondual and highly abstract. Because so little can be said about it, what is said is both accurate and extremely abstract; there are very few hooks for imagery or conceptualization. In this sense, it is akin to Mary Daly's Verb of Verbs or other abstract ultimates found behind the male deity deconstructed by feminist theology. The greatest difference is that in Buddhism, such discourse is the foundation for more concrete imagery of Buddhas and Buddha activity, rather than the distillation from a critique of more conventional language.

Dharmakaya as source takes form in *sambhogakaya* and *nirmanakaya. Sambhogakaya* is usually translated as "bliss-body" or "enjoyment-body," but these literal translations convey almost nothing in English. I would argue that the term is more accurately, if less literally, translated as "mythic manifestation of Buddhahood," if the term "myth" is understood as "sacred presence" about which neither truth nor falsity is at stake and which has utility as model and inspiration for human Buddha activity. These "sacred presences" are much more tangible than is the abstract *dharmakaya.* They are somewhat human in form, though they can have anatomical features, such as multiple heads and the like, not usually sported by mortals. Traditionally, the *sambhogakaya* Buddhas cannot be seen by ordinary human beings, but are visible to highly realized human beings. Fortunately, their mythic form has been captured for us ordinary human beings in art and, thus, can readily be contemplated. Their form can also be seen esoterically in visualization meditations, common in Tantric Buddhism. In such visualization meditations, they can be the model for one's own enlightened being, which slowly emerges as one identifies with a specific *sambhogakaya* Buddha. If one does not have the energy to engage in visualization practices, one could also approach these mythic Buddhas and bodhisattvas through ritual and veneration, though that technique will probably not result in human Buddha activity as quickly as will visualization meditations.

For feminist theology, two generalizations about *sambhogakaya* Buddhas are important. First, they are imagined in both female and male sexes. (Since these *sambhogakaya* Buddhas do not observe gender roles, I emphasize their anatomical maleness and femaleness.) Buddhism bears out the generalization that whenever "anthropomorphic" imagery is used about Ultimate Reality, both feminine and masculine images are commonplace unless something has gone wrong. Thus, even nontheistic symbol systems bear out this generalization. Second, though these *sambhogakaya* Buddhas and bodhisattvas look like deities, they are nontheistic or mythic. Inherent existence would never be attributed to them, for they arise out of the Emptiness (*sunyata*) of *dharmakaya* and return to that Emptiness. Yet such mythic beings have carried both an esoteric and an exoteric religious system of great popularity and depth. Such information is important to feminists struggling to reconstruct a vibrant and compelling set of symbols on the base of a deconstructed abstract Ultimate. If even a nontheistic religion like Buddhism constructs anthropomorphic and gynemorphic models of enlightenment, feminist theology, growing out of a theistic base, will undoubtedly also need such mythic images. On the other hand, Buddhism clearly shows that it is possible to celebrate such myth-models without reifying them, which has always been the pitfall of theistic anthropomorphism and sometimes seems to overtake feminist theology as well.

～ Vajrayogini and Tara: Two Buddhist "Goddesses"

To see in practical concrete terms how the *sambhogakaya* forms are used in Vajrayana Buddhism, let us look at two very important and popular female *sambhogakaya* forms, one of them exoteric, the other esoteric. It is important to remember that neither of these "goddesses" was found in early layers of Buddhist tradition, that they each patronize a complete myth, ritual, and meditation system for those who practice their *sadhana*s as a spiritual discipline, and that the assertion of their independent, reified existence apart from Emptiness would be incomprehensible in the context of traditional Buddhist thought and practice.

Tara, the Savioress, is certainly one of the two most popular meditational deities of Tibet. According to Stephen Beyer, one seldom finds a Tibetan shrine that lacks her icon,[5] though it may be surrounded by many other more esoteric *yidam*s.[6] She is widely prayed to and contemplated by practitioners of every level and lifestyle, and her *mantra*[7] is one of the best known and most widely used. Initiation to practice her *sadhana* (spiritual discipline) is widely available, and its practice is encouraged for virtually anyone.

Her well-known story is told on two levels. Though she is said now to be both an advanced bodhisattva and a fully enlightened Buddha, like all such beings, she was once an ordinary human who aroused the "thought of enlightenment" (*bodhicitta*) and practiced the various disciplines for many eons. Taranatha, an important Tibetan teacher, wrote in 1608 the text that has become a standard "history" of Tara. He relates that eons ago, a princess named Moon of Wisdom made extensive offerings to the Buddha of that eon and to his entourage for a very long time. Finally, for the first time, *bodhicitta* arose in her. Then the monks present suggested, "If you pray that your deeds accord with the teachings, then indeed on that account, you will change your form to that of a man, as is befitting." After a long discussion, she told them, "In this life, there is no such distinction as 'male' and 'female' . . . and therefore attachment to ideas of 'male' and 'female' is quite worthless. Weak-minded worldlings are always deluded by this." Then follows her vow:

> There are many who wish to gain enlightenment in a man's form, and there are but few who wish to work for the welfare of sentient beings in a female form. Therefore, may I, in a female body, work for the welfare of beings right until Samsara has been emptied.[8]

It is also said that she originated from the tears of Avalokitesvara, the male bodhisattva of compassion who appears as the female Kuan-yin in East Asia. It is said that Avalokitesvara wept when he saw that no matter how many beings he saved, countless more still remained in *samsara*. A blue lotus (also held by Tara) grew in the water of his tears, and Tara was born on that lotus.[9]

Her appearance and activities, frequently described in Sanskrit and Tibetan poetry, are well known and widely contemplated. The best-known set of descriptions is the "Praise in Twenty-One Homages," which gave rise to several traditions of *thangkha* paintings, in which a central figure of Tara in her most familiar form is surrounded by twenty-one smaller figures of Tara representing all the activities she undertakes. This set of praises is found in *sadhana*s composed for meditation on Tara as one's *yidam* (deity contemplated in meditation practices) and has been widely commented upon.[10] Rather than trying to summarize these praises, or even to summarize a complete description of Tara, I will quote two verses from one of the many devotional poems composed in her honor. This description includes some of her most important features and explains their symbolic meaning, important to the *yidam*'s form or appearance. Though this quotation is not from a *sadhana*, the description is congruent with the form that would be used for self-visualization of oneself as Tara when meditating using her *sadhana*.

> On a lotus seat, for pure understanding of emptiness,
> Emerald-colored, one-faced, two-armed girl,
> In full bloom of youth, right leg out, left drawn in,
> Uniting Method and Wisdom—homage to You!
>
> Prominent, full breasts, treasures of undefiled bliss,
> Face with a brilliant smile like a full moon,
> Mother with calm-mannered, wide, compassionate eyes,
> Beauty of Khadira Forest—to You I bow! [11]

Not explained in the text is Tara's green color. Though there are Taras in other colors as well, the Green Tara is the most popular. In Tantric symbolism, green is the color of the Action Family, of those Buddhas and bodhisattvas who specialize in the Wisdom of All-Accomplishing Action. This color is consonant with Tara's constant activity to help and save beings. Thus, it is often explained at a Green Tara initiation that her *sadhana* is especially recommended for active people who have major projects under way.

Much of the devotional poetry written to Tara praises her for her many activities. A standard repertoire of activities attributed to her includes saving people from the eight great dangers. Though there are some variants in some lists, or sometimes more than eight dangers from which Tara rescues, a standard list of the eight includes fire, water, prison, bandits, elephants, tigers (or lions), snakes, and evil spirits.[12] One can appreciate these as troublesome mundane dangers that would worry anyone in the environment of ancient India. Tara is very accessible; she helps people with these everyday worries and does not confine her help to so-called spiritual matters. If one wishes, one can interpret any of the eight dangers in a spiritual way, which was sometimes done by devotees singing her praises.[13]

Among the many stories of how Tara rescued her devotees, I find two narrated by Taranatha especially appealing and whimsical. She saved a devotee from bandits in the following fashion. She appeared in a dream to the master Sanghamitra, telling him to study Mahayana teachings. He set out to go to Kashmir, but on the way he was captured by bandits, who said that they needed to worship Durga (a popular Hindu goddess) by offering her warm human blood. They took him to a Durga temple "like a charnel ground." He prayed to Tara, and the Durga image spontaneously split into many pieces. The bandits became frightened and ran away from him. How she saved from tigers is even more intriguing. Master Buddhadasa traveled through an empty town with many tiger dens. When he inquired, he was told that the tigers ate humans every day. "Therefore, great compassion arose in him." He walked toward the tigers, prayed to Tara, and sprinkled water over which he had recited mantras. "Through this, the tigers became of peaceful mind; thereafter they did no harm to living creatures but stopped eating and passed away." Things ended well for the tigers, who were reborn in a more fortunate existence in which, presumably, they could subsist as vegetarians.[14] The gentleness of Tara, the peaceful *yidam*, could not be more graphically demonstrated.

The red, semi-wrathful Vajrayogini or Vajravarahi—sow-headed, dancing on a lotus, corpse, and sun disk—is much more esoteric. She is undoubtedly the most important female *yidam* of the *anuttarayoga* tantras, the highest and most esoteric class of tantras, according to most classification schemes. In these tantras, she is celebrated both as the central *yidam* of her own extensive *sadhana* and as the consort of major male *yidam*s, such as Cakrasamvara and Hevajra. Her initiation is much more difficult to receive than is Tara's and her practice much more restricted because, as a semi-wrathful *yidam*, she can arouse emotions that may overwhelm a student not ready to take on her wild, untamed, fierce energy or her "transcendental lust." Therefore, commentaries about her are more restricted to the oral tradition.

*Thangkha*s and line drawings of Vajravarahi are relatively standard.[15] In the *sadhana* text itself, as is always the case, the meaning of each aspect of her form is explained, since the meditator visualizing herself as Vajrayogini is not especially trying to become a red sixteen-year-old, but to take on and manifest the qualities implicit in her form. Thus, for example, she wears a garland of fifty-one freshly severed heads, which represents wearing out the habitual patterns of grasping and fixation. She also carries a hooked knife and a skullcup filled with blood or *amrta* ("deathless"—a liquid much used in Tantric ritual liturgies). She holds the *khatvanga* staff in the crook of her arm. She is naked and wearing bone ornaments. She dances on a corpse, a sun, and a lotus.[16] She is surrounded by four dakinis almost identical to her in form, but in appropriate colors (blue, yellow, red, and green) for the sphere of the *mandala*[17] they embody. Thus, her practice involves a complete universe in which all five of the basic energies so important to Vajrayana Buddhism are roused and transmuted.

Because practicing with Vajrayogini as one's *yidam* is considered relatively advanced and dangerous, she is not usually regarded as a savior and one does her practice not for relative benefits but for the ultimate *siddhi*—enlightenment. Therefore, her praises talk of her as promoting, often in terrifying fashion, the states of mind that overcome confusion and clinging. A number of these praises have been translated and ably commented upon in a very illuminating article by Chogyam Trungpa. A few of them will suffice to connote Vajrayogini's immensely compelling, highly charged, and provocative iconography. They also communicate well her activities to promote enlightenment. One praise comments on the meaning of her sow's head as well:

> Your sow's face shows nonthought, the unchanging *dharmakaya*,
> You benefit beings with wrathful mercy
> Accomplishing their welfare with horrific accouterments,
> I prostrate to you who benefit beings in nonthought.

The efficacy of her wrathful actions is evoked in many praises.

> Naked, with loosed hair, of faultless and terrifying form
> Beyond the vice of the *klesas*, you do benefit for sentient beings.
> You lead beings from the six realms with your hook of mercy,
> I prostrate to you who accomplish Buddha activity.

A concluding praise links her with Prajnaparamita, the Mother of all Buddhas. This certainly sums up the meaning and purpose of her fierce form and activity, which summon primordial energies in the practitioner, familiarize the practitioner with them, tame them, and harness their energy—very quickly and effectively, it is hoped.

> Prajnaparamita, inexpressible by speech or thought
> Unborn, unceasing, with a nature like sky
> Which can only be experienced by discriminating awareness wisdom,
> Mother of the victorious ones of the three times,
> I praise you and prostrate.[18]

Both of these anthropomorphic representations of enlightenment are central to Vajrayana Buddhism. As anthropomorphic representations that can be visualized and related with, they demonstrate more readily than does philosophy the nature of enlightened mind, which, according to Vajrayana Buddhism, is always there waiting to be realized. If gentle Tara's smile does not push one over the brink from confusion to enlightenment, perhaps Vajrayogini's fang-filled grimace will. But clearly, in consonance with the command not to denigrate women,[19] Vajrayana tradition claims that these wonderful female *yidam*s demonstrate to the seeker the nature of her or his own mind in its unfettered form as readily as their male counterparts might.

∿ Sambhogakaya *and* Nirmanakaya

The *nirmanakaya* is seemingly the most immediate and ordinary manifestation of Buddhahood. Usually translated as "transformation-body" or "apparition-body," it is commonly understood as Buddhahood in human form, an Enlightened One. All forms of Buddhism recognize that there has been and will be a series of *nirmanakaya*s, but most forms of Buddhism expect them to be rather rare and, in a certain sense, regard them as another variety of mythical Buddha, an earthly rather than a heavenly mythic Buddha. Tibetan Vajrayana Buddhism does not. A realized human being or recognized teacher is understood to be a *nirmanakaya* Buddha. While some forms of Buddhism invoke a heavily docetic mode when telling stories of the *nirmanakaya* Buddhas, as if they were literally "apparitions," Tibetan Buddhism stresses the human[20] birth, life, education, accomplishments, teaching, and death of a *nirmanakaya*.

Accomplishing the *nirmanakaya*, which is possible for any being possessing the "precious human birth,"[21] brings the energy of *dharmakaya* and *sambhogakaya* down to earth, so to speak. The way in which human potential for spiritual realization is connected with the abstract, neuter, nonpersonal *dharmakaya* and the sacred presence of *sambhogakaya* Buddhas is instructive for those concerned with Goddess theology. Following *trikaya* theory, a "goddess" could be either the myth-model or her human embodiment, and both arise from and dissolve into *dharmakaya*.

Dharmakaya is conceptualized as all-pervading and found in all phenomena, which is the source of the common Mahayana Buddhist statement that Buddha is present in a grain of sand and that virtually any human activity can be the trigger for enlightenment. *Dharmakaya* is present in human beings as *tathagatagarbha*, often translated as "Buddha nature," the "Buddha within,"[22] or the "enlightened gene."[23] Therefore, when the focus shifts from the historical Buddha to the nonpersonal neuter source of enlightenment, the emphasis shifts from one historical person to the potential of each and every embodied human being. Buddhahood ("Buddha" simply means "awake" or "enlightened") is not the possession of one quasi-mythical person who lived a long time ago, but the potential of each human being and the resource coursing through all of experience and the phenomenal world, linking them all and us all in our most primordial and essential characteristic. That resource is activated by the sacred presence of *sambhogakaya* Buddhas and bodhisattvas. They are myth-models in the sense that they are not external beings to be worshiped but the anthropomorphic or gynemorphic form of *dharmakaya* and, hence, of one's own enlightened experience. As such, one identifies with them in a series of powerful meditations and contemplations, gradually interfusing their form into one's own. Therefore, according to *trikaya* doctrine, mythical manifestations of Buddhahood help in training and encouraging human beings, endowed with inherent Buddhahood, to manifest themselves as *nirmanakaya* Buddhas.

It is interesting and instructive to consider the links between gender symbolism associated with the mythical Buddhas and bodhisattvas and the sex and gender of the Buddhist practitioners who take them as myth-models. As has already been made clear, *sambhogakaya*s take both female and male forms, but these myth-models themselves do not conform to gender roles, either divine or human. That is to say, as is typical of symbol systems that include goddesses, goddesses are not confined to the human female gender role. (The label "Mother Goddess" as the generic label for all female personifications of divinity could not be further from the mark.) There is little, if any, gender-linked specialization associated with either female or male *sambhogakaya*s. Nor is there any link between the sex of a myth-model and the sex of the human being who is assigned to contemplate a specific *yidam* in his or her *sadhana* (spiritual discipline). Men are often assigned to visualize themselves as a female Buddha and women to visualize themselves as male; the reverse of each practice is equally common. In the system with which I am most familiar, everyone, woman or man, first identifies with a powerful female *sambhogakaya*. That visualization is followed by a practice involving a couple in sexual union, but along the way, male myth-models are also introduced to both women and men, without regard for the physiological sex of the meditator.

∿ Nirmanakaya *and* Guru:
Some Feminist Assessments

As already has been made clear, the point of *trikaya* theory and the meditations involving *sambhogakaya* Buddhas is their ability to serve as *upaya*, as tool and technique that enables those endowed with the "enlightened gene" to realize the *nirmanakaya* and to develop their human potential. Those humans who are recognized as having done so are honored by their communities as "living Buddhas," as *guru*s. Because

Vajrayana Buddhism depends heavily on oral tradition and a direct student–teacher relationship, the guru is extremely important in this form of Buddhism. In fact, the guru is so important that he or she is sometimes considered the fourth object of refuge, in addition to the Buddha, the dharma (teachings) and the *sangha* (community)[24] and the avenue of access to the three major objects of refuge.

The guru has this position of honor because, according to Vajrayana Buddhism, spiritual truth cannot be captured in words, so that reading or memorizing the dharma that has been written in books is no guarantee of realization and insight. The scholar may have all the right words, but may have totally missed the sense of those words, to use a distinction familiar to Vajrayana Buddhism. A guru is someone who has not only mastered the words of the tradition but has thoroughly incorporated their meanings into her or his being; because of that she is competent to guide the spiritual search of her students. Because her understanding reduplicates that of the Buddha, in essence, not necessarily in form or content, she is a lineage holder, whose job it is to keep the teachings not only pristine but up to date. The lineage holder must interpret the teachings in the idiom of the day, perhaps crossing cultural frontiers to do so. The lineage holder also trains the next generation of students and certifies those whose level of spiritual understanding is sufficient to make them lineage holders as well.

From the student's side, this relationship is extremely intense and personal, though not necessarily in conventional ways. Devotion is the proper attitude with which to regard the wondrous guru. The importance of these gurus is explicitly recognized in Buddhist meditation liturgies and religious art. Daily chants include an invocation to and a recitation of the lineage of gurus, from one's own guru back to sect founders and the Buddha. Gurus, like *yidam*s and Buddhas, are frequently the subject of Buddhist religious art and meditation. The lineage is sometimes portrayed in the form of a lineage tree, a great tree in whose branches sit all the gurus of the lineage, surrounded by the Buddhas, bodhisattvas, *yidam*s, and protectors, with the sacred books also supported by the tree. Prostrations are done before this lineage tree containing all the objects of refuge. Given the centrality of the guru in the spiritual life of the student and the intensity of the devotion that is cultivated and recommended, it is provocative to suggest that, in the forms of Buddhism that regard the guru so highly, the guru is a nontheistic, functional equivalent of the deity of theistic religions.

If society followed symbolism, one would expect that about equal numbers of women and men would be recognized as such leaders and gurus. But this has not been the case throughout Buddhist history. A woman such as Yeshe Tsogyel can be recognized and venerated as a guru. Vajrayana Buddhism places no theoretical limits on the achievements of those humans who take rebirth in the female form of the "precious human body." But, however many numberless women may have activated their "enlightened gene" and manifested Buddha activity, *very few of them have been recognized and honored as gurus* by their contemporaries. As a result they have had few students and little impact on the shaping and articulation of their tradition.

That gurus and teachers currently are almost always men, and have been throughout Buddhist history, is thoroughly androcentric and completely disempowering for women, in the same way as is the male monopoly on images of deity in monotheism. The lack of female presence in the lineage supplications, on the limbs of the refuge tree,[25] and on the teaching throne from which living teachers teach, reinforces and drives home the shame of being female in patriarchy. It is living proof that Buddhist institutions do not respect and nurture the Buddha embryo present in women in the same way that they nurture the Buddha embryo present in men.

One can shed many tears and write many pages concerning the patriarchal and androcentric institutions and record-keeping practices that have tainted and corrupted Buddhism historically. On the other hand, for Buddhism, history is not normative or exemplary, so Buddhists cannot cogently call upon the authority of tradition or the past in maintaining Buddhist patriarchy. In fact, in one apocryphal story the Dalai Lama is reported to have told a woman questioning the Buddhist record, "That's history! Now it's up to you." That story can and should also be reversed. We can say to the leaders of Buddhism, who deserve the respect they have earned, "Now it's up to you! Recognize and empower female gurus!" The deliberate cultivation of female gurus and teachers is the most critical agenda facing contemporary Buddhists and the single most important requirement for achieving a genuinely post-patriarchal Buddhism. This is equally true for those forms of Buddhism that do not revere the guru so formally, for the teacher is always central to the transmission of Buddhism from generation to generation.

Fortunately for Buddhism, it is currently meeting a movement seeking liberation that is its own equal, though not its duplicate. As Buddhism came West, for the great good fortune of both movements, its first decades of relatively widespread acceptance in the West coincide with the growth of feminism as a strong spiritual force in the West. As a result, the initial generation of Western Buddhists includes many, many women who are Buddhists themselves, first and foremost, who see their main function not as enabling male practitioners but as developing their own Buddha nature. Were it not for the magic of timing, of the simultaneous arrival of many Asian Buddhist teachers and a generation of Westerners steeped in feminist values, Buddhism would have little possibility of being liberated from its sexism by Western feminism. Tibetan Buddhism has a term for such a mutually appropriate synchronicity—"auspicious co-incidence."

Completing *trikaya* theory through cultivating the presence and teaching authority of female *nirmanakaya*s would have a more powerful impact in ending definitively the shame associated with being female in patriarchal culture and undoing the scapegoating of women for samsaric existence than would any other act or symbol. Seeing a woman on the guru's throne, teaching the dharma and granting initiations and blessings, would be powerfully transformative for both men and women. For men, the experience of devotion to a *female* guru, accompanied by all the longing and yearning that characterize nontheistic guru devotion, would undo the negative habitual patterns, learned in early childhood under patriarchal child-rearing practices, that scapegoat women for the limitations and finitude of life.[26] Here would be a woman undoing *samsara* for the male by her teaching presence. For women, this presence will be affirming, empowering, and encouraging in a way that nothing else can be. At last Buddhist women will have the same kind of role model that Buddhist men have always had! For both genders, it will be definitively, incontrovertibly clear that there is no shame in being female, that it's okay to be a woman.

Completing current forms of Buddhist theory, however, will not be the only blessing that comes with the presence of female teachers. Sometimes Buddhists imagine that Buddhism after patriarchy is merely a matter of equal rights. It is imagined that things will end when women regularly take on the teaching role in Buddhism and that these women will do nothing more than continue to present the same messages that the male teachers have always presented, that only their form and presence, but not their message, will be different. That such women will present *only* the same messages seems unlikely, however. It seems unlikely that males speaking out of patriarchal conditions have said everything that needs to be said about liberation. It seems unlikely that, when women finally participate in Buddhist speech, they will not add to the sum total of Buddhist wisdom about liberation. For a genuinely post-patriarchal Buddhism will include the one thing that Buddhism has always lacked—large numbers of well-trained, thoroughly practiced, articulate women *who are not male identified*. Certainly the example of Christianity, in which feminist analysis is far more developed than in Buddhism, strongly suggests that the androgynous voice does not merely amplify what had always been said, but adds to it significantly. And this androgynous voice *will* be articulated, whether or not the Buddhist authorities recognize it as the wisdom of the Buddha.

CHAPTER 14

The Feminine Principle
in Tibetan Vajrayana Buddhism:
Reflections of a Buddhist Feminist

THIS CHAPTER INVOLVES an exciting development for me, because it links my personal meditation practice and my professional interests in a new way.[1] I chose this topic so that I could comment on my acquaintance with the practice of the *sadhana* (meditation-liturgy) of Vajrayogini, which I began doing about a year ago. Traditionally it is said that this practice, which is somewhat advanced, involves developing the "feminine principle." The *sadhana* of Vajrayogini is an important traditional practice in Tibetan Vajrayana Buddhism, especially within the Karma Kagyu lineage with which I am affiliated. My teacher, Chogyam Trungpa, Rinpoche, only assigns this practice to the student after considerable experiences with formless *samatha-vipashyana* practice (somewhat similar to Zazen) and after completing *ngundro* (the Vajrayana preliminaries consisting of one hundred thousand prostrations, one hundred thousand repetitions of a hundred-syllable *mantra*, one hundred thousand *mandala* offerings, and one million recitations of guru homage). Typically, it is also one's first *sadhana*, or so-called deity-yoga (*yidam*) practice. Vajrayogini is called "the glorious co-emergent Mother"; she is female in her iconography and visualization, and her practice develops one's awareness of and appreciation for "the feminine principle" in oneself and the world. Such development is considered necessary before doing *sadhanas* connected with the masculine principle, at least according to the tradition in which I am being trained.

When I began to do this practice, naturally I was eager to explore it, since it is so important to the Kagyu lineage. However, I also had lingering questions and doubts about the relevance of dividing reality into "a feminine principle" and "a masculine principle," as is typical in Vajrayana

Buddhism. This skepticism directly derived from feminism, which remains central in my value system. I wanted to explore all my doubts and questions, including the meaning of the terms "masculine" or "feminine principles" in Vajrayana Buddhism in the context of my experience with the *sadhana* of Vajrayogini. As one works slowly with the oral tradition and the practice, one realizes one is working with materials quite different from conventional patriarchal gender roles, psychological archetypes, or sex-linked psychological traits or experiences. However, rather than beginning by presenting the feminine or masculine principles in Tibetan Buddhism, I want first to retrace my disillusionments with other variants on the theme of feminine and masculine principles.

For years, I have been deeply concerned with basic questions about the feminine principle, and my early seminars and publications about the "divine feminine" and the Goddess, though not Buddhist, essentially have been on the same topic. I have also realized that, though I approach this topic with hesitancy and ambivalence, I am also drawn to it willy-nilly from almost every perspective. It is my hope, therefore, that I can raise into sharp focus basic questions about "the feminine principle," even if much of my discussion is quite open-ended.

My exploration focuses on the essential claim of Vajrayana Buddhism regarding masculine and feminine principles. The tradition claims that the teachings and the practices involve and promote a *balance* of masculine and feminine principles in the phenomenal world. Is that really so? Three questions must be dealt with to determine whether the traditional claim has merit. First, is it relevant or useful to talk about feminine or masculine principles at all? Second, what would a *balance* of masculine and feminine principles involve? Finally, how would such a balance be manifested *in the phenomenal world?*

Why do we need to differentiate experience into a masculine and a feminine principle? Why do so many traditions do so? Is it helpful or oppressive to do so? In my own life and work, I have both questioned the validity of such differentiation and attempted to foster a positive feminine principle. In my youth, what was called the feminine principle, or "true womanhood," was mainly an attempt to discriminate against my intelligence and to convince me to be satisfied with subservience. On the basis of that experience, I saw no reason to rally to defend *that* version of "the feminine principle." I turned instead in defense to notions of "common humanity" beyond female and male, a common humanity that recognized that there are no significant differences between women and men. But at the same time, and not completely consistently, I also developed a rationale for the need specifically to study women, and I became very interested in goddesses and the divine feminine. I was also very uneasy about conventional versions of "androgyny," which seemed to be only an invitation for women to become male-identified, something I resisted, though I have developed alternative definitions of androgyny.

Though it was difficult to pinpoint my frustration and dissatisfaction with these conventional and culturally familiar examples, I now realize I was much more concerned about an imbalance *between* the masculine and feminine principles than about the actual *presence* of a feminine principle per se. That imbalance manifests itself in two ways, both of which are found in most or all Western versions of the feminine or masculine principles. They are imbalanced due to an implicit or explicit hierarchy of the two principles. They are also imbalanced because of a common assumption that men should embody the masculine principle and women should embody the feminine principle. But the tendency of religious symbol systems to find a masculine and a feminine principle in experience is so widespread that we have no choice but to discuss and utilize these ideas. But we must also maintain a critical perspective because they have so often been used in ways that do not enhance human goodness and wholeness.

If we must deal with masculine and feminine principles because they are there, the most critical question is whether significant examples of such symbolism involve *balance* between feminine and masculine principles. The most critical criterion for *balance* between the masculine and the feminine principles is freedom from the expectation that there is or should be identity between symbolic or mythological masculine or feminine principles and male or female human bodies. When I talk about feminine or masculine principles. I am always talking about what might roughly be called "mythological or symbolic" images or psychological traits that are not sex-linked. It is important to stress this preliminary distinction between feminine or masculine principles and male or female persons, because the two are so frequently equated. Having stressed that distinction, we can return to the question of the usefulness of dichotomizing experience into masculine and feminine principles.

This critical perspective will be applied first to the three major Western concepts of the feminine principle: classical traditional Western monotheism, Jungian psychological constructs, and contemporary feminist counterimages.

Technically speaking, there is no feminine principle in Western religions at the orthodox level. The three great "reforms" of the initial Western religious imperative (monotheism, divine transcendence over nature, and abolition of divine gender) so successfully scuttled the idea of a divine feminine that the slogan "Trust in God—She will provide" is a radical teaser, while the slogan "Trust in God—He will provide" would be only mainstream conventional piety, somewhat saccharine and unnoteworthy. Monotheism, one of the great inventions of Western religious thought, was supposed to ensure the recognition of the *one* power behind the *many* forms. This one power is supposed to transcend sex altogether. The most common reply to feminist requests for female god-language is to reply that such language is trivial and unnecessary. "God is neither male nor female. He is beyond sex altogether." Nevertheless, "he," and all its variants, is conventional, while "she," and all its variants, including a female priest-hood, is anathema, or at least unconventional. I have often suggested that such a technique for transcending sex does not really transcend sex at all. It is a divinization of masculinity and a demonization of feminity. There-fore, though in conventional Western religious mythology, the feminine principle technically is not recognized, frequently it crops up as a shadow, a demonic other, or a seducer. Sometimes it emerges as a legitimate "mys-tical" or esoteric component of Western religious imagery. The extent to which this attenuated version of the feminine principle is aberrant in world religions is only beginning to be recognized by scholars and mystics of Western traditions. Most other world religions do have a significantly more developed feminine principle.

In Western thought, psychology is a recent invention and has emerged as a likely refuge for the feminine principle. Jungian psychology especially has called for a revalorization of the feminine "unconscious." Stressing a limited androgyny for psychologically mature persons and the importance of the dark and banished "other" feminine qualities of the psyche, Jungian thought has often inspired self-development and served as a corrective to the one-sided, masculine emphases of mainstream Western mythic imagery. Recently, however, some have argued that, despite the Jungian highlighting of the banished, dark, feminine qualities, Jungian thought does not contain much *balance* of masculine and feminine principles. "Light" and "conscious" male attributes remain "good." Furthermore, they are said to be much more appropriate for men than for women. The existence of "dark" and "unconscious" female attributes is recognized, and these attributes are said to be elemental. But men's and women's psyches are not thought to have similar relationships to these "light mas-culine conscious" and "dark feminine unconscious" qualities. Further-more, a relative valuing and disvaluing of these respective principles continues, despite Jungian recognition of the importance of both to psy-chological life.[2]

Having found much Western mythology and psychology disappointing in these matters, it is not surprising that many people have turned to a nontraditional version of the feminine principle. The feminist spirituality movement is the only Western religion that avowedly and openly emphasizes a feminine principle. Many segments of the contemporary feminist spirituality movement, however, do not seek or value a *balance* of feminine and masculine principles either. Frequently, their elevation of the feminine principle also involves denigration of masculinity, seeing it as a defective, unfortunate, or maimed condition. So, rather than being an *alternative* to conventional spirituality, the feminist movement often functions as conventional spirituality, *in reverse*, by affirming a feminine principle at the cost of the masculine principle.[3]

Thus, all the major contemporary Western mythological or psychological systems with which I am familiar fail to have an equalizing *balance* between masculine and feminine principles and tend to use familiar examples of feminine or masculine principles competitively and oppressively. No matter which way the labels are attached, a "good–bad" duality predominates. Additionally, men and women are supposed to be like "the masculine" or "the feminine," respectively. In such a system there will always be "winners" and "losers," and it will be difficult for anyone to feel spiritually whole. It is easy to see why an interest in a feminine principle could be tempered with caution or skepticism about the idea of dividing experience into a duality that is seen as "female" and "male."

I have found, however, an equally balanced duality of feminine and masculine mythic images compellingly attractive when the feminine principle is dignified and healthy. Though I am not convinced that women manifest the feminine principle more than they manifest the masculine principle, or any more than men can manifest the feminine principle, it does seem clear to me that women's psyches (and men's also) simply do better, simply are healthier and saner when both are deeply imbued with mythic images of a dignified feminine principle. I would like to look more deeply into the reasons for this sense of well-being that goes with a truly balanced expression of feminine and masculine principles by considering more carefully their duality, interrelationship, and unity.

In stressing the "common humanity" underlying masculine or feminine principles, I had originally misdiagnosed the problem. The problem is not the duality of the principles, but the *way in which that duality is handled*. In fact the problem with the Western versions of feminine and masculine principles is not that they are too dualistic, but that they are not dualistic enough. It is the lack of appreciation for duality, distinction, and differentiation that manifests itself as the imbalance between the masculine and feminine principles.

The major mythological image of contemporary Western religious tradition, as we all know, is a single Supreme Being, of no gender in pristine theology but of decidedly masculine gender in popular imagination. The *singularity* of this Supreme Being, otherwise known as monotheism, has resulted in a belief that oneness is superior to duality or multiplicity. Because of the monolithic emphasis on monistic unity, duality is reduced to oneness, usually by the attempted elimination of part of the duality. We could ask why the feminine principle rather than the masculine principle was eliminated in the attempt to purge multiplicity or duality from the mythic system and to reform the core myth into *monotheism*. But continuing tendencies of Western monotheism, including the repeated re-emergence of a covert divine feminine, point to the fact that duality, distinctiveness, and differentiation cannot be eliminated in order to reduce everything to oneness.

The importance of *appreciating* duality, multiplicity, and the specific qualities of each separate element is at the heart of my answer to the question of the relevance and usefulness of feminine and masculine principles. If the distinctiveness of each specific element is not destroyed when over-arching unity is recognized, then the feminine and masculine principles can complement rather than compete with each other. In fact, no image more effectively promotes this simultaneous appreciation of duality and unity than that of complementary but distinctive female and male mythological images, such as are found in Vajrayana Buddhism, with its great appreciation for both the Many and the One. I will return to the images utilized by this tradition later. Here I want to point out that there is *a way* to experience the feminine principle, not merely as something with which we are stuck, often oppressively. Properly understood, it could be a tremendous resource.

However, simply acknowledging the duality of feminine and masculine principles is not enough. If we emphasize their duality but do not see them *in balance*, oppression will result. To me, the single most important requirement for balance between feminine and masculine principles is their primordial and elemental co-equality. A *balance* of feminine and masculine can in no way involve a *hierarchy* of *one dominating the other*. In other words, the mere inclusion of a feminine image beside or along with a masculine image does not necessarily imply a balance between them. We could simply have an image of "He" and "His consort," an image that is quite prevalent in many religious and mythic contexts, including even the Jungian context, in my view. This image in no way connotes or communicates a balance of feminine and masculine elements, despite the inclusion of a feminine image. Two popular images from Western culture will help us see clearly the difference between an androcentric imbalance of female and male energy and a truly co-equal balance of male and female energies.

Some of the space probes of the middle to late seventies involved placing objects on spacecraft that could perhaps be found at some point by beings from other civilizations in our galaxy or perhaps other galaxies. These objects were selected to impart information about our world to an unknown world and, presumably, were carefully chosen to reveal essential features about our civilization. A metal greeting card placed on spacecraft Pioneers 10 and 11 uses mathematical symbols to locate the earth, the sun, and the solar system. Most of the card, however, features a prominent portrayal of a man and a woman, nude, done as a simple line drawing. The placement of the couple alongside the mathematical diagram that illustrates the distances between parts of the galaxy, is such that the eye is drawn toward the male figure as the prominent or dominant one. To further encourage this impression, he is drawn facing and looking straight ahead, one arm raised (in greeting?). She, meanwhile, already off to the side and with the abstract diagram drawing attention away from her, is slightly turned toward the man. Her face and eyes are also turned toward him, definitely not looking directly into whatever world faces her.[4] Thus, though both masculine and feminine principles are recognized, he is oriented to the world and she is oriented to him. Reminiscent of the stereotypical politician-and-his-wife, minister-and-his-wife, or professional-and-his-wife, this intergalactic greeting card does not portray *balance* and *co-equality*, however much it mirrors our world.

Balance involves images that convey strength, independence, interdependence, complementarity, and co-equality. The feminine and masculine principles both can and do function independently of each other and, when they come together, together-yet-separately, the two-in-one complement each other in forming another larger whole, but they do not overpower each other. Neither principle exists essentially or primarily "for" the other, but insofar as each one is for the other, they are equally for each other.

To return to the previous example and my own spiritual practice, I can now take up the inevitable question: Does Vajrayana Buddhism actually speak of the feminine and masculine principles in this balanced way? I have not yet been able fully to answer that question, though my acquaintance to date with the teachings and practices has not presented anything that makes me want to end my exploration. I have also begun to feel that I am *at last* working with a tradition that does not use images of masculine and feminine principles in hierarchical or oppressive ways. Furthermore, the "edge" quality of not having definitive answers to my questions about the use of feminine and masculine principles in Vajrayana Buddhism seems to be a healthy insecurity, fundamental to practice and the effort to wake up.

A very important motif in Vajrayana Buddhism is the way in which experience is divided into complementary dualities associated with feminine and masculine principles. The basic pair is space and form, accommodation and specific, definite action, emptiness and bliss or energy, or, more classically put, *prajna* and *upaya* (discriminating awareness wisdom and skillful action or compassion). In addition, many more esoteric pairs are found in the oral tradition: sun and moon, red and white, vowels and consonants, liquor and meat, ritual bell and scepter, left and right, and so on. Two things are striking about all these pairs. Clearly, they are dyadic unities, not hierarchic dualisms or monolithic entities. In addition, without the code of the oral tradition, relying only on conventional thinking, it would be hard to find a logic whereby one represents the feminine principle and the other the masculine. Space, accommodation, emptiness, and *prajna* (discriminating awareness wisdom) constitute the feminine principle. They provide the opportunity for their counterparts to arise. Form arises out of emptiness, compassionate skillful activity out of wisdom, and bliss or energy out of accommodation. Without this feminine element the masculine one could not arise; together they form the enlightened world. So, transcendent Wisdom, *Prajnaparamita,* is literally "Mother of all the Buddhas" because Buddha activity arises out of, results from, and is born from Wisdom. Distinct yet together, they are enlightenment, transcending but not abolishing duality.

A feminist untrained in meditation might become upset with these associations, interpreting them as an indication that the feminine principle accommodates and enables the masculine, which is thought to be more important. She might be led to feel that once again the masculine uses the feminine. However, someone trained in meditation understands and appreciates the significance of space, of background, of emptiness. She knows that it is literally true that action depends on space, that foreground depends on background. She also realizes that, if anything, action is the "easier" part. Learning to recognize space, to do nothing, to develop discriminating awareness wisdom is the "harder" part of meditation training and enlightened activity. It is said that once unobstructed space—vision unclouded by conventionality and discursiveness—is developed, then appropriate action develops spontaneously and blissfully. On the other hand, though Wisdom provides the ground for Enlightened Activity, Enlightened Activity completes the dyadic unity. Without Enlightened Activity, Wisdom is sterile, possibly destructive. Space and activity are not being ranked; their temporal relationship, their complementarity and co-necessity are being recognized. Before there can be a child, there must be a mother.

But why is space feminine and activity masculine? Why not the other way around? And isn't that description similar to the Western "active and passive"? Anyone who meditates knows that space and passivity are not the same thing at all. In any case, space is highly positive in Buddhist thought whereas passivity is of questionable value in Western thought. Why do space and accommodation go with the feminine principle? Although the association seems intuitively correct to me, I do not think it occurs because women's psyches are more in tune with the feminine principle. Rather, I think it occurs for the same reasons that in the *I Ching* solid lines represent masculine and broken lines feminine. The anatomy of sexuality and reproduction would make it difficult to reverse the symbolisms. However, in Vajrayana Buddhism this symbolism is not used to teach that "anatomy is destiny," limiting the individual female or male practitioner to experiencing or manifesting only one part of the dyadic unity.

Another important representation of the feminine and masculine principles in Vajrayana Buddhism involves the "mythological" realm of the *daka*s, *dakini*s, *yidam*s, *dharmapala*s, and so on. They are important in the *sadhana* practices of Vajrayana Buddhism and are familiar to anyone knowledgeable about Tibetan art, since they are often portrayed on the *thangkha*s or in statue form. Not yet having been introduced to the oral traditions of most of these "mythological" figures, I do not have the same personal experience with them that I do with the co-emergent Mother Vajrayogini and with the symbolisms associated with the feminine and masculine principles outlined above. Nevertheless, because so many people look at and speculate about these figures, I want to offer some preliminary comments, addressing the themes of this chapter.

In the artwork portraying these figures, the balance between feminine and masculine can be seen in the fact that all species of beings in this "mythological" universe occur frequently in both sexes, unlike the inhabitants of many Western mythological universes, both serious and popular. The dance poses, ornaments, dress, implements, and the like, of the males and females are similar or identical. Both females and males are often pictured alone, without a mate, and when they appear singly, the females and males are identical in the strength, energy, and attraction with which they are portrayed. These beings also consort with each other, quite literally, and such imagery is frequent. There are several typical poses, but all of them involve a couple, seen from the female's back and the male's front. Both faces are visible, by the device of having the female's head flung back in the extreme.

For years, I have contemplated this image and wondered if it is androcentric. Are we seeing a dyadic unity, or are we seeing Him and His consort? This is a critical question. As partial answer, I have tried to imagine other ways of portraying the same image, with no success. Since, for the other meanings of the image to be conveyed, the pose must be sexual, a simple, side-by-side front forward view would not work. A joined sexual pose meant to be viewed from the side would not show faces, which would lose full expression. A sexual pose viewed from the side, but with both heads turned to face the viewer?—not much passion would be conveyed by that pose. Her front and his back?— if he is taller he would hide her completely. The only other option I can think of is the widely adopted Hindu Tantra image of the female sitting on a prone male. But this icon conveys, and is meant to convey, the passivity of the masculine principle and the activity of the feminine principle, which is not part of Buddhist Tantra. So there may not be any other options.

But it is not clear to me whether the classical image is an androgynous or androcentric image. My suspicion that it is slightly androcentric increases when He becomes multi-headed, multi-armed, and multi-legged while She retains one head, two arms, and two legs. I cannot recall any images in which this situation is reversed. On the other hand, since he is Skillful Means, Compassionate Activity, perhaps he needs as many arms as possible, whereas Enabling Wisdom needs no elaboration. Without the oral tradition, I remain only on the "edge" of understanding. Looking at *daka*s, *dakini*s, and *yidam*s in art books is, as I already emphasized, a vicarious, exoteric relationship with these beings. One truly comes to know and to become one with them in doing *sadhana* practices. Since I know only a small portion of this oral tradition, I cannot present many generalizations.

Questions about how women and men actually do these practices brings us to the third critical question concerning whether the feminine and masculine principles are balanced *in the phenomenal world*. In doing *sadhana* practice, the question of balance concerns, first, the ways in which male and female practitioners are taught to relate with these "mythic" beings. For the Vajrayogini *sadhana*, the instructions are identical for women and men. Both develop a deeper understanding of the feminine principle. At this time, I do not know much about the details of *sadhana*s involving a male *yidam*, or a couple, but both men and women are given both male and female *yidam*s. Men who practice, for example, Vajrayogini *sadhana*, must learn to visualize themselves as female, and women learn to visualize themselves as male in *sadhana*s involving male *yidam*s. Both also learn to visualize the dyadic unity of the consort-couple—an intriguing proposition. In the not too distant future I hope to learn more about this type of *sadhana* practice. Though it is difficult to gain much specific information about how to do these practices, I have heard several important Karma Kagyu teachers emphasize that the practices are identical for both women and men and strive to develop "feminine" and "masculine" energy in both. The Dalai Lama also made a similar statement.[5]

Though the practices one does and the eventual enlightened manifestation of both principles are not different for women and men, still, as students-in-training, perhaps women and men respond differently to their *yidam* practices. I have not conducted any surveys on this question, and I believe it would be difficult to isolate differences based on gender from other factors such as personality (one's Buddha family in Vajrayana terminology[6]), experience, education, and so on. However, I would like to offer some impressions from my own experience.

I know that for me it is deeply satisfying and confirming to do a practice focusing on this version of the feminine principle. It is both confirming and comforting to have this relationship with Vajrayogini. It is like remembering or meeting again one's true self. I do not know if this sense of solace and relief is intensified because of my personal experience of being a Western woman who grew up with no satisfying, strong, and positive feminine imagery. It should also be very clear that when I speak of such solace and comfort, I am not describing a cozy, comfortable situation. The energy of *sadhana* practice can be devastating and bleak, but filled with truth.

I also do not know if men experience the same solace in meeting Vajrayogini. Often it strikes me that for men there may be more of a shock, a discovery of something different, and a consequent passion toward her. Both responses would seem to have a deep impact on one's conduct in the phenomenal world. For me, the masculine principle becomes much more palatable and delightful when one is also working with a feminine principle, whereas things become sour when I am limited to working with only masculine imagery. For example, before I began to practice the Vajrayogini *sadhana*, sometimes when I did another *sadhana* by myself, I simply changed the "Hes" to "Shes" out of simple frustration and deprivation. Now I no longer feel any desire to do so. However, I want to be careful to clarify that even though I may find working with the feminine principle more comforting than a man may, that does not seem to be evidence for a claim that men are more in tune with the masculine principle and women the feminine principle. I do not feel that I manifest the feminine principle of space more than I manifest action, or that I have more sense of space than do men. I certainly would not look with favor upon a claim that I am, or will be, less capable of skillful action because that is connected with the masculine principle.

In sum, I feel strongly that the masculine and feminine principles would quickly become oppressive if it were asserted that women are or should be more like the feminine principle than like the masculine principle, or that they should or do manifest the feminine principle more than men do. Manifesting *balance* in the phenomenal world has to do with fostering the full development of both women and men, not with limiting them to mirroring half the picture. And I am cautiously optimistic that the Vajrayana Buddhist tradition manages to do just that.

CHAPTER 15

"I Will Never Forget
to Visualize that Vajrayogini
Is My Body and Mind"

THIS CHAPTER[1] CONTINUES a discussion begun at the annual meeting of the American Academy of Religion in New York City in 1979.[2] It is an attempt, within the limits of a secret tradition of initiation stretching back at least a thousand years and across the cultural frontiers of north India, Tibet, and North America,[3] to discuss my acquaintance with Vajrayogini as *yidam*, as my body and mind, as well as the body and mind of the phenomenal universe.

In this chapter, I will reflect on the contrast and continuity between what was presented six years earlier and my situation in 1985, when this chapter was written. That 1979 paper is in some ways very strange, though it has remained one of my favorites. The word "Buddhism" does not appear in the text; nevertheless, it was my first Buddhist paper. It consisted of two parts. The first is an experiential discussion of finitude and suffering as major challenges to feminist theological theory. The second part is an attempt to illustrate the discursive theological points I was making by reference to an extended contemplative description of the Hindu Goddess Kali, my favorite Hindu goddess then and now.[4] The first part is basic Buddhism—what I had been learning through *samatha-vipashyana* (mindfulness-awareness) meditation and the study of basic dharma (truth). The latter part looks both backward and forward—back to my articles on Hindu goddesses as a resource for Western feminism,[5] and forward, in that the description of Kali now reads to me remarkably like a description of a *yidam* in a *sadhana* (liturgical text).

When I wrote that earlier paper in 1979, I was about to go off to the three-month meditation and study intensive known as "seminary" in Buddhist jargon. After seminary, one begins the practice of the Vajrayana

preliminaries and then, after completing *ngundro* (Vajrayana foundations),[6] one may begin the practice of the *sadhana* of Vajrayogini as one's
yidam. I did not yet know, when I wrote that earlier paper, so much
between the worlds, that a mere eighteen months later Vajrayogini would
become my *yidam*. Sometime during seminary I did figure out that we
Kagyu Buddhists do as a serious main practice the *sadhana* of a female
yidam, which may partially explain why I practiced my Vajrayana preliminaries so intensely. The fact that I could have gone as far as I did without
realizing that eventually my main practice would involve a female *yidam*
shows how secret these practices are. It also explains why I will not guess
at this point, in this context, what the practice connected with Vajrayogini's consort will involve or bring up. But I also marvel that there is
something so organic, such a natural unfolding in the three-*yana*[7] journey,
that, on the basis of the training I had already undergone, I was trying to
construct some sort of *sadhana* for myself. I was trying to take the next
step in the journey out of longing and my academic knowledge, without
even knowing that that's what I was doing.

When I evaluate these experiences, I see a tremendous difference
between what I was attempting in my earlier paper and what is available
to me as I write this chapter. For me, initiation into Vajrayogini practice
was an incredible relief. In fact, I would say that with the transmission of
this practice I found what I had been seeking but always missing by a
slight margin in my previous studies of and contributions to feminist theology. I did not know that anywhere in the modern world such practices
were available in an unbroken line of oral transmission. No longer was I
confined to art books, mythology collections, and my own imagination,
coupled with my solitary contemplations and occasional writings. Here
was an authentic lineage of oral transmission introducing me to myself
and to the world as the body and mind of Vajrayogini—this incredibly powerful, magnetizing red woman dancing on a corpse, sun, and lotus seat,
naked, sixteen years old, wearing out the *samskaras* (habitual intellectual
patterns) of egoistic grasping and fixation pictured as a garland of fifty-one
severed heads, holding in her two hands a hooked-knife and a *kapala*
(skullcap) filled with blood-*amrta* (liquor of deathlessness), and so on. The
details of her iconography mean much more to me and are infinitely more
vivid than were my earlier musings on Kali, but to quote the *sadhana* text,
"to speak is violation. . . . If this discipline is spoken of immediately I die
and rot." Therefore I am not at liberty to quote long sections of the text or
give a long description and explanation of her iconography.[8] But I have
never met anyone else like her and, if I do not forget, she is my body and
mind, and the body and mind of the phenomenal world.

Instead, what I can and want to do is to present some information about the meditative and ritual practices connected with Vajrayogini and to interweave this information with some sense of my appreciation of these practices. This appreciation is based on my experience that, unlike the theology and symbolism connected with some other religious symbol systems heavily invested in feminine imagery, the symbolism and theology of Vajrayogini in particular, and the feminine principle of Vajrayana Buddhism in general, are quite compatible with feminism. In fact, as already discussed in previous chapters, I have found them more healing, more compelling, and more cogent than some aspects of feminist theology.

When I received the transmission to become Vajrayogini and to practice her *sadhana*, I was stepping into an old communal tradition. I received transmission from a (male) guru with whom I would trust my life and my sanity, who is himself inseparable from the female *yidam* Vajrayogini—a set of teachings I still try to comprehend completely. He had done this practice himself and had transmitted it in Tibet. He began to transmit the practice to Western students in 1977. By 1981, I was still among the first three hundred Westerners to receive the practice from him. Transmission involved a magical and unexpected combination—trust and assurance, combined with a genuine transmission into feminine energy personified in Vajrayogini. I had already begun to trust Buddhism unconditionally as something that provided an important ingredient missing in all previous academic and religious training. But I still thought that my search for a trustworthy, dignified, and empowering set of symbols, myths, and icons involving female presence would go on alone. Then things came together in a way that I suspect many feminists still trying to reconstruct a broken lineage may well envy. I experience in Vajrayogini practice an impressive, all-encompassing, and empowering representation of enlightened mind in female form. Because this was transmitted to me by a genuine spiritual master, I do not have to struggle to reinvent the wheel, discovering Kali or whatever, and then to spin out some personal private interpretation. And I do not have to be alone or in an artificially separated community to express all this richness.

One of my great joys is that I can tap into the energy of the lineage of transmission and do the practice of Vajrayogini communally with both women and men. Participation in an old, well-established tradition that does not offend my feminist sensibilities, a tradition that offers modest spiritual guidance, and that provides some community, is a special privilege. However, it must also be pointed out that the understandings and practices that I describe so enthusiastically and with such appreciation are much more available to me than they were or are to many generations of Asian Buddhist women. The impact of feminism on first-generation Western Buddhism, though largely unnoticed and ignored, has been profound. It has been said, accurately, that the most significant difference between Asian and Western Buddhisms is that in Western meditation halls, one sees both women and men practicing. That is an all-important difference. Without it, Buddhism is not worth transmitting to the West. Thus, the poignancy, urgency, and potential of first-generation Buddhism in the West are explosive.

Probably the most complete experiences of my life have been occasions of doing the *sadhana* of Vajrayogini in group practice, an opportunity I do not get often because of my geographic isolation from other Buddhists. These experiences are especially intense at Fire *Pujas* ("ritual services") at which a group of senior Vajrayogini students do the practice in a special way, very intensively, for eight or more days. There is nothing like the deep chanting, bells and drums sounding precisely when they should, fire-light blazing with offerings, liturgical text, and ongoing visualization. The group becomes as one; subtle shifts in energy are experienced by all and the chanting deepens, slows down, or speeds up as one; eventually there is even unity with the phenomenal world and some response and interaction with it, as is claimed in all the books we historians of religions read about shamanism.

I am trying to say, impressionistically, because it is difficult to be direct and discursive, that when a ritual or spiritual practice is genuinely transmitted and practiced something really happens. One is not merely putting in time in a mechanical kind of way. Meditative rituals, properly done under the proper guidance, are genuinely transformative. They do not function merely to relieve the imagined anxieties of anthropological subjects written about by sociologists or anthropologists of religion. The lesson is clear: as highly trained scholars of religion, we need to stop assuming that reductionistic explanatory modes utilizing economic necessity, sociological need, or psychological trauma explain what happens in a profound ritual context.

Why, some scholars might ask at this point, am I so elusive and indirect in my discussion of *what* happens, so protective of the mysteries? I have addressed the necessity of such secrecy and carefulness in another context.[9] Here let me say only that it is necessary and completely comprehensible if one has any glimmering of understanding of the nature of oral transmission and oral traditions and of the process of spiritual transformation. It is also important to state that, despite the immense methodological difficulties engendered by this fact, there is a level of understanding beyond which observation and reading cannot carry one. Participation—complete participation—is a prerequisite. Thus, at a certain level, this chapter will fail. No matter what I say about Vajrayogini practice, most of its power and meaning will be missed by non-initiates. Nevertheless, an initiated scholar can say quite a bit; furthermore, I believe something is thus communicated that cannot be communicated by an uninitiated scholar.

Vajrayogini is a major *yidam* for Kagyu Buddhists, often the first major *yidam* whose *sadhana* is assigned to the student. The performance of the *sadhana* becomes a meditation-ritual. I use the term "meditation-ritual" to refer to the fact that the practice involves chanting of the liturgical text combined with use of ritual gestures (*mudras*), playing of musical instruments, making offerings, and the use of a rather complicated shrine with many ritual implements upon it. But this ritual process, which can be rather impressive when seen from the outside, is *upaya* (a skillful method) for generating meditative states of mind, both during actual practice sessions and in daily life. Thus, much more than "ritual" as performance of gestures is occurring. The ritual is accompanied by continuous visualization practice, which could never be fathomed or experienced by the uninitiated. The two parts of the practice are equally essential and mutually enhancing; knowledge of one without the other would be quite misleading. This meditation-ritual continuously involves the "three gates" to the phenomenal world—body, speech, and mind—which are basic categories in Tibetan Buddhism. Body is involved through the continuous use of the meditative posture and frequent use of *mudras*, speech through chanting or subvocal recitation of the *mantra*, and mind through the numerous visualizations that are generated in practicing a *sadhana*. What is observable is a small part of the entire process, which is both meditation and ritual, perfectly enmeshed with one another.

When doing a *sadhana*, the above-described type of practice, called *utpattikrama*, or development-stage, or simply "form" practice, is begun, ended, and interspersed with periods of formless practice, or *sampannakrama*, fulfillment stage. This simple sitting practice is similar to basic foundation practices of all schools of Buddhism. The two, *sampannakrama* and *utpattikrama*, must always be properly balanced; despite the vivid power and attraction of the ritual-liturgical side of *sadhana* practice, by itself such practice would be quite unbalanced and spiritually counterproductive.

Such practice is demanding and time-consuming. The full practice, done only twice a month, usually takes six to eight hours. Called "Feast Practice," it involves an additional elaborate liturgy and meditation-ritual and a festive meal at which *torma* (the *upaya* substance representing skillful means and the masculine principle, made essentially of barley flour) and *amrta* (the *prajna*, substance representing wisdom and the feminine principle, made of liquor) are consumed with other food, often to the accompaniment of music, poetry readings, spontaneously written group poems, and dancing. However, the daily practice, with its alternating *sampannakrama* and *utpattikrama*, is itself time-consuming and demanding. No matter the shortcuts and abbreviations possible, it really can't be done in any adequate fashion in less than two hours. A two-hour session does not allow any significant period of time for mantra-recitation. To complete the practice and proceed to Fire *Puja*, one must complete a million rnantra-recitations. One cannot just do the *mantra* without the accompanying liturgy and *sampannakrama*s. So completing the practice takes time and effort.

Then comes "Amending the Mantra" Fire *Puja*—a practice to amend all one's mistakes while doing the first million *mantra* recitations. This Fire *Puja* involves eight days of extremely intensive practice at which one's understanding of the phenomenal world and the self usually increases significantly. So one wants to do more Fire *Puja*s. In 1984, my community began to practice a more advanced version of the Fire *Puja*—the Four *Karma*s Fire *Puja*—which involves beginning to learn about the elemental cosmic energies of pacifying, enriching, magnetizing, and destroying. This practice is also done in eight days that stretch one beyond preconceived limits. One goes back for more because the word "realization" becomes less foreign and exotic.

This *sadhana* is a *yidam* practice to which one is initiated only after considerable preparation and only after developing significant devotion to the guru, seen as inseparable from the *yidam* and the only possible means of introduction to the *yidam*. A *yidam* is a nontheistic deity and a personal deity, which is why *sadhana* practice is called "deity-yoga" in some books. Both the term "nontheistic deity" and the term "personal deity" need some explanation. Visually, *yidam*s are anthropomorphic, but often highly unusual in appearance. They are vivid primary colors, usually unclothed, but decorated and bejeweled, often with multiple arms or heads. To those relatively unschooled in Vajrayana Buddhism, the *yidam*s are primarily accessible through books on Tibetan art. From these art books one can gain some intuitive hints about *yidam*s, but the accompanying explanations are often vague or even misleading. *Yidam*s are one of the major subjects of the *thangkha*s (religious paintings) and the *rupa*s (literally "form," a religious sculpture) collected by Western lovers of Tibetan art. However, someone who approaches *yidam*s exoterically, through published art, should be aware that the art is created as a support for visualizations and is not intended to be an "art object." Tibetan religious art portrays not only *yidam*s but also gurus and *dharmapala*s (protectors) as well as other visual representations of the spiritual universe of Vajrayana Buddhism. It is relatively easy to tell them one from another once one learns the language, but it could be confusing to the outsider.

A *yidam* is a nontheistic deity.[10] But how can this be? One of the basic claims of all forms of Buddhism is nontheism—lack of belief in or reliance on an external creator and savior. And isn't the phrase "nontheistic deity" an oxymoron?

By "deity" is meant that a *yidam* is an anthropomorphic representation of enlightened mind—one's own inherent potential for realization and Buddhahood. It could also be said that, in some sense at least, a *yidam* is also a self-revealing and self-correcting projection. By "nontheistic" is meant that this representation is not regarded as an external reference point, as any kind of objectively, externally existing reality, or as a savior. Rather these *yidams*, despite their splendor, are an aspect of *upaya* or skillful method; they quickly bring the practitioner to realization of her own enlightened mind. They are also at the *sambhogakaya* (enjoyment body) level, the intermediate "mythic" level of the *trikaya* (triple body of Buddha) between the absolute level of *dharmakaya* (truth body) and the relative and compassionate existence of *nirmanakaya*—the form-body of enlightened mind in actual human existence as the guru. Thus, important teachings about the unity of guru and *yidam* become more comprehensible. The relationship between *dharmakaya* and *sambhogakaya* is well expressed by a line in the text: "though *dharmakaya* is indivisible like space, *rupakayas* [form bodies] appear individually like colors in a rainbow." They exist; they are very real in the experience of a practitioner, but they do exist as solid, independent, objectively real forms. Vajrayana Buddhism is very interesting in this regard, since the possibility of "deity" is not introduced at all until quite late on the path of spiritual development. A student of Vajrayana Buddhism will never hear of it at the *hinayana* stage and only barely or vaguely at the *mahayana* stage. That the notion of "deity" is brought up only well after the student should no longer be capable of objectifying the deity as a solidly existing independent form or external savior is one of the most skillful aspects of Vajrayana Buddhism's *upaya* (skillful means).

Finally, in the Vajrayana one meets the *yidams*. Why bring up deity at this point? An anthropomorphic representation of enlightened mind is quite helpful and relevant spiritually. Every detail of Vajrayogini's iconography means something, much as I saw significance in the details of Kali's portrayal in my 1979 paper. But with Vajrayogini I am not guessing or going solely on my own intuitions. She is my body and mind, as the text says. Thus, deity in Vajrayana is an anthropomorphic representation of one's own enlightenment and of the enlightenment of the whole phenomenal world. In the practice one relates with oneself as Vajrayogini and with the world as Vajrayogini. The text states that out of emptiness "instantly I arise as the Jetsun Vajrayogini with a red body, with one face and two arms, and so on. Other parts of the text state that "in the space in front appear clearly the five *devis* [goddesses] of the Jetsun Vajrayogini *mandala*" and so on. *Yidam* practice is in many ways the ultimate combination of the power of concrete symbolism and the power of abstraction beyond conception. This combination is, of course, in the service of one's personal transformation toward enlightenment by means of seeing oneself and the world as Vajrayogini—female, red, two-armed, one-faced, bone-ornamented, dancing, girdled by the oceans.

The epithets go on and on, arising with luminosity out of emptiness. Thus, a *yidam* is a personal deity, not in the sense that ultimate reality is personal, as in theistic religions, but rather that this nontheistic deity is intimately related with oneself as one's body and mind as well as one's world. Seeing oneself and one's world *as yidam*—as an anthropomorphic representation of enlightened mind—is a very interesting and useful practice, though by no means introductory or easy.

At this point a historic event involving Vajrayogini practice is occurring. It is being transmitted from Asian culture to Western culture. Someday students will do historical research on this transmission, just as people now study the transmission of Buddhism from India to the rest of Asia. I feel that scholars should not let this historic event slip by unnoted but should be examining this phenomenon as it occurs. As previously stated, this is an old, well-established practice, undoubtedly constructed and preserved mainly by men, many of them monks. It is interesting that such people—mainly monastic males—would determine that the first *yidam* practice should involve a female *yidam* and the development of one's feminine energy. It is worth pointing out the fact that a new religious development is occurring here, now. This is probably the first time that this practice has been done so extensively by lay people and by women. At this point almost everyone in my *sangha*—Vajradhatu—is a householder, and at least half of the *sadhakas* (*sadhana* practitioners) are women—a fact that is much noted and commented on. What happens when large numbers of laywomen practice a spiritual discipline largely designed by and for men? For that matter, what happens to Western men, raised in a chauvinistic culture, who find themselves being asked to develop their feminine energy and feminine being as an essential stage of their spiritual development? The practice is identical for women and men. Are the effects similar or different?

I cannot say since I have not done the kind of research that would yield such answers. Furthermore, in this context, I do not wish to divulge what male friends have told me about their experiences of being Vajrayogini, beyond saying that they find it a positive experience. As a feminist, I cannot help but feel strongly that such a practice could be a wonderful skill-ful means (*upaya*) for undoing a bias toward male superiority. Thus *yidam* practice, combined with the continual emphasis on gentleness and non-aggression—which in the Buddhism I experience is *not* something preached by men but practiced by women—does not provide a very viable basis for male chauvinism. Indeed, in my experience, though Buddhist men often have many misguided notions about feminism, they are not chauvinistic compared to the norm.

Women seem to do very well with the practice, as evidenced by their large numbers in the ranks of senior students. In fact, a widespread impression in the Vajradhatu *sangha* is that women are, typically, much better practitioners than men. One wonders, then, why, historically, their avenues to practice have been largely blocked, but discussion of that topic is a different paper. Not only are women now highly regarded as practitioners, but Buddhist women are generally much stronger and more self-determining than is the Western cultural stereotype. Many of them are not only senior students but also highly regarded teachers and meditation instructors. Though the record of accomplishment is less impressive, there is also a widely perceived need for and some success at having women in important administrative positions in Vajradhatu.

I will turn now to a discussion of the effects I experience from this practice, insofar as I can determine them. Some of the effects are what I expected; others are quite surprising. First, it is important to state that, however compelling and entrancing Vajrayogini practice may be (and it is experienced that way by virtually all students), this practice is not a relief from one's painful and troublesome patterns. Instead they become vivid because one is so much more sensitive. That too is a virtually universal experience. *Samsara* (cyclic existence) must be worn out; it cannot simply be repressed, and the wear and tear can be overwhelming. The obvious enthusiasm I express for this practice should not be confused with the idea that it brings a one-sided happiness, a dualistic happiness opposed to dualistic sorrow. Rather, by bringing up and including everything, this, like all genuine spiritual practices, begins to take one beyond that distinction altogether. Second, as I expected, I find it incredibly empowering to have a practice of a female *yidam*. Though I have now chanted the liturgy literally hundreds of times, it is a rare occasion when I am not aroused and moved by some part of the text and the practice, despite real experiences of boredom and tedium.

Much of the power of the experience relates to Vajrayogini's femininity and the way that empowers me. She is so strong and beautiful, so fierce and compassionate; she permeates everything; she is my body and mind.

This empowerment, however, involves a subtle edge. It is important to be clear about what is being empowered, what is being undercut, and how Vajrayogini's femininity relates to both. The point *of yidam* practice is *definitely* not to empower one's *samsaric* ego, one's conventional habitual patterns. As much as possible, I arise out of emptiness as Vajrayogini, that is, as all that *she* symbolizes—not as Rita Gross, feeling empowered by identification with a powerful transcendent other. She empowers me—but not me as any conventional or limited identity whatsoever. She empowers me as seed of enlightenment, no one in particular, neither female nor male, neither feminist nor nonfeminist, and yet without limit.

What is the link between the empowerment involved in Vajrayogini's femininity and what she empowers or does not empower? This practice was not designed to solve the problems inherent in Western patriarchal religion—even though it has done that for me. Why was it able to do so? I believe that healing has something to do with both the misery of being female (or male) in the context of patriarchy and with the power of non-patriarchal, nonsexist anthropomorphic symbolism. It is impossible to avoid anthropomorphic and, therefore, genderized representations of ultimate reality. Under patriarchal monotheism, we have lived for millennia with a supposedly nongenderized but highly male deity. Clearly, most feminist theology agrees that this is not healthy. It is not so clearly agreed that a better set of anthropomorphic symbols is essential to the healing process, but I have always found them to be completely necessary and more useful than conceptual abstractions, even though they are so difficult to find. Then I was introduced to Vajrayogini.

However, though Vajrayogini does empower me as female, clinging to that empowerment and fixating on it would undo much of that attainment from a Buddhist point of view. Though this practice heals, to some extent anyway, it also constantly pulls one further rather than encouraging one to rest where one is. Thus in a sense, a feminist comforted by this practice, will also be pulled beyond feminism, which *does not mean* that one is no longer a feminist. It only means that one no longer creates an "ego" (used in the Buddhist sense of a defense mechanism against basic existential groundlessness) out of being a feminist. That is quite simple, liberating, and useful.

Lastly, I did not expect that combined with the sense of empowerment would come so much longing for completion and going further, such longing to meet the consort and to unite with the phenomenal world, such longing to learn more about the compassionate activity that is spacious wisdom's partner. This feeling developed slowly and organically, almost unnoticeably; it only became apparent and vivid after I completed the counted practice and began to do Fire *Puja*s. This development makes a lot of sense to me when I think about the unfolding of the path. Developing one's feminine energy is understood as developing the space in which enlightened activity can arise. Besides empowerment, that feels like devastation, which is precisely what is happening to ego or conventional mind and beliefs or any finite resting point on which one might attempt to land. Having opened up and given up at least to some extent, one has gone through an important process—and then there is the waiting and the longing, which feels to me precisely right. At this point I am curious to find out what it will be like to meet and become Vajrayogini's consort in addition to being her, for clearly, one does not stop being Vajrayogini when one takes on the Cakrasamvara practice.

In conclusion, I will summarize some of my central impressions of being a woman initiated into this particular tradition involving the feminine principle. First, I feel extremely lucky to have had the karmic connections to find an unbroken lineage of transmission into such a spiritual discipline as the practice of Vajrayogini. The solace of being able to share communally with both women and men and to experience the leadership of teachers whom I feel to be trustworthy is one of the great joys of my life. I am so glad that I do not have to invent spiritual disciplines adequate to a feminist, so unrelievedly, one-pointedly glad, that nothing I could say would convey the gratitude.

Second, I feel both privileged and burdened to be among those preserving this tradition and establishing it in the West. It is awesome to realize that a spiritual practice of such power and relevance, which arose in India more than a thousand years ago and survived only in Tibet for many hundreds of years, is now being transmitted to and possibly preserved in one's own culture. It is exciting to be one of the little cogs, one of the few out of the millions in America, involved in that process. Most of us senior students feel that this particular generation of student-practitioners is critical in history. How did it happen that out of the devastation of Tibet came a teacher who could speak extremely accurately to the Western world and that we several hundreds are among his senior students who will be important in establishing or destroying Vajrayana Buddhism in the West? If there are miracles, that is a miracle—or else it is *karma* and *karma* actually operates, rather than being merely an Indian concept. Who knows?

Finally, I personally feel very strongly about the "auspicious coincidence" (*tendril*) of Buddhism and feminism in and the West.[11] Time does not diminish my sense of urgency regarding this confluence of events. For the first time in many millennia, we have the chance to combine a deep spirituality with a nonsexist, egalitarian access to that spirituality. For

Buddhism, even Vajrayana Buddhism, despite the importance of Vajra-yogini, does not present such a historical model. Fewer, many fewer, among the senior students, perceive this need not only to establish Vajrayana Buddhism in the West but to establish it in a definitively non-sexist way. So all the communal joy I tried to convey in this paper also has its lonely side.

CHAPTER 16

Life-giving Images in
Vajrayana Buddhist Ritual

A S A HISTORIAN OF RELIGIONS, I am sensitive to the centrality of ritual in religion and in no way sympathetic to the usual Western ratio-
nalist disregard for ritual. Nevertheless, both as a religious studies scholar
and as a Buddhist, I must begin by saying that ritual is not as central to
Buddhism as to most other religions. To be certain, many rituals with a
great deal of local color have developed in the many cultures to which Buddhism has spread. For example, in Theravada Buddhist countries temporary monastic ordination serves as a boy's initiation ritual; in East Asian
countries, Buddhists hold a virtual monopoly on death and mourning rituals; and colorful chanting ceremonies have developed in all the varying
monastic practices of Buddhism. Thus, clearly, Buddhism is not immune
to ritual, despite its decisive claim that meditative awareness and equanimity alone, not ritual performances, bring release from suffering.

From my perspective as a Western feminist Buddhist, however, these
traditional rituals are not, for two reasons, the appropriate focus for my
discussion of how women might transform Buddhist ritual. First, many of
these rituals are more part of Asian cultures than Buddhist ideology and
are not being transmitted to Western students. Thus, the problem of how
women might transform Buddhist rituals intersects with the issue of what
is Asian and what is Buddhist in the forms of Buddhism being taught to
Westerners today. Unraveling Buddhism from Asian culture will undoubtedly be a major concern of Buddhists for some time to come. It is not
appropriate for me to suggest how traditional Asian rituals that are not
part of the Buddhism in which I am being trained might be adapted and
transformed by women, though Asian Buddhist feminists would undoubt-

edly take a keen interest in that problem. Second, even in Asian cultures, ritual is not central to Buddhism; meditation is.

Thus, it would seem appropriate that I should take up that which is central to Buddhism, whether Asian or Western, and ask whether and how one could discuss feminist transformations of the key Buddhist ritual—meditation. Though meditation is not exactly a ritual, nevertheless to the observer, and even to the practitioner, it has some kinship with ritual. One observes people in a very specific posture, often in very precise spatial arrangements vis-à-vis each other and a shrine. Sometimes meditators engage in verbal utterances and predetermined, very precise movements. From the outsider's point of view, such behavior might well look like ritual, although meditation would be an unusually boring ritual to watch. From the insider's point of view, however, what counts is the mental state of one-pointed concentration, calm abiding, and clear awareness that ideally accompany the verbal utterances and the movements.

This emphasis on the mental state of the meditator is what makes meditation only akin to ritual, rather than just another ritual. In ritual, the major emphasis is on the correct performance of the movements, not on the mental state of the ritual performers, even though an important side effect of ritual is social and individual transformation of consciousness.[1] Several classical ritual settings will demonstrate this claim. For example, in a traditional Jewish synagogue, it only matters that the service is proceeding correctly; individuals often come and go as they need to and converse with each other during nonessential parts of the service. (In fact, in some situations, women, who previously did not read Hebrew and couldn't participate in the service fluently often spent the majority of the time chatting when they infrequently attended synagogue services.) In Vedic-inspired dimensions of Hinduism, correct performance is paramount and, again, individuals may come and go, so long as the ritual goes on. Most decisively, one of the many controversies in early Christianity concerned whether the state of mind of the officiating priest determined the efficacy of the Mass. The winners were those who claimed that it did not, so long as the Mass was correctly celebrated.

I am most familiar with Buddhist meditation in the Vajrayana traditions associated with Tibet, having experienced more than twenty years of meditation practice within that tradition. In Vajrayana Buddhism, there are two types of meditation—formless and with form. Formless meditation is more basic and more pervasive, found in all forms of Buddhism, whereas meditation with form is more restricted. Formless meditation, usually a meditation using the breath as a reference point, has only slight affinity with ritual, as usually understood, since verbal utterances and movement are minimal or nonexistent. Meditation with form, however, is closer to ritual, both to the observer and to the participant. In Tibetan Buddhist *sadhana*s, or services, the participants may chant for long periods of time and often use complex hand gestures, sometimes with, sometimes without ritual implements. An elaborate, precisely arranged shrine is integral to the *sadhana*, and during more complex versions of the *sadhana*, such as feast practice, a ritual leader manipulates various objects on the shrine. Sometimes even dress is ritually controlled, as in the Four Karmas Fire *Puja*, in which participants all dress in the color appropriate for the section of the *mandala* and the Buddha family to which that day's meditation is dedicated.

Clearly, such behavior looks like ritual and is interesting enough to observe that commercial videotapes of some *sadhana*s are available. Such videos, however, always pare the ritual down to the more colorful moments, since it is unlikely anyone not participating would be willing to watch such a video all day. In addition, a video can capture only the outer form of this ritual. The *visualizations* that accompany the words of the chant and the ritual gestures and give them meaning are essential to the ritual; without knowledge of the visualizations, one cannot understand much about the words and the gestures. (To compensate for this lack, some videos and books try to portray the visualization as a picture, somewhat like the captions in a comic book, above the meditator's head.) Thus, clearly the ritual emphasis on correct praxis only partially accounts for what happens when performing a *sadhana*; meditation, with its emphasis on a focused and stable mind, is essential to *sadhana*. For these reasons, I referred to *sadhana* practice as meditation-ritual in the previous chapter and suggest that same understanding here.

Except as an initiated participant, it is quite difficult to understand such meditation-rituals accurately, even if one has the *sadhana* text in one's hands. These rituals are said to be self-secret, that is, incomprehensible apart from the oral instructions given by the initiating guru and one's own practice of those oral instructions. I have found this to be the case over and over in the *sadhana*s that I have practiced, which presents another obstacle to this discussion. How can I talk about self-secret meditation-rituals with people who have no access to the oral instructions and no experience practicing them? And how can I do so without violating my own vows to maintain secrecy about them? For the *sadhana* texts proclaim that if I discuss their contents with those not properly initiated, I will immediately "die and rot" myself!

I have decided to solve this dilemma by discussing the most public aspect of Tibetan Vajrayana ritual, namely, the icons of the *yidam*s (meditation deities or anthropomorphic representations of one's own innate enlightenment). As mentioned before, the meditator visualizes throughout the performance of a *sadhana*, and as an aid to forming and stabilizing the visualization, two-dimensional and three-dimensional icons of the *yidam* that is the meditational focus of the *sadhana* are usually found on the shrine and the meditator's *puja* table. Though these icons are painted or cast as ritual tools, not as art objects; are supposed to be used only in a sacred manner; and cannot be accurately understood apart from the oral commentaries, outsiders to the world of Tibetan ritual probably are more familiar with these icons than anything else. Countless art books and some museum exhibits have made these icons relatively available even to those who will never use them in their intended ritual context.

When one looks at these icons, regular patterns begin to emerge relatively quickly. The *yidam*s are humanlike in shape, though they may have multiple heads, eyes, arms, and, more rarely, legs, and they are painted in vivid colors (usually blue, red, green, yellow, black, or white). They routinely appear in both sexes. Typically, they sit, in meditation posture or in the relaxed teaching posture (with one leg drawn up and the other extended), or they dance. Rarely do they simply stand still. Their hands hold ritual implements or form *mudra*s (hand gestures). They are bejeweled and richly garbed with scarves, crowns, and skirts, though they are also usually semi-nude to the waist, whether male or female. Their demeanor is classified into three types—peaceful, semi-wrathful, and wrathful. Obviously, the peaceful *yidam*s smile calmly, while the wrathful *yidam*s generally look like someone you would not want to meet alone at night unless you knew the password. Both female and male *yidam*s appear as both peaceful and wrathful. The male and female *yidam*s may appear independently or together, but when they appear together, they appear as a couple in sexual union, the famous *yab-yum* icon. Not surprisingly, given what I have said about *sadhana* practice, every detail means something, and those meanings are communicated in the *sadhana* text itself and in the oral commentaries, both of which are restricted to initiated practitioners.

I have been doing *sadhana* practice since 1981, when I received the *abhisekha* (literally "sprinkling" or initiation) of Vajrayogini. Vajrayogini is a semi-wrathful female *yidam*, red and dancing, carrying a skullcap filled with blood, a hooked knife, and holding a *khatvanga* (a staff with three prongs at the top.) After completing the required number of *mantra* recitations and the fire *puja*s of this *sadhana*, I received the *abhisekha* of Cakrasamvara in 1986 and have since completed the *mantra* recitation and fire *puja*s of that practice as well. The Cakrasamvara *sadhana* is actually a *yab-yum* practice, since the blue Cakrasamvara is visualized in sexual union with Vajrayogini. She holds the same dancing pose as when one practices her *sadhana*, but now she is joined with Cakrasamvara. He crosses his arms behind her back and holds the primary Tantric ritual implements, a bell and a *vajra* scepter in his hands. (This gesture, one of the most profound in Tantric sign language, symbolizes the co-emergent union of wisdom and compassion, which are also the feminine and the masculine principles.) These have been my major *sadhana*s, though I have received many others since then and have practiced some of them, including Manjusri, Green Tara, Kalachakra, and Vajrakilaya more sporadically.

Because all these icons are quite available publicly and because I am personally immersed in the symbolism and the practice of each of these *yidam*s, I will discuss the possibilities and the problems presented by these ritual icons for a Buddhist feminist seriously concerned with how these meditation-rituals might transform and be transformed by women. I will not discuss any images that I have not lived with and practiced with for years; in fact the visions behind these words are all *thangkha*s (paintings on cloth bordered by brocades, with a silk curtain that can be used to cover the painting when outsiders are present) and *rupa*s (literally, "form," the word used for a three-dimensional icon) in my personal collection. I have been oriented to the visual arts throughout my life. (When I was a child I drew non-stop and thought I would become an artist, and I have published several articles on how Hindu icons could inspire Western feminist theologians.) I have a long-standing and deep appreciation of the Indian understanding that revelation occurs as readily through the sense of sight[2] as through the sense of hearing, that pictures and statues are no less (and no more) reliable than books and words as media for communicating the uncommunicable Beyond at the heart of all religions. Hence I have no sympathy for the monotheistic command not to make "graven images" and its frequent diatribes against "idols" (pictures and statues of the divine). Given this orientation, I have found immense comfort in these Buddhist icons, which have been literally life-giving, but, as a feminist, I, have also found significant problems with some of them.

In my own practice I work with these icons both formally and informally. The formal practice involves the meditation-ritual of *sadhana* practice, either in my elaborate and complete Tibetan-style shrine room at home, or in my childhood home, a twenty-by-twenty foot log cabin with no modern conveniences other than electricity, where I do the required solitary retreats. (The *mantra* recitations that count toward completing the practice of Cakrasamvara, Vajrakilaya, and several others must be done in strict solitary retreat. Therefore, I have spent about three months at that cabin doing *sadhana* practice in recent years. I take great delight in the integration of my strange life represented by my doing these traditional Tibetan meditation-rituals in the locus of my culturally and financially deprived childhood, in the very place in which I was indoctrinated with a rigid, bigoted form of monotheism.)

The informal practice involves the constant visual reminder of icons placed at critical spots around my home. For example, as I write, I glance repeatedly at the beautiful icon of Manjusri, bodhisattva of wisdom, with his delicate golden face and feminine torso, holding a flaming sword in one hand, with the other hand in a teaching *mudra*. Vajrayogini dances on my coffee table and Green Tara holds forth on the mantlepiece and on my dresser. My best *thangkha*, a Kalachakra *yab-yum*, holds the place of honor in the living room, which hosts a total of five *thangkha*s. Thus, I have literally surrounded myself with visual cues and reminders of the sacred universe I inhabit as a Vajrayana Buddhist and draw much comfort and inspiration from this immersion in space filled with ritual icons. (Perhaps the fact that I am a solitary practitioner, that no one else within a hundred miles does these practices, helps explain why I have emphasized this informal practice of visual cues and reminders.)

The peaceful male and female *yidam*s appearing by themselves have brought only solace and comfort to me. Though Green Tara is perhaps the most popular deity in Tibetan Buddhism, her practice is not emphasized by my teacher and I do not perform her *sadhana* very often. But her icon was the first I acquired, when I had just begun meditation practice, and her beauty and her smiling face, on two *thangkha*s and two *rupa*s, have been with me for twenty years. Manjusri is quite emphasized by my teacher, especially for people involved in intellectual pursuits and study, so I have practiced a short Manjusri *sadhana* much more frequently. But he is more important to me in informal practice. For as long as I have had a computer, more than ten years now, he has sat by my computer and watched over all my writing, including *Buddhism after Patriarchy*.

Vajrayogini, whose practice I have done for thousands of hours, has perhaps been the most comforting of all, for, as a longtime critic of male monotheism and longtime advocate of use of Indian imagery of female deities to re-imagine Western religions,[3] I was more than ready for a spiritual discipline in which the imagery of a strong, fiery, fierce, beautiful female was so predominant. This practice is especially empowering because, like all more advanced *sadhana* practices, it involves self-visualization of oneself *as* the deity. Therefore, she is no imagined external presence but my own body and mind.

Understandably I was eager, but also somewhat apprehensive, to take on the same kind of practice regarding a male *yidam* when the time came to begin the next *sadhana* in the sequence of practices. The next two *sadhana*s usually practiced involve a *yab-yum* visualization. I have also done thousands of hours of Cakrasamvara practice by now, though I am relatively inexperienced still with the practice of Vajrakilaya. I was apprehensive because of apparent androcentrism in the icon, a problem over which

I brooded long before the *sadhana* text and the oral commentaries were available to me, as was narrated in the previous chapters.

Now, with the text and the oral commentaries, as well as the icon, before me, I am in a much better position to evaluate whether or not androcentrism lurks in this picture. My conclusion is that the oral commentaries definitively lay to rest any androcentric or male-dominant interpretations of the icon and the text to which one might fall victim (or which some others might hope to find). But the text that I use (which is only one of many versions of the Cakrasamvara *sadhana*), definitely has androcentric overtones. And I can no longer avoid the conclusion that the icon, in its usual form, is also somewhat androcentric.

Since the icon is available to the public while the text is not, let me focus on the icon. Whether in its two- or three-dimensional form, the icon presents her back and his front to the viewer. She is often significantly smaller and often has only two arms, whereas he may have as many as twelve. (In the version of the practice that I do, each has only two arms. In my Kalachakra *thangkha*, he has four faces and she one; he has twenty-four arms and she eight.) Sometimes, when she is not a distinctively different color from him, as in the Vajrakilaya icon, in which case both are blue, she is barely distinguishable in the tangle of arms, faces, and bodies. (That problem does not occur in Cakrasamvara practice; he is blue, she is red.) So that one can see her face, especially in *thangkhas*, her head is flung back and twisted in an impossible pose that some of us have begun to call "the broken neck" syndrome.

Outsiders have long interpreted this icon as a statement that she is merely an instrument or extension of him, rather than a being in her own right. For example, at the conference on *Buddhism after Patriarchy*, held in Toronto in 1995, a young scholar tried to argue that Indian images of divine androgyny, including the Vajrayana *yab-yam* icon, could never be liberating for women because of their androcentrism. Like many feminist critics of other religious feminists who work within a traditional religious framework in spite of its tendencies toward male dominance, she viewed the tradition as static and unchangeable. But she made a more significant error; she knew nothing of the oral commentaries on how to practice with this icon and was uninterested in hearing that they did not corroborate her interpretation. I believe that the same problem is responsible for the depressing conclusions regarding the status of women in Tantric Buddhism put forth by the eminent scholar David Snellgrove.[4]

Perhaps the most important instructions one receives when learning to do Cakrasamvara practice, and presumably, any self-visualization of a *yab-yum* deity, is that one does *not* visualize oneself as the male with an external consort. One is the whole *yab-yum* icon, both female and male, though even some practitioners, usually men, make the mistake of thinking that once they finish Vajrayogini practice, in which their self-visualization is female, they "get to be a guy." I have sarcastically suggested that such a misunderstanding would reduce the practice to something like "*vajra* and *ghanta* (bell and scepter, the primary implements for Tantric practice) in hand, consort on penis, ready to rock and roll." When confronted with this stark caricature, they usually laugh and quickly retract their version of the practice.

That one does not visualize oneself as a male with an external consort is in accord with the widespread Vajrayana Buddhist understanding of the co-emergence, inseparability, nonduality, and equality of the masculine and feminine principles. However the icon may look to an uninitiated outsider, in Vajrayana symbolism, the relationship between the masculine and feminine principles is not hierarchical. One sees this more clearly when one remembers that the right hand is masculine and the left feminine, that the scepter is masculine and the bell feminine, and that in Tantric ritual, they are always used together as equal mates. Even more forcefully important is the fact that wisdom and emptiness are regarded as manifestations of the feminine principle, while compassion and skillful means are regarded as manifestations of the masculine principle. One of the most important goals of Mahayana and Vajrayana Buddhism is the simultaneous development of wisdom and compassion, which are never ranked hierarchically.

Not only are the feminine and masculine principles equally emphasized; they are also inseparable. Even when the female or the male *yidam* appears alone, her or his consort is represented in a covert manner. For example, the *khatvanga* that Vajrayogini carries represents her consort Cakrasamvara. Such knowledge makes impossible the claim made by some that Indian images of divine androgyny are always androcentric.

It should also be emphasized that men and women both perform this practice, arising as Cakrasamvara and Vajrayogini *yab-yum*, in exactly the same manner. It is crucial to understand that Vajrayana practice never suggests that men embody the masculine principle while women embody the feminine principle, since this point is often lost on outsiders. Each individual, whether male or female, needs to develop *both* wisdom and compassion; women do not specialize in wisdom nor men in compassion. Since *sadhana* practice is regarded as *upaya*, as a skillful means to quickly develop enlightened qualities, especially wisdom and compassion, in the practitioner, it is clear that one would not regard Cakrasamvara as somehow more important that Vajrayogini, or oneself as Cakrasamvara but not Vajrayogini when doing this practice.

Nevertheless, I also have reached the reluctant conclusion that the usual icon of Cakrasamvara and Vajrayogini does not portray their equal importance as clearly as it might. The visual representation of them is somewhat androcentric, and I believe that the icon and the oral commentaries are somewhat at odds with each other. However, I view this visual androcentrism not as a deliberate attempt to thwart female practitioners and aid male practitioners but as an unfortunate side effect of the lack of feminist consciousness in Buddhist tradition and the fact that most authors of *sadhana* texts and most *thangkha* painters have been men.

What can be done? Admittedly, one faces a difficult technical problem. How can one simultaneously portray sexual union and the faces of the deities? At one point, represented in an earlier chapter in this section, I believed that the conventional icon solved the problem in the best way that could be done, since I believed that seeing the deities' full faces was essential. The only other way to portray both sexual union and the faces of the deities would be to show their bodies in profile with their heads turned toward the viewer—hardly a convincing pose for sexual passion. But especially as I spent long, demanding days in strict retreat in my cabin practicing the self-visualization of Vajrayogini and Cakrasamvara *yab-yum*, I became less and less satisfied with the standard portrayal of Cakrasamvara and Vajrayogini, though the power of practice was overwhelming. I found myself using a modern greeting card with exquisite faces that avoided the "broken neck" syndrome and really featured both faces well, rather than a traditional *thangkha*, as the support for my visualization. I found myself turning my *rupa* sideways on the shrine and I found myself focusing a lot on the space between their bodies, as well as the place of union (*rupa*s are anatomically correct). I was clearly experiencing what Robin Kornman, a friend, translator, and fellow practitioner, pointed out as the inevitable inadequacy of the visual form, since one is *not* looking at them when doing the practice, but *is* them—something that is impossible to portray visually. Nevertheless, why should the visual representation be androcentric?

For years, I tried, somewhat timidly, to discuss these issues with male leaders of Tibetan Buddhism, but either my concerns were dismissed or I was told that it is impossible to change traditional forms—a claim that I reject as a religious studies scholar. One Rinpoche told me that he understood my problem but that men had the same problems with Vajrayogini practice, so everything was even, equal, and fair—a comment I now regard as quite superficial. Meanwhile, I continued to dream of a *thangkha* that portrayed the *yab-yum* from the side, the partners of equal height, gazing intently into each other's faces—a mutually empowered passionate couple, as I later put it to the artist who will finally execute the *thangkha* for me. (In fact, I had wanted their heads to be the cover design for *Buddhism after Patriarchy*, but the press did not have an artist who was up to the task of making the design.) I had given up the notion that one needed to see their full faces, now convinced that profiles could also express passion and that, whatever its drawbacks, my suggested design at least avoided andro-centrism, which I regard as quite misleading. (In part, I probably reached this conclusion after years of gazing at two paintings of the Hindu couple, Radha and Krishna, that adorn my bedroom wall. They are not portrayed in sexual union, and one sees their bodies almost in full frontal position, but they turn their heads to gaze intently into one another's eyes—pas-sionate profiles.)

I had heard of a woman *thangkha* painter in Boulder who had done another innovative *thangkha*. Jetsun Kushalo, a Sakya woman guru, had commissioned her to do a *thangkha* that reversed the usual *yab-yum* image, so that one saw her front and his back—an image that is quite rare. I was intrigued with the idea, but knew that that wouldn't solve my prob-lems, since I have never believed that role reversal is the solution to fem-inist issues. For several years, I contemplated asking this artist to paint my envisioned *thangkha*, but somehow the timing was never right and I always put off the phone call.

Then, in fall 1995, things came together. I was determined to meet a young woman teacher, Khandro, Rinpoche, a Rinpoche of the same lin-eages as my own teacher, who had been getting rave reviews from Bud-dhist women whom I respect deeply. So I traveled to Boulder for the single purpose of meeting her. And I was determined one last time to bring up the issues that I had found no male teacher willing to take seriously. Whereas male teachers had usually given me about fifteen minutes, she had set aside an hour for our audience. Our meeting is probably the most empow-ering encounter I have ever had. Already familiar with my work, she said over and over that feminism is necessary and *she* gave *me* a gift, which she said was to thank me for my work, to encourage me to continue, and to indicate that she would do anything she could to help me. This is one of the greatest honors I have ever received; even the most laudatory book review is not anywhere nearly as important to me!

Though I had many questions, the most important to me was the old question of *yab-yum* visualizations. Using my hands to represent the deities, I explained my problems and my proposed *thangkha* to her. She also began using her hands and immediately tried out the various visual-izations. Reaching her decision quickly, she asked my to try not to use my proposed visualization during practice, at this point in time, but also to proceed with having the *thangkha* painted. I asked her why not to use the alternative visualization during practice and she replied that at this point, I was only working with thoughts anyway, so their content didn't matter too much.

I was extremely excited to have a positive response to my proposed *thangkha* and called the *thangkha* painter, Cynthia Moku immediately. She was enthralled with the idea and relieved that I had already received Khandro Rinpoche's blessing for the idea, since she would not have been willing to execute such an unconventional *thangkha* only on her and my authority. It became clear to me why earlier I had not felt that the timing was right for approaching the artist. Another lesson in the virtues of trusting intuition!

And so she is now in the process of executing the *thangkha;* my vision will take form and become visible to my eyes. To the best of my knowledge, this will be a new image in the repertoire of Tibetan Buddhist images, and I believe that this will be a historic *thangkha.* (Recently the artist told me that she had been discussing the project with a male Tibetan lama, who immediately became very enthusiastic, saying that "you'd be able to see better with that visualization.") It all seems so simple, so obvious, in hindsight. Yet in the 1300-year history of Tibetan Buddhism, no one has thought of this alternative, or at least no one has given it form. Perhaps what the world needs most is more feisty feminist women who won't take no for an answer!

I will conclude by drawing some generalizations regarding how women might transform ritual and how ritual transforms women from my experience. First, the creativity of women working together is wonderful. Khandro Rinpoche, the guru, Cynthia Moku, the artist, and I, who went through a lot of turmoil in the process of giving birth to the vision, will together make something new and profoundly useful.

I am also delighted with the demonstration of the truth of a claim I have been making in the Buddhist world for years—women teachers who understand feminism *will* make a difference. For years I have claimed that the single biggest problem in contemporary Buddhism is a lack of female teachers, only to be dismissed by most of my Buddhist compatriots, who claim that the teachings are the same teachings whether they are spoken by a man or a woman and that, therefore, the sex of the teacher is irrelevant. Since I have already published a complex argument refuting this stereotypical view,[5] in this context I need only point out that, quite clearly, a woman Rinpoche conversant with feminism *did* make a big difference in my story, and does make a big difference to many Buddhist women. Though many of the senior teachers in the Buddhist organization to which I belong are women, Khandro Rinpoche, is the first female guru and lineage holder we have encountered. And, obviously, she is not merely doing and saying only the same things male teachers say, though she presents the gender-neutral teachings of Buddhism in ways that both men and women appreciate. But, in addition, she holds audiences for women at which, unlike male teachers, she owns up to the fact that in the relative world and in a patriarchal system, women do have a more difficult time than men. (Male teachers tend to respond to such questions by saying that gender is irrelevant to the dharma, or basic teachings, and that Buddhism is about working with our own habitual patterns rather than blaming suffering on factors outside ourselves.) She now has a wildly enthusiastic following among Buddhist women and is clearly touching women in ways that had not happened before.

Regarding my experience, I believe that what is most instructive is the manner in which, on the one hand, I have struck out on my own into uncharted territory, but on the other hand, I have worked with tradition and traditional authorities. It is clear from the manner in which I work with images, especially in my informal practice of surrounding myself with icons and immersing myself in their contemplation, that I am striking out on my own. There is a good deal of personal appropriation in my informal practice, and I believe this personal appropriation is essential for feminists at this point in history. Clearly, my new *thangkha* is the product of years of working alone, on my own, engaging in personal appropriation and creativity.

But, as much as possible, I also want to work with tradition and traditional authorities, for two reasons. First, in my view, genuine spiritual breakthroughs are so rare that completely rejecting traditional religions because they are tainted by patriarchy is fairly dangerous spiritually and may leave one more bereft than ever. Just as some feminists choose to trust their own creativity as they reject traditional religions, I choose to trust my own ability to sift the wheat from the chaff and to forge a union between feminism and the invaluable spiritual insights of a long-standing, well-tested spiritual discipline.

My second reason for making the choice to work with tradition and traditional authority as much as possible has everything to do with Buddhist ideas of *upaya*, or skillful means, of taking the actions that are most likely to get the job done. My feminist view is that a feminist society is more likely to come about if feminists work within institutions, such as the traditional religions, rather than abandon them for less frustrating, clearly feminist alternatives. The *thangkha* that I envisioned will have far more impact on Buddhism because it is being done within the system than it would have if I had simply hired an artist to do my bidding. And I believe that the story of the long process I went through to finally bring my vision into the realm of form demonstrates that not all traditional religious authority systems are unworkable. But one does need a good deal of patience and persistence.

Notes

~ *Chapter 2*

1. Paul J. Griffiths, *Christianity through Non-Christian Eyes* (Maryknoll, N.Y.: Orbis Books, 1990), 190.

~ *Chapter 3*

1. This use of the terms "head" and "heart" is modeled on Wendy O'Flaherty's use of these terms in her book *Other People's Myths: The Cave of Echoes* (New York: Macmillan, 1988).

2. Rita M. Gross, "Female God-Language in a Jewish Context," in *Womanspirit Rising: A Feminist Reader in Religion*, ed. Carol P. Christ and Judith Plaskow (San Francisco: Harper & Row, 1979), 169–73.

3. For examples, see Rita M. Gross "Steps Toward Feminine Imagery of Deity in Jewish Theology," in *On Being a Jewish Feminist: A Reader*, ed. Susannah Heschel (New York: Schocken Books, 1983), 234–47; and Rita M. Gross, *Buddhism after Patriarchy: A Feminist History, Analysis, and Reconstruction of Buddhism* (Albany, N.Y.: State University of New York Press, 1993), 125–35.

4. This understanding of the process of ego formation can be studied more fully in Chogyam Trungpa, *Glimpses of Abhidharma* (Boulder, Colo.: Prajna Press, 1978).

5. William E. Paden, *Religious Worlds: The Comparative Study of Religion* (Boston: Beacon Press, 1988), 35–49.

6. Ninian Smart, "Comparative-Historical Methods," in *The Encyclopedia of Religion* (New York: Macmillan, 1987), 3:572.

7. Rita M. Gross, "Religious Diversity: Some Implications for Monotheism," *Wisconsin Dialogue* 9 (1991), 35–48.

∾ *Chapter 4*

1. For example, see Paula Caplan, *Lifting a Ton of Feathers: A Woman's Guide to Surviving in the Academic World* (Toronto: University of Toronto Press, 1993).

2. Just as material conditions in the workplace are important in other fields, so too are they in academic life. The "chilly climate" for women is a well-documented phenomenon, and it is a testimony to women's determination and commitment to their work that so many have survived what has often been a hostile and exclusionary work environment.

3. Karen McCarthy Brown, "Heretics and Pagans: Women in the Academic World," in *Private and Public Ethics: Tensions between Conscience and Institutional Responsibility*, ed. David G. Jones (New York: Edwin Mellen Press, 1978).

4. Thomas S. Kuhn, *The Structure of Scientific Revolutions* (Chicago: University of Chicago Press, 1962), 52–91. See also the preceding chapter in this volume, "Why Me? Reflections of a Wisconsin Farm Girl Who Became a Buddhist Theologian When She Grew Up."

5. Rita M. Gross, "Female God-Language in a Jewish Context," in *Womanspirit Rising: A Feminist Reader in Religion*, ed. Carol P. Christ and Judith Plaskow (San Francisco: Harper & Row, 1979), 167–73; and "Hindu Female Deities as a Resource in the Contemporary Rediscovery of the Goddess," *Journal of the American Academy of Religion* 46 (1978): 269–91.

6. Rita M. Gross, *Feminism and Religion: An Introduction* (Boston: Beacon Press, 1996), 5–16.

7. However, despite the supposed preference for outsiders, certain positions, especially those in Islamic studies and Jewish studies almost always go to insiders. In East Asian studies likewise, many "native speakers" are hired. Ironically, it is in South Asian studies, both Hindu and Buddhist, devoted to the study of cultures and religions so long colonized by Europeans, that the strongest academic bias against insiders is found. The claim that Hindus and Buddhists are academically incompetent to study and teach their own religions may well be a lingering colonial bias. Finally, the academic world still prefers to hire men with androcentric worldviews to teach "malestream" culture over hiring women and men with feminist values to teach human culture and history. The bias against insiders does not seem to apply when androcentrism is the insider perspective.

∾ *Chapter 6*

1. From a statement widely circulated among Western Buddhists as a Tibetan prophecy: "When the iron bird flies, the dharma will come to the land of the red people." The authenticity of this statement as a Tibetan proverb is being investigated.

2. For an overview of the major events, see Sandy Boucher, *Turning the Wheel: American Women Creating the New Buddhism* (Boston: Beacon Press, 1993). For a report on the conference with the Dalai Lama, see Surya Das, "Toward a Western Buddhism: A Conference with His Holiness the Dalai Lama," *Shambhala Sun* 2, no. 1 (June 1993): 42–43. For a report on the Spirit Rock conference, see "No Picnic at Spirit Rock: Power, Sex and Pain in American Buddhism," *Shambhala Sun* 2, no.

5 (May 1994): 40–45, 52–53. My source for the most recent conference with the Dalai Lama is a personal communication from Dr. Judith Simmer-Brown. For two thought-provoking articles on the complexities of the issue, see Stephen Butterfield, "Accusing the Tiger: Sexual Ethics and Buddhist Teachers," *Tricycle* 1, no. 4 (Sept. 1992): 46–51; and "No Right, Nor Wrong: An Interview with Pema Chodren," *Tricycle* 3, no. 1 (Fall 1993): 16–24. The next few issues of *Tricycle* also contain revealing letters to the editor after each article.

3. For full discussion of this point see my *Buddhism after Patriarchy: A Feminist History, Analysis, and Reconstruction of Buddhism* (Albany: State University of New York Press, 1993), 32–40.

4. Forms of Buddhism that do not have the same understanding of the teacher–student relationship do not face the same problems in differentiating devotion from imitation and hero worship. For further discussion of the teacher–student relationship in Vajrayana Buddhism, see Chogyam Trungpa, *Journey Without Goal: The Tantric Wisdom of the Buddha* (Boulder, Colo.: Prajna Press, 1991), 55–63.

5. Chogyam Trungpa, *Shambhala: The Sacred Path of the Warrior* (Boston: Shambhala, 1988), 134–48.

6. This distinction between authority and power, which is used by anthropologists, is quite useful. Authority is the formal, publicly recognized right to make decisions and be obeyed. Power involves the informal, unacknowledged processes by which decisions are often, in fact, made.

7. The person behind the title is the eldest son of Chogyam Trungpa, Rinpoche, the founder of Vajradhatu. This title was conferred on him in May 1995 in Halifax, Nova Scotia, in a formal enthronement ceremony. Before that time, he was known for many years as the Sawang Osel Rangdrol. He became the head of Vajradhatu in 1990 immediately after the death of the Vajra Regent Osel Tendzin.

~ Chapter 7

1. For example, see articles by Ian Harris in *Religion* 21 (1991): 101–14; *Journal of Buddhist Ethics* 1 (1994): 46–59; *Religion* 25 (1995): 199–211; and *Journal of Buddhist Ethics* 2 (1995): 173–90.

2. Joanna Macy, *World as Lover, World as Self* (Berkeley, Calif.: Parallax Press, 1991); see also *Dharma Gaia: A Harvest of Essays on Buddhism and Ecology,* ed. Allen Hunt Badiner (Berkeley, Calif.: Parallex Press, 1991); and *Buddhism and Ecology,* ed. Martine Batchelor and Kerry Brown (London: Cassell, 1992).

3. Harold Coward, "New Theology on Population, Consumption, and Ecology," *Journal of the American Academy or Religion* 65, no. 2 (Summer 1997): 259–73.

4. Rita M. Gross; see chapter 9 below.

5. Christopher S. Queen and Sallie B. King, *Engaged Buddhism: Buddhist Liberation Movements in Asia* (Albany: State University of New York Press, 1996).

6. Richard H. Robinson and Willard Johnson, *The Buddhist Religion: A Historical Introduction,* 4th ed. (Belmont, Calif.: Wadsworth Press, 1997), 62–67.

7. R. A. Stein, *Tibetan Civilization* (Stanford, Calif.: Stanford University Press, 1972), 62; and David Snellgrove and Hugh Richardson, *A Cultural History of Tibet* (Boulder, Colo.: Prajna Press, 1968), 31–32.

8. Snellgrove and Richardson, *Cultural History*, 144–45; and Sir Charles Bell, *The Religion of Tibet* (London: Oxford University Press, 1968), 42.

9. Arthur Wright, *Buddhism in Chinese History* (New York: Atheneum., 1968), 74–76.

10. Ibid., 36–41.

~ *Chapter 8*

1. This chapter was a talk first given at the San Francisco Zen Center in April 1993 in a series of talks on American Buddhism. It has been significantly revised and updated for publication.

2. A lineage chant invokes the generations of Buddhist teachers through whom one's own specific traditions and practices have been passed down, at least mythically, throughout the generations, from the Buddha to one's own teacher. In my liturgical tradition, the lineage supplication is part of the morning liturgy.

3. *Midrash* is the Hebrew term for the extended, contemporary, and sometimes fanciful interpretations of scripture that have characterized Jewish ways of working with traditional texts for almost two millennia. The literal meaning of the text is put on hold to mine it for a reading of its contemporary significance.

4. In my tradition, a refuge name is given to a newcomer to Buddhism when one receives the Triple Refuge, otherwise known as the Refuge Vows, from one's preceptor and formally becomes a Buddhist. It is said to highlight one's style of working with oneself.

5. Traditional Buddhism encourages practice of the "two accumulations"—the "accumulation of merit" and the "accumulation of wisdom." Without the accumulation of wisdom, enlightenment is impossible, as the accumulation of merit brings only good karma and fortunate rebirth. The traditional division of labor between lay and monastic practitioners encouraged laypeople to practice the accumulation of merit by supporting monastics. In some future rebirth, this accumulation of merit would lead to a life in which the accumulation of wisdom could be approached more directly by practicing a monastic lifestyle.

6. This phrase was popularized by Chogyam Trungpa, whose first book bore that title. The phrase is used to refer to the fruitional practice of maintaining ongoing mindfulness, awareness, and tranquillity in the midst of the ordinary daily activities that one participates in after the end of periods of formal meditation. Such meditation in action is far more basic to the Buddhist vision than is formal meditation practice, but, as is often said, "Without meditation, there can be no meditation in action."

7. Buddhism is a nontheistic religion that declares that its adherents may find refuge in three things: the Buddha as example; the dharma, or teachings, as trustworthy guidance; and the *sangha,* or community, as source of psychological comfort and feedback.

8. For more extended discussion, see my *Buddhism after Patriarchy: A Feminist History, Analysis, and Reconstruction of Buddhism* (Albany: State University of New York Press, 1993), 257–69.

9. Though not without problems, Miranda Shaw's book *Passionate Enlighten-*

ment (Princeton, N.J.: Princeton University Press, 1994) is the most detailed account to date of such relationships as they are recorded in Indian Vajrayana texts.

~ *Chapter 10*

1. *Tulkus*, believed to be the reincarnation of a deceased teacher and also an incarnation of one of the Buddhas or bodhisattvas of the huge Mahayana Buddhist pantheon, are commonly picked in early childhood and trained to be the spiritual head of a monastery or group of monasteries. This practice is well developed in Tibetan Buddhism; the *Dalai Lama* is the most famous such person.

~ *Chapter 11*

1. The phrase "Don't lead, don't follow" is sometimes regarded as pith meditation instruction for relating with thoughts in meditation practice. Thoughts cannot be suppressed or repressed, but one does not encourage them to arise or linger with them once they do arise. Rather, one returns immediately to one's focal point for developing meditative awareness, usually the breath. Though it is always claimed that meditation instruction cannot really be learned from a book (and that is also my experience), several accurate published accounts of meditation instruction do exist. For the technique with which I am familiar, see Chogyam Trungpa, *Shambhala: The Sacred Path of the Warrior* (Boston: Shambhala, 1988), 37–41.

2. Shunryu Suzuki, *Zen Mind, Beginner's Mind: Informal Talks on Zen Meditation* (New York and Tokyo: Weatherhill, 1970), 102–3.

3. Ibid., 103.

4. Ibid.

5. Ibid.

6. Many Buddhist practices are done a hundred thousand times as a formal way of completing that practice before moving on to another formal practice.

7. Rita M. Gross, *Buddhism after Patriarchy: A Feminist History, Analysis, and Reconstruction of Buddhism* (Albany: State University of New York Press, 1993), 146–51.

8. The most famous discussion of this thesis is found in Rosemary Radford Ruether, "Misogynism and Virginal Feminism in the Fathers of the Church," in *Religion and Sexism: Images of Women in the Jewish and Christian Traditions*, ed. Rosemary Radford Ruether (New York: Simon & Schuster, 1974), 150–83.

9. While it is too soon to tell if a similar pattern will emerge with Western Buddhism, the enormous popularity of Tsogyel Rinpoche's book *The Tibetan Book of Living and Dying* (San Francisco: Harper & Row, 1992) indicates that Westerners may be hungry for the Buddhist way of dealing with impermanence and death.

10. Lynn White, "The Historical Roots of our Ecological Crisis," *Science* 155 no. 3767 (1967): 1203–7.

11. Carol P. Christ, *Laughter of Aphrodite: Reflections on a Journey to the Goddess* (San Francisco: Harper & Row, 1987), 226–27.

12. Rosemary Radford Ruether, *Gaia and God: An Ecofeminist Theology of Earth Healing* (San Francisco: Harper & Row, 1992), 139–40.

13. Suzuki, *Zen Mind*, 102–3.

~ *Introduction to Part 3*

1. See Rita M. Gross, "Female God-Language in a Jewish Context," in *Womanspirit Rising: A Feminist Reader in Religion*, ed. Carol P. Christ and Judith Plaskow (San Francisco: Harper & Row, 1979), 167–73; and "Steps Toward Feminine Imagery of Deity in Jewish Theology," in *On Being a Jewish Feminist: A Reader*, ed. Susannah Heschel (New York: Schocken Books, 1983), 234–47.

2. For more information on this topic, see Rita M. Gross, *Buddhism after Patriarchy: A Feminist History, Analysis and Reconstruction of Buddhism* (Albany: State University of New York Press, 1993), 102–14, 192–206; and Judith Simmer-Brown, *Dakini's Warm Breath: Feminine Principle in Tibetan Buddhism* (forthcoming).

~ *Chapter 12*

1. Rita M. Gross, *Buddhism after Patriarchy: A Feminist History, Analysis and Reconstruction of Buddhism* (Albany: State University of New York Press, 1993), 146–51, 280–88.

2. This chapter was initially prepared for a panel investigating this thesis at the annual meeting of the American Academy of Religion in November 1993.

3. The phrase "precious human body" is integral to Buddhism, as indicated in earlier chapters. Without the human body, enlightenment is difficult or impossible to attain, and it is generally understood that the body is the basis for being able to practice spiritual discipline. Since meditation practices that include the body are the basis for transcending samsara, or conventional living, one has more grounds for being suspicious of the thesis that an emphasis on transcendence is also inevitably anti-body.

4. For example, see the best-selling, highly accessible popular interpretation of Tibetan Buddhism intended for Westerners, *The Tibetan Book of Living and Dying*, by Tsogyel Rinpoche (San Francisco: Harper & Row, 1992).

~ *Chapter 13*

1. Rita M. Gross, "Female God-Language in a Jewish Context," in *Womanspirit Rising: A Feminist Reader in Religion*, ed. Carol P. Christ and Judith Plaskow (San Francisco: Harper & Row, 1979), 167–73.

2. Rita M. Gross, "Hindu Female Deities as a Resource in the Contemporary Rediscovery of the Goddess," *Journal of the American Academy of Religion* 46 (1978): 269–91.

3. Paul J. Griffiths, *Christianity through Non-Christian Eyes* (Maryknoll, N.Y.: Orbis Books, 1990), 136.

4. In some Tantric imagery, the personification of *prajna*, Manjusri, carries a sword, which cuts through dualistic fixation or, alternately, cuts both elements of a dichotomy. "The sword of *prajna*" is a favorite image for the process of letting go of false dichotomies and dualisms.

5. Stephen Beyer, *The Cult of Tara: Magic and Mystery in Tibet* (Berkeley: University of California Press, 1973), 55.

6. *Yidam* is the term used for a *sambhogakaya* manifestation that is one's "meditation deity," the focus of one's self-visualization in so-called deity yoga.

7. A *mantra* is a short verbal formula, repeated over and over in meditation, that captures verbally the essence of the *yidam* and stabilizes one's meditation on that *yidam*.

8. Taranatha, *Origins of Tara Tantra*, ed. and trans. David Trios Templeman (Dharamsala, India: Library of Tibetan Works and Archives, 1981), 11–12.

9. Martin Willson, *In Praise of Tara: Songs to the Saviouress* (London: Wisdom Publications, 1986), 125.

10. Ibid., 105–66.

11. Ibid., 301.

12. Ibid., 190–93.

13. Ibid., 305–6.

14. Ibid., 191–93.

15. Tsultrim Allione, *Women of Wisdom* (London: Routledge & Kegan Paul, 1984), 30; and Chogyam Trungpa, "The Vajrayogini Shrine and Practice," in *The Silk Route and the Diamond Path: Esoteric Buddhist Art on the Trans-Himalayan Trade Route*, ed. Deborah E. Klimberg-Salter (Los Angeles: UCLA Art Council, 1982), 234.

16. Allione has some discussion of meanings that can be attributed to some of her implements and aspects of her pose (*Women of Wisdom*, 31–34). See also Trungpa, "Sacred Outlook: The Vajrayogini Shrine and Practice," in *The Silk Route and the Diamond Path: Esoteric Buddhist Art on the Trans-Himalayan Trade Route*, ed. Deborah E. Klimberg-Salter (Los Angeles: UCLA Art Council, 1982), 238–40. Another description of Vajrayogini and the meaning of her implements, in her role as consort of Cakrasamvara, is found in Kazi Dawa-Samdup, *Sri Cakrasamvara-Tantra: A Buddhist Tantra* (1919; reprint, New Delhi: Ditya Prakashan, 1987), 20–21.

17. A *mandala* is the mythic universe which a *yidam* inhabits and which the meditator visualizes. It consists of a circle or a square oriented around the center and protected by boundaries, with gates in the cardinal directions.

18. Trungpa, "Sacred Outlook," 238–40. For additional praises, see that article, which also provides extensive commentary on these praises, which would be quite opaque otherwise.

19. One of the *samaya* obligations taken on by a practitioner of Vajrayana Buddhism, though not of other forms of Buddhism, includes a vow not to denigrate women "who are nature of *prajna* and *sunyata*, showing both."

20. Some first-time readers of Tibetan hagiographical literature might question this claim, since the literature does include frequent "miracles." Such events do not contradict the humanity of the main characters, but are based on other Tibetan

and Vajrayana beliefs, concerning the ability of an "accomplished human" (*siddha*) to control the elements. For further discussion of this motif, see my article on Yeshe Tsogyel, "Yeshe Tsogyel: Enlightened Consort, Great Teacher, Female Role Model," in *Feminine Ground: Essays on Women in Tibet*, ed. Janice Dean Willis (Ithaca, N.Y.: Snow Lion, 1989), 11–32.

21. All forms of Buddhism regard human rebirth as extremely auspicious, in part because only in the human realm, but not in the realm of the "heaven dwellers" or in any other realm of sentient existence, is enlightenment possible. Tibetan contemplations encourage one to treasure this "precious human birth" and to use it wisely before all-pervasive impermanence takes its toll. Since other Buddhist contemplative exercises that foster detachment by focusing on the foulness of the human body or on a rotting corpse are better known to Western students of comparative religion, it is important to clarify that one needs the "precious human body" to engage in such contemplations.

22. S. K. Hookham, *The Buddha Within* (Albany, N.Y.: State University of New York Press, 1991).

23. This colloquial translation of the term *tathagatagarbha* is from the oral teachings of Chogyam Trungpa.

24. These are the Three Jewels, or the Three Refuges, the most basic elements of Buddhism and the focus of the refuge ceremony, in which a non-Buddhist, by going for refuge to the Three Jewels, becomes a Buddhist.

25. Yeshe Tsogyel is found on the Nyingma lineage tree and is supplicated in lineage chants, the only exception to this generalization of which I am aware.

26. Gross, *Buddhism after Patriarchy*, 234–40, 249–55.

~ Chapter 14

1. This chapter was initially written for a presentation at a conference on women and Buddhism at the Naropa Institute in July 1982; it was originally published in the *Journal of Transpersonal Psychology* 16, no. 2 (1984): 179–92.

2. See the work of Naomi Goldenberg, especially her book *Changing of the Gods: Feminism and the End of Traditional Religion* (Boston: Beacon Press, 1979). For a clear example of this trend in Jungian thought, see Erich Neumann, *The Origins and History of Consciousness* (New York: Pantheon Books, 1954), 5–143.

3. The writings of Mary Daly, especially *Gyn/Ecology: The Metaethics of Radical Feminism* (Boston: Beacon Press, 1978), illustrate this brand of feminist reversal. For shorter statements, see Charlene Spretnak, "Feminist Politics and the Nature of Mind," in *The Politics of Women's Spirituality*, ed. C. Spretnak (New York: Doubleday Anchor Books, 1982), 565–73; and Grace Shinell, "Women's Collective Spirit: Exemplified and Envisioned," in ibid., 510–28.

4. The *Smithsonian* magazine shows a photograph of the greeting cards (no. 9, 1978, p. 41).

5. See D. R. Komito, "Tibetan Buddhism and Psychotherapy: Further Conversations with the Dalai Lama," *Journal of Transpersonal Psychology* 16, no. 1 (1984): 1–24.

6. This traditional Tibetan teaching regarding basic psychological traits is

unlike Western psychologies and very useful. See Chogyam Trungpa, *Journey Without Goal: The Tantric Wisdom of the Buddha* (Boulder, Colo.: Prajna Press, 1981), 77–85; idem, *Cutting through Spiritual Materialism* (Berkeley: Shambhala, 1971), 217–43. See also Thinley Norbu, *Magic Dance: The Display of the Self Nature of the Five Wisdom Dakinis* (privately published; P.O. Box 146, New York, N.Y. 10002).

∼ Chapter 15

1. The title of this chapter is a quotation from an important section of the *sadhana* of Vajrayogini. This vow is part of self-empowerment done on feast days which occur on the tenth and twenty- fifth days of the lunar calendar. This paper was originally presented at the annual meeting American Academy of Religion in 1985 and was originally published in the *Journal of Feminist Studies in Religion* 3, no. 1 (1986): 77–89.

2. The presentation referred to in this comment was subsequently published as "Suffering, Feminist Theory and Images of Goddess," *Anima* 13 (Fall 1986): 39–46.

3. The Karma Kagyu lineage of Vajrayana Buddhism traces itself to Tilopa (999–1069), an east Indian yogi who is said to have had direct encounters with Vajrayogini. The teachings were transmitted to Tibet by Marpa the Translator (1012–1097), who made three long trips to India to learn the teachings. Marpa's chief disciple, Milarepa (1040–1123), transmitted them to Gampopa (1079–1153), who is generally considered to have systematized the Kagyu order. Thereafter the teachings were transmitted from generation to generation by the major leaders of Kagyu order, most of whom are part of the line of so-called reincarnating lamas. Thus, Chogyam Trungpa, who is one of the leading figures responsible for the transmission of Vajrayana Buddhism to the West, is the eleventh in the line of Trungpa *tulkus* ("emanation bodies"). Born in east Tibet in 1939, he was recognized in infancy and raised to be supreme abbot of a group of monasteries. After the Chinese takeover of Tibet, he fled and eventually came to the United States in 1970. The story of his lineage is both historical and mythic: historical in the sense that these people existed in space and time; mythic in that these biographies are direct models and inspiration to the student.

4. The best discussion of Kali's mythology is found in David Kinsley, *The Sword and the Flute* (Berkeley: University of California Press, 1975). An excellent selection of devotional poems to Kali is Rampradad Sen, *Grace and Mercy in Her Wild Hair* (Boulder, Colo.: Great Eastern Books, 1982). The iconographic representation of Kali that I used as a visual aid during my presentation, a devotional poster in my collection, has been reproduced in Rita M. Gross, "The Second Coming of the Goddess," *Anima* 7, no. 1 (Fall 1979): 55.

5. Rita M. Gross, "Hindu Female Deities as a Resource for the Contemporary Rediscovery of the Goddess," *Journal of the American Academy of Religion*, 46, no. 3 (Sept. 1978): 269–91; eadem, "Steps Toward Feminine Imagery of Deity in Jewish Theology," in *On Being a Jewish Feminist: A Reader*, ed. Susannah Heschel (New York: Schocken Books, 1983), 234–47.

6. *Ngundro* practice consists of one hundred thousand prostrations accompa-

nied by one hundred thousand recitations of the refuge formula, one hundred thousand repetitions of the one-hundred-syllable *mantra,* one hundred thousand *mandala,* and one million repetitions of the guru-homage formula. See Judith Hanson, trans., *The Torch of Certainty* (Boulder, Colo.: Shambhala, 1977).

7. In Tibetan Buddhism the various stages of spiritual path are seen as a gradual unfolding. The three *yanas* are *Hinayana* (convention vehicle), *Mahayana* (greater vehicle), and *Vajrayana* (indestructible vehicle).

8. The most extensive description of Vajrayogini in English, including extensive quotations from the *sadhana* text and an extensive discussion of Vajrayogini's iconography, is found in Chogyam Trungpa, "Sacred Outlook: The Vajrayogini Shrine and Practice," in *The Silk Route and the Diamond Path: Esoteric Buddhist Art on the Trans-Himalayan Trade Routes,* ed. Deborah E. Klimberg-Salter (Los Angeles: UCLA Art Council, 1982).

9. Rita M. Gross, "Initiation and Oral Tradition in Tibetan Vajrayana Buddhism," unpublished manuscript.

10. For additional information on this point, as well as on Vajrayana Buddhism in general, I highly recommend Chogyam Trungpa, *Journey without Goal: The Tantric Wisdom of the Buddha* (Boulder, Colo.: Prajna Press, 1981).

11. This concept is developed in my *Buddhism after Patriarchy: A Feminist History, Analysis, and Reconstruction of Buddhism* (Albany, N.Y.: State University of New York Press, 1993), 215–21.

~ Chapter 16

1. It might seem strange to claim that psychological transformation, whether individual or collective, is a side effect of ritual. Very often individuals report experiences of greatly heightened consciousness during ritual, and effective rituals can promote or even create group cohesion. Yet these transformations are the *effect* of ritual being performed precisely and regularly, whether or not the ritual happens to be inspiring on any specific occasion. In this sense, individual or social transformation is a side effect of ritual performance, rather than the reason for such performance.

2. For an excellent discussion, see Diana Eck, *Darshan: Seeing the Divine Image in India* (Chambersburg, Penn.: Anima Books, 1985).

3. Rita M. Gross, "Female God-Language in a Jewish Context," in *Womanspirit Rising: A Feminist Reader in Religion,* ed. Carol P. Christ and Judith Plaskow (San Francisco: Harper & Row, 1979), 167–73; eadem, "Steps Toward Feminine Imagery of Deity in Jewish Theology," in *On Being a Jewish Feminist: A Reader,* ed. Susannah Heschel (New York: Schocken Books, 1983), 234–47.

4. For a discussion of his conclusions, see my *Buddhism after Patriarchy: A Feminist History, Analysis, and Reconstruction of Buddhism* (Albany, N.Y.: State University of New York Press, 1993), 105–8.

5. Ibid., 249–55.

Index